IRISH heRalbRy

Irish Heraldry

A Brief Introduction

Written and Illustrated by

Nicholas Williams

evertype

2017

Published by Evertype, 72 Woodgrove, Portlaoise, R32 ENP6, Ireland. *www.evertype.com.*

First edition 2017. Also published in Irish by Evertype, ISBN 978-1-78201-139-2

Editor: Michael Everson.

A catalogue record for this book is available from the British Library.

ISBN-10 1-78201-192-7
ISBN-13 978-1-78201-192-7

Typeset in JansonText and ceanannas by Michael Everson.

Cover: Michael Everson and Nicholas Williams.

Printed by LightningSource.

For

DOMINICA LUCY PERPETUA

Foreword to the 2001 Irish-language edition

It is clear from their surviving seals that the Normans introduced heraldry into Ireland. When the English administration decided to put the practice of heraldry here on an official footing Bartholomew Butler was made King of Arms in 1552, an appointment which founded the Heraldic Office. When Edward MacLysaght was appointed Chief Herald of Ireland in 1945, the heraldic officers were obliged thereafter to use Irish as the principal language in documents published by the Office of the Chief Herald. This obligation would have presented little difficulty to his generation, raised as they had been with a thorough grounding in the national language, if only the necessary references works in Irish had been available. Unfortunately such works were not forthcoming.

Now at last this splendid book in Irish by Nicholas Williams of University College, Dublin, fills the gap, dealing as it does with the heraldry of Ireland and containing a comprehensive heraldic vocabulary. The author and publisher are to be congratulated for providing the general public with an opportunity to enjoy the riches of our heraldic tradition through the medium of Irish.

This book will be a valued addition to the shelves of those who are interested in this aspect of our national heritage.

Dómhnall Ó Beaglaoich
formerly Chief Herald of Ireland

Table of Contents

List of Figures

00.00: Heraldry

Few topics are as interesting as heraldry, although it is necessary to expend a certain amount of effort before one can enjoy it fully. The following pages contain a description of heraldry in general and of the heraldry of Ireland as a subdivision thereof. This book first appeared in Irish, and in it much of the recently systematized heraldic vocabulary of Irish appeared for the first time. In this edition, an English translation of the Irish, every attempt has been made to keep the contents as simple as possible so that the average reader may find it of interest.

Corporate heraldry is perhaps the sort of heraldry that is most usually seen in Ireland, that is, the heraldry of towns and cities, counties, colleges, universities and other public bodies. In Dublin, for example, the arms of the various local authorities can be seen on lamp-posts, litter bins, etc. In the country coats of arms can often be seen on the border between one county and another and on roads into many of the towns. Other institutions, colleges, schools, etc., display their arms at the entrance to them, on their stationery and on the uniforms of their students.

Personal heraldry is perhaps the aspect of heraldry that is most popular. Since many people believe that a particular coat of arms belongs to a surname, they think that somebody needs only to discover which arms belongs to his surname, for him to possess a coat of arms. This view is a fallacy, however, but unfortunately there do exist "heraldic" companies that are more than willing to take advantage of such a mistaken opinion. Such firms produce "arms of the surname" on plaques, and so forth and they encourage people to buys such arms to hang on the wall of their houses (§30.00).

00.01: The origin of heraldry

In order to understand the right to a coat of arms, one needs to go back to the origin of heraldry in the early middle ages. It seems that heraldry first appeared in the second half of the twelfth century, simultaneously it appears, throughout western Europe. Some commentators believe that the the beginnings of heraldry coincided with the invention of the closed helmet. Before that it would have been possible to recognize a knight on the battlefield or in the tournament. With the advent of the closed helmet, however, he was no longer recognizable and it became necessary to identify him by other means. Knights therefore began to paint distinctive patterns on their shields. Soon the same patterns began to be shown on the caparisons of the knights' horses and upon their surcoats. It is from the latter use that the expression *coat of arms* derives.

At first the patterns drawn on shield were very simple, for exaample, animals or bold geometric shapes. Since it was essential that the designs should be as visible as possible, the knights used only the brightest colours. The rules that deal with the correct use of the various tinctures are still valid in heraldry today (§05.06).

Since heraldry began as a means to distinguish one knight in armour from another, each coat of arms must originally have belonged to only one man. When a knight died, however, his heir would have adopted his father's arms, in the same way that he would have adopted his father's other feudal rights and obligations. Gradually therefore arms began to be associated with a particular family, although at any one time the arms had only one owner. This dichotomy is still a feature of heraldry, namely that a coat of arms belongs at any time to one armiger, but if the matter is examined over several generations, the arms belong to a family rather than to one inidividual.

> NOTE: It has been more recently suggested that heraldry had a rather different genesis, and that arms were first seen on banners and on seals. This may indicate that arms had their origin in the civil realm rather than with a miliatry milieu. This view holds that armorial bearings were first used among the nobility in Flanders and that some of them may have originated in the court of Charlemagne. This rather revisionist view of the origin of armorial bearings has not yet been widely accepted.

00.02: The beginnings of heraldry in Ireland

The Normans introduced heraldry to Ireland two generations after the beginnings of heraldry in England and in the other countries of western Europe. It appears that heraldry in Ireland developed in step with other places. Tournaments in particular greatly influenced the development of heraldry. We know from French sources that the Anglo-Normans in Ireland held tournaments. Morevoer the Annals of Inisfallen recount that in the year 1284 Donnchad Ó Briain killed Cennétig the son Brian in a joust. It would appear then that jousting was also practised among the Gaelic Irish at that period. Unfortunately the remains of Anglo-Norman heraldry still remain to be exhaustively studied. Moreover there are significant gaps in the heraldic records of the early centuries.

Wax seals are a very useful source of information for the history of heraldry. Although heraldic seals had been in use in other countries from the beginning of the thirteenth century, the earliest surviving heraldic seal from Ireland dates from 1347.

We know that some of the Norman nobility who came to Ireland in 1169 possessed armorial bearings. Strongbow, for example, appears to have used the arms of the de Clares (§07.04). Irish knights are occasionally mentioned in medieval rolls of arms, for example, Walter Burke, Earl of Ulster (†1271), Theobald Butler, Chief Butler of Ireland (†1285) and Maurice Fitzgerald, fourth Earl of Kildare, who took part in the siege of Calais (1345-1348) (FCA: 38, 27, 87). The earliest surviving example of Norman heraldry in Ireland is the statue of Thomas de Cantwell (†1319) in Kilfane, County Kilkenny, which was carved *ca* 1260. Cantwell's arms (*Gules five annulets* [...] *and a canton ermine*) can be clearly seen on his long narrow shield.

It is clear that some of the Anglo-Norman nobles were very interested in the use of armorial bearings. An obvious example is James Butler (†1452), fourth Earl of Ormond, who is usually known as the White Knight. He granted land to the College of Arms in London and he was given permission by Henry V to appoint John Kitely as Ireland King of Arms (§28.01).

Probably he best sources for the development and particular nature of Irish heraldry are carved tombs and other carvings. In this context the sketches made by Du Noyer of arms on Irish tombstones, now preserved in the Royal Irish Academy, are important. A definitive study of the arms that can be seen in Trim, County Meath, was published by Elizabeth Hickey in the years 1982-84. Occasional accounts of heraldic tombstones, etc. are to be found in various journals concerned with Irish local history.

01.00: When did the Gaelic chieftains adopt heraldry?

It is likely that heraldry did not emerge until the invention of the closed helmet. We know that the Gaelic Irish wore Norman style armour as early as the battle of Athenry in 1316. Few of them had adopted heraldry by that date, however. Heraldry was essentially a feudal phenomenon. This was the social system practised by the Normans before they came to Ireland and which they introduced into the country. Within the feudal system a vassal possessed his land from his feudal lord and he was bound thereby to render his lord military service. When a man died, his eldest sone inherited both his land and his feudal rights and obligations. A man's coat of arms was one of such feudal rights.

Gaelic society was very different. In the Gaelic system land did not pass from father to son, but rather was held in common and belonged to the entire agnatic kindred, that is, to the brothers, uncles and cousins of the chieftain. The position of chief did not pass to the oldest son, but to the most suitable male relative. If the Gaelic chieftain could not say that his kindred's lands was his own property, he could hardly claim to possess armorial bearings either.

Although the Normans brought both heraldry and feudal practice to Ireland, by the fourteenth century the Anglo-Normans were becoming Gaelicized and Gaelic speech and customs were strengthening among them. In the year 1351 William O'Kelly issued an invitation to the poets of Ireland to come to his house in Gáille to celebrate a feast in his compary. The long poem by Gofraidh Fionn Ó Dálaigh *Filidh Éireann go haointeach* ('The poets of Ireland to one house') describes the occasion in detail. Although Ó Dálaigh gives meticulous description of both the feast itself and the house of O'Kelly, there is no mention anywhere in the poem of anything even vaguely heraldic. The same can be said of *Caithréim Thoirdhealbhaigh*, a prose texts written at some time in the period 1345-1360 and which deals with the wars of the O'Briens of Thomond in the thirteenth and fourteenth centuries. In the work there is a long description of Donnchad MacConmara and his men arming themselves for battle (1309). Every part of the armour and equipment of the heroes is described but there is no reference to armorial bearings on either shield or banner. As late as 1562 the Lord Deputy FitzWilliam writing to William Cecil says that the Gaelic chieftains of Ireland are still reluctant to adopt heraldry.

One might surmise therefore that the differences between Anglo-Norman society in Ireland and that of the native Irish was so great, that it would fruitless to look for examples of heraldry among the Gaelic chieftains. It seems, however, that from the beginning of the Norman presence in Ireland there were Gaelic chiefs who had close relations with the Anglo-Normans and who in consequence deliberately imitated their customs. Cathal Crobhdhearg O'Connor (§01.01) can be numbered among such chieftains and the MacCarthy family of Munster (01.04). Moreover, as we have seen, the Anglo-Normans themselves became Gaelicized and it was not long until the two groups in various formed a single community. If some of the native Irish were reluctant to adopt heraldry, other Gaelic chieftain seem to have used armorial bearings from the thirteenth and fourteenth centuries onwards.

01.01: Heraldry among the Gaelic chieftains in the thirteenth century: Cathal Crobhdhearg O'Connor

There is an entry in Thomas Jenyns' book, an Anglo-French roll of arms from *ca* 1410, which mentions *Charles à la maine rouge d'Irland fondeur de l'Abbey de Liske* 'Charles of the Red Hand of Ireland, founder of the Abbey of Liske'. The work tells us that the arms in question are *Argent a red hand issuing from the sinister side of the shield* (PO 902). It is likely that *Charles à la main rouge* is a direct translation of Cathal Crobhdhearg 'Cathal/Charles of the Red Hand'. Cathal was a brother of Rory O'Connor, the last high king of Ireland. He was king of Connacht for a long period and he died in 1224. The abbey of Lough Key was founded *within* his territory in 1215, and it is therefore probable that *Liske* in the roll of arms is a misreading for **Loghke* or something similar. The actual founder of the abbey of Lough Key was Clárus Mac Maoilín, the archdeacon of Elphin.

It should be noted, however, that the arms ascribed by Thomas Jenyns to Cathal Crobhdhearg are not the arms usually borne by the O'Connors of Connacht. It is nonetheless that the customary arms used by the O'Connors of Connacht are surmounted by an arm in the crest, that is to say, above the shield itself. An arm in armour grasping a sword can be seen in the crest of both O'Connor Don and O'Connor Sligo (IF: 212).

It is remarkable that armorial bearings should be ascribed to a Gaelic chieftain as earliy as the first quarter of the thirteenth century. It should be remembered, however, that Cathal Crobhdhearg had close dealings with King John who recognized his claim to be king of Connacht. Moreover Cathal held some of this territory in virtue of a charter from John, and his son and successor, Henry III. It is known that Cathal Crobhdhearg deliberately imitated the Anglo-Normans in other ways as well. Although the beginning of the thirteenth century is extremely early for armorial bearings among the native Irish, it is probable that the evidence of the Jenyns' roll is trustworthy in this matter.

01.02: Gaelic heraldry in the fourteenth century

Although Gaelic chieftains used seals to authenticate documents, etc., for their seals carry non-heraldic ornamentation for the most part. There was, however, a seal used by Hugh "the Fat" O'Neill (Aodh Ramhar Ó Néill). Hugh was chief of his kindred from 1345 till his death in 1364. His shield, which unfortunately went missing in the nineteenth century, showed a shield charged with a right hand couped. On each side of the shield were depicted a fabulous animal (a wyvern possibly) and the words S[*igillum*] *Odonis Regis Hybernicorum Ultonie* 'The Seal of Aodh Ó Néill, king of the Gaels of Ulster' was written round the edge.

Hugh O'Neill had close relations with the Anglo-Normans. In the first place he was made chief of his kindred by Ralph de Ufford, Justiciar of Ireland, when the latter deposed Henry O'Neill, Hugh's cousin. Hugh also introduced succession by primogeniture into his kindred, a practice which lasted until the end of the fifteenth century. Moreover Hugh is mentioned in a proclamation which Edward III sent to the nobility of Ireland, requesting them to join him in an expedition against the Scots.

The arms which Hugh adopted were based on pre-heraldic symbolism. It is certain that the red hand was a badge of Cineál Eoghain from the earliest period, although the family of the Magennis sometimes claimed that they had the exclusive right to used the symbol. It is also worth noting that that Hugh O'Neill's arms on the seal are identical with the arms ascribed to Hugh O'Neill, Earl of Tyrone by manuscript GO 32 in the Dublin Genealogical Office (*ca* 1585), namely *Argent a right hand couped at the wrist gules*. The O'Neills of Tyrone were accustomed to add further charges to that shield from the end of the sixteenth century onwards.

01.03: The banners of O'Connor Faley and O'Dempsey

An Anglo-Norman document of July 1355 tells us that the clergy and laity of the diocese requested the bishop of Kildare to excommunicate the O'Connor Faley and O'Dempsey and their people, because they were attacking their country daily. The document says that the Gaelic chieftains attacked and plundered the Anglo-Normans with a great host and *vexillis explicatis* "with banners unfurled". It is not possible to say what kind of banner the attackers are said to have carried here. Since, however, it is certain that heraldic guidons were in used by the Gaelic chieftains by the sixteenth century (§01.10), it is not unlikely that heraldic banners are intended in this present case. If so, heraldry seems to have been employed by the O'Connor Faley and O'Dempsey by the middle of the fourteenth century.

01.04: MacCarthy Mor

Dermot O'Connor asserts *ca* 1714 that Donal Roe MacCarthy, king of Desmond, granted a particular crest to the O'Dineens (Creast: *lámh armtha le rulla parsment airna thabhairt dó le Domhnall Roe Mac Cárthadh, rígh Deasmhumhan* 'Crest: an arm in armour with a roll of parchment, given to him by Donal Roe MacCarthy, king of Desmond'). Donal died in 1302, a date which is rather early in this contexts (though it is later than Cathal Crobhdhearg; §01.01). If O'Connor is not mistaken, the MacCarthys were granting a crest to their followers at the beginning of the fourteenth century. If so, heraldry was being practised by the MacCarthys for some time before that again. It should be pointed out, however, that the crest over the helmet was a recent innovation at the beginning of the fourteenth century (§19.01). If heraldry was indeed in use by the MacCarthys at this period, they were up to the minute with their heraldry as well.

It is apparent from Goghe's map of 1567 (§01.10) that the arms of the MacCarthy consisted of *a stag passant*. A stag passant are the arms ascribed to the Province of Munster by a European armorial as early as *ca* 1440 (§24.08) and it would seem that those arms are themselves based on the armorial bearings of the MacCarthys. This is perhaps further evidence that the MacCarthys practised heraldry at an early date.

Those Gaelic chieftains who began the practice of heraldry early usually had close relations with the Anglo-Normans. This was certainly the case with the MacCarthys. Cormac MacCarthy (†1359) was a close associate of the Anglo-Normans and their government in Ireland. Cormac assisted the Justiciar, Sir Thomas de Rokeby, against another member of the MacCarthy family, Dermot mac Dermot. As a reward Cormac received a grant of extensive territory in Muskerry and Castlemaine from Edward III. Cormac's son Donal was confirmed in possession of the territory at a later date by the Duke of Clarence, the Lord Deputy. When Donal died in 1392, the title and lands of MacCarthy Mor were inherited by primogeniture in the feudal custom until 1508. It would seem that the MacCarthys had adopted aspects of feudal practice including heraldry as early as the beginning of the fourteenth century.

In spite of what has been said above, it is possibly unwise to rely entirely on what Dermot O'Connor says about the crest granted by Donal Roe. Donal's seal survives and there is no evidence for his use of heraldry on it. The figure of the chief appears on one side of the seal, but he has neither helmet nor shield. No armorial bearings are shown on the caparison of his horse either.

01.05: Richard II in Ireland

Jean Froissart gives an interesting account in his chronicle of the visit of Richard II to Ireland. Froissart obtained his information from Henry Kyrkestede, the king's squire. When Richard was in Ireland (1394-95), four important Gaelic chieftains swore allegiance to him and the king made knights of them all. The four chiefs concerned were O'Neill, "king of Meath", O'Brien of Thomond, Art MacMurrough, "king of Leinster", and O'Connor, "king of Connacht." Kyrkestede knew Irish well and he was given the job of teaching the four chieftains the customs and manners of chivalry. Froissart mentions the arms of Kyrkestede himself (*Argent a chevron gules between three torteaux*). He does not, however, mention the arms of any of the four chieftains. O'Neill already had armorial bearings (§01.02). It seems likely that the other three received arms at this period, if they were not already armigerous.

Under the year 1392 Froissart mentions *Chandos le Roi d'Irlande*, that is to say 'Chandos, Ireland King of Arms'. If Froissart is correct, it seems that he is referring to Sir John Chandos (†1369), a private herald, who was appointed

Ireland King of Arms after that date. If such an office existed during the reign of Richard II (1377-99) and if Ireland was his heraldic province, it is probable that he came to Ireland with the king. At all events we know that John Othelake, March Herald, the private herald of Roger Mortimer was in Ireland at this period (§28.01). Roger was the heir presumptive of Richard II, until he was killed by the O'Briens in Kells in 1398. If arms were devised for the Gaelic chieftains during Richard's Irish visit, it is likely that there were heraldic experts in the king's entourage who were able to do the work.

01.06: Gaelic heraldry in the fifteenth century: some chieftains of the Irish Midlands

There are a group of Gaelic chieftains from the Irish midlands, Offaly and Westmeath for the most part, who are ascribed armorial bearings that are remarkably similar to one another. Among such chiefs one can include MacEgan, O'Kearney (the Fox), MacAuley, Keogh, O'Shiel (physicians to MacCoughlan), Brennan, O'Daly, and Crosbie. All these are ascribed variants of the same arms: *Argent a lion rampant gules and in chief two right hands couped of the same*. It seems likely that these arms are all in conscious imitation of further arms, that is to say the armorial bearings of Talbot and O'Neill respectively.

John Talbot, Lord Furnivall, was one of the Talbots of Malahide, County Dublin, although he was himself born in England. He came to Ireland in 1414 as Lord Deputy. He wielded power in the country until 1447, although he was in constant conflict with James Butler, Earl of Ormond, who has been mentioned above (§00.02). By right of his wife Talbot claimed the western portion of the territory of the de Lacys in Westmeath, and he attempted to exercise that right soon after his arrival in Ireland. According to the annals he plundered the O'Dalys in 1415 and they and other families in the region yielded to him. More than one coat of arms is ascribed to the Talbots, but the basic coat is *Argent a lion rampant gules* (BGA: 995).

It is probable that the Gaelic nobility of the Midlands of Ireland, MacEgan, O'Kearney, etc., started to use the Talbot arms in the period *ca* 1415 onwards. Although red hands were added to the arms thereafter, is seems that at first the chieftains used the coat of arms of their feudal lord itself as a sign that they had sworn allegiance to him. There is some evidence to suggest that *Argent a lion rampant gules* was the coat of arms used at one time by some of the Gaelic families in the midlands. Those arms are still part of the arms of O'Melaghlin, for example (IF: 217), one of the most important chieftains in Westmeath. It is interesting to note also that *Argent a lion rampant gules* are also the arms ascribed by Kennedy to the Carolans, a family long associated with Meath and with Dease in Meath (K: 68, 39).

In the year 1425 Owen O'Neill, the most powerful man of his kindred at the time, swore allegiance to Henry VI, king of England, and to the Earl of Ulster.

In spite of that oath, however, he marched south in 1430 and burnt western Meath. Many Gaelic chieftains yielded to him: O'Connor Faley, O'Madagan and O'Melaghlin, for example. Many of the Anglo-Norman families of the midlands yielded to him also, Plunketts, Nugents and Herberts, for example. Had it not been for the castles and strong walls of the towns of Meath, O'Neill would have reached Dublin itself. That expedition of Owen O'Neill was an unprecedented occurrence.

Since a red hand was the only charge in the arms used by the O'Neills at that time, it is not unlikely that MacEgan, O'Kearney and other chieftains after O'Neills expedition added red hands to their arms, which already contained the lion rampant gules of the Talbots. They would have realized after 1430 that they owed allegiance to two feudal masters, one Gaelic and one Anglo-Norman and therefore that they should indicate the fact in their armorial bearings.

The above is pure speculation, of course, but it bears the signs of veri-similitude. If there is any basis to the hypothesis, that it would seem that coats of arms were beginning to be used by some Gaelic chieftains in the period 1420-35. John Talbot powerful in Ireland during the lifetime of James Butler, though the two of them were in constant conflict. James Butler himself was very interested in heraldry, but if so, such was hardly exceptional for an Irish noble-man of Norman origin at the period. It seems that heraldry was flourishing in Ireland in the early fifteenth century. We should not therefore be astonished if some of the Gaelic nobility adopted heraldry at this period.

01.07: Gaelic and Anglo-Norman knights at the siege of Rouen

We learn from the Annals of Connacht for the year 1419 that 720 men accompanied Thomas Bacagh Butler, the son of the Earl of Ormond, to France in order to assist the English king, Henry V, against the king of the French. Half bore red and half bore white shields. They included noblemen both of Gaelic and of Anglo-Norman origin and according to the Annals a pestilence killed many of the "Irish". It would seem that the author here believed that the two groups, Anglo-Normans and Gaels, formed a single community. The rolls of arms tell us what was the coat of arms born by James, the Earl of Ormond himelf, at the siege of Rouen (FCA: 27). If the knights of Anglo-Norman origin had armorial bearings at the siege of Rouen, it is very likely that some of the Gaelic knights had coats of arms as well.

01.08: The tomb of O'Kane in Dungiven

A tomb can be seen in the ruins of the conventual church in Dungiven in County Derry. On it can be seen the figure of a knight lying under a canopy and at his shoulder the arms of O'Kane are carved in the stone. It used to be thought that the tomb was of Cooey na nGall O'Kane (†1385). It is now generally believed that the tomb is of a later date (though it was restored in the nineteenth century) and dates from the second half of the fifteenth century. This tomb is therefore evidence that the O'Kanes practised heraldry *ca* 1450-1500.

01.09: Kavanagh's heraldic seal

Our next piece of evidence for the practice of heraldry among the Gaelic nobility is a heraldic seal belonging to Donal Reagh MacMurrough Kavanagh, which is preserved in the National Library of Ireland. The seal dates from the year 1475. The shield is charged with a lion passant and a lion as supporter appears on either side. The same seal matrix produced the seal that was used on an agreement between Pierce Butler and Donal Reagh's grandson, Murrough Kavanagh, which was made in 1525.

01.10: The sixteenth century onwards

From the sixteenth century onwards the use of heraldry becomes more frequent among the Gaelic nobility. A letter sent in August 1537 by Magnus O'Donnell, lord of Tirconnell, to Leonard Grey, the Lord Deputy, can be found in the English state papers. The letter was sealed with wax and a lion and a right hand are visible on the wafer. Although the matrix has been awkwardly used, it seems that the design of the seal was a heraldic one. Moreover it appears that the lion and dexter hand are related to the arms used at one time by the O'Donnells, namely *Sable two lions combatant between in chief a dexter hand between two mullets and in base another mullet all argent* (BGA: 748).

In 1542 Sir John Travers, Master of Ordnance in Ireland, when fighting against some Gaelic chieftains, was able to take from them two guidons. He obtained the first in O'Kane's castle on the River Bann, and the second he sezed from the MacDonnells. The first of the two guidons carried the armorial bearings of Maguire ("a horseman armed after the ires facion"), even though it was in the possession of the O'Kanes. The second guidon bore the arms of MacDonnell apparently, for ""a sheype [ship] without a tope" was among the charges to be seen on it.

E. C. R. Armstrong examined the fiants of Queen Elizabeth I in the Public Record Office in the early years of last century, before they were destroyed. Among the fiants he found a number of documents of submission signed by Gaelic and Anglo-Norman leaders. A few of the Gaelic chieftains sealed their documents with heraldic seals, Turlough O'Brien (Toirdhealbhach Ó Briain), for example, Conall Molloy and Fehin O'Farrell Boy. The arms of the O'Briens of Inchiquin could clearly be seen on the seal of Turlough O'Brien, that is, *Quarterly 1 and 4 three lions passant in pale 2 Three piles converging at the base 3 A pheon.*

In 1567 John Goghe published his map of Ireland. The arms of several nobles of Anglo-Norman origin can be seen on it, for example, the earls of Ormond, Leinster, Desmond and Clannrickard. The arms of two Gaelic chieftains appear

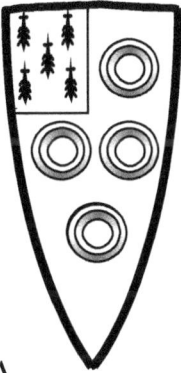

A.

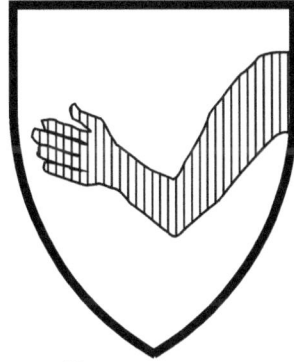

B.

C.

D.

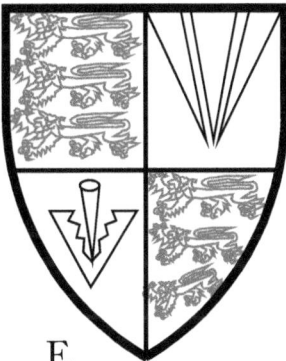

E.

A. Arms of Thomas Cantwell (Cantwell Fada), Kilfane, Co. Kilkenny

B. Arms of Cathal Crobhdhearg O'Connor (after Foster)

C. Seal of Hugh "the Fat" O'Neill (Aodh Ramhar Ó Néill) (†1475)

D. Seal of Domhnall Reagh MacMurrough Kavanagh (1475)

E. Arms of Turlough O'Brien (Toirdhealbhach Ó Briain) from his seal (c. 1585?)

Figure 1

on the map also, MacCarthy Mor, that is, the Early of Clancarty (*Argent a stag passant gules*) and O'Brien, Earl of Thomond (*Gules three lions passant in pale argent*) (FNMI: 4 i: 5).

Du Noyer cites a few examples of arms used by Gaelic noblemen on tomb dating from the 1680s. A fair number of arms borne by Gaelic chieftains can be found in two manuscripts in the Dublin Genealogical Office, that is, GO 32 and GO 34, both dating from the end of the sixteenth century. GO 34 was compiled *ca* 1590 and the following arms are cited in it: O'Donnell, Earl of Tirconell; O'Brien, Baron Ibrickan; and O'Neill, Baron Dungannon. GO 32 was composed *ca* 1595-97 under the direction of Christopher Ussher, Ulster King of Arms. The following arms are cited in it: O'Brien, Baron Inchiquin; Donogh O'Brien, Earl of Thomond; Donal MacCarthy Mor, Earl of Clancarty; and Hugh O'Neill, Earl of Tyrone.

01.11: Epilogue

It should be pointed out that as far as the latter cases are concerned, the arms are not grants. It is clear that the chieftain had long been in possession of their armorial bearings. It seems reasonable to assume, therefore, that the Gaelic nobility usually had adopted arms long before the first reference to them. Let us not forget that Dermot O'Connor claims that Donal Roe MacCarthy (†1302) granted a crest to the O'Dineens (§01.04). If what O'Connor says is true, then arms or at least parts of them were being granted by Gaelic chieftains to their followers as early as the beginning of the fourteenth century. In spite of the MacCarthys' close relations with the Anglo-Norman colony, it would seem that their heraldic activity was wholly independent from the Crown.

Although it is likely that further evidence about Gaelic heraldry remains to be gleaned from the rolls of arms preserved in England and elsewhere, the outlines of the question are already clear. The native Irish did not adopt heraldry all at once, but rather gradually, one chieftain after another according to varying circumstances. Cathal Crobhdhearg, if the evidence is trustworthy, was using arms as early as *ca* 1215. We have no further evidence until the beginning of the fourteenth century, when it appears that heraldry was being practised by a few Gaelic chieftains. It also seems that the Gaelic revival of the from the end of the thirteenth century onwards to some degree hindered the adoption of heraldry by the native Irish. At any rate, heraldry does not seem to have been a common practice among the Gaelic nobility until the fifteenth century at the earliest. By the beginning of the sixteenth century feudalism was undergoing radical change, and the social differences between the Gaelic nobility and the Anglo-Norman settlers were less than ever. At that point the way was open to the practice of heraldry among the native Irish.

02: Native symbolism
02.00: Gaelic banners before the advent of the Normans
It is apparent from Irish literature, that the native Irish had a system of symbols long before they adopted heraldry. In the work known as *Cogadh Gaedhel re Gallaibh* (eleventh century), for example, the banners of the men of Bréifne are mentioned: *agus deich meirge agus trí fichid orra do dhearg agus do bhuidhe agus d'uaine agus do cheineál gacha datha um an meirge síthe sárshuaithnidh séanta saineamhail rug buadh gacha catha ... meirge órghráineamhail Fhearghail Uí Ruairc* 'there were among them seventy banners of red and yellow and green and of every kind of colour on each long very distinctive blessed particular banner that had been victorious in every battle... the gold-spangled banner of Fergal O'Ruairc'. It seems that O'Ruairc's banner was semé with small golden charges of some kind.

Geoffrey Keating believes that the native Irish had always used heraldry. In *Foras Feasa* ii. 13 when speaking of the battle Battle of Mag Rath (634) , he says that each commander had his own *suaitheantas* 'badge' and that each company marched into battle under the *suaitheantas* of their commander. Keating implies that the purpose of the different banners was to enable the historians to recognize the various heroes in the heat of battle. It would seem tht the customs of medieval knights and their heraldic practice lie behind these statements of Keating's. Moreover Keating cites from a poem beginning *Tréan tiaghaid catha Conghail* 'Mightily advance the squadrons of Conghal' a quatrain which described the banner of Conghal Claon. The banner according to the poem was identical with the banner of Conor mac Neasa, king of the Ulaidh:

Leomhan buidhe i sróll uaine,	['A yellow lion in green satin,
Comhartha na Craobhruaidhe,	the symbol of the Red Branch,
Mar do bhí ag Conchobhar cháidh,	as borne by noble Conor,
Atá ag Conghal ar congbháil.	is held aloft by Conghal.']

Although the poem in its entirety forms part of the *Battle of Mag Rath*, it is likely that the poem is later in date than the prose tale. The prose tale was probably composed *ca* 1200. The verse may be late enough to have been influenced by Gaelic heraldry.

02.01: Gaelic heraldry and the synthetic history of Ireland
If, as Keating asserts, the Irish had long borne heraldic banners or *meirgí*, there was a good reason for the practice. The Irish began to use armorial bearings in imitation of the Children of Israel: *Is imchian ó do thionnscnadar Gaedhil gnáthughadh na suaitheantas ar lorg chloinne Israel lér gnáthuigheadh san Égipt iad ré*

linn Ghaedhil do mharthain, an tan bhádar clann Israel ag triall trés an Muir Ruaidh agus Maoise 'n-a ardtaoiseach orra 'Long ago did the Gaels begin to practise arms following the Children of Israel, who used arms in Egypt, while Gael Glas was alive, when the Children of Israel were marching through the Red Sea under the command of Moses'.

It was widely believed in the middle ages that the tribes of Israel had coats of arms. There are references in the book of Numbers (10:11-27) to the muster of the various tribes under their own banners. Moreover Jacob likens his sons to animals (Genesis 19:3-27). These two passages were conflated and the arms of the twelve tribes resulted.

There is, of course, no basis to the fiction that the Israelites had coats of arms, though it was widely believed in places well into the nineteenth century (see K: 67, for example). On the other hand Keating mentions the matter quite deliberately. In medieval England people believed that heraldry first emerged duing the Trojan War, in order to distinguish the Greek commanders from each other and from the Trojans also. According to the synthetic history of Wales and England recounted in the twelfth century by Geoffrey of Monmouth, for example, the people of Britain descended from a Trojan called Brutus. Geoffrey tells us that Brutus fled from the fall of Troy and sailed westward and northward, until he landed in Totnes in Devonshire. Britain (*Britannia* in Latin) takes its name from Brutus, the Trojan refugee. Moreover, according to Geoffrey, Brutus and his followers introduced heraldry into Britain. Keating inserts his own narrative concerning the origins of heraldry into his history, for the express purpose of demonstrating that Irish heraldry has a biblical basis through Gael or *Gadelus*, the ancestor of the Irish, and is thus older than the heraldry of the English and Anglo-Normans.

It should incidentally remembered, that the Irish word *meirge* 'banner', to which reference has been made above, is not a native term; rather it has been borrowed from Old Norse *merki* 'flag, banner'. Although *meirge* itself is a borrowing, much of what was displayed upon pre-heraldic Gaelic banners is native enough. It is probable also that many of the distinctive charges in Gaelic heraldry are in origin Celtic and pagan in origin.

02.02: Celtic iconography and Irish heraldry

It is remarkable how frequently one meets certain charges in Gaelic heraldry that are not anywhere near as common in English heraldry or the heraldry of continental Europe. Among the living creatures that occur commonly in the heraldry of the Gaelic chieftains one might mention the boar, the stag, the hound, the salmon, the serpent and the lizard. Among other frequent charges one might cite the sun, the human hand and arm and various species of tree. These are sufficiently common in Gaelic heraldry to make it unlikely that their frequent attestation is coincidental. All the items mentioned so far are aspects of the pagan iconography of the Celts of Ireland, Britain, and continental Europe. They are often met with in the surviving remains of the pre-Christian cultic art of the Celts and have often been described by archaeologists.

It appears that the Gaels always had a pagan iconography and that elements of it survived down to the fourteenth and fifteenth centuries, when it was put to a new use, namely as charges in the coats of arms being adopted by Gaelic chieftains at the time. Mention has already been made of the red hand, the ancient symbol of Cineál Eogain, which was seen for the first time in the coat of arms of Hugh O'Neill (§01.02).

The survivals from ancient Celtic iconography give a distinctive personality to Gaelic heraldry, but there are other features which should be mentioned here. It is remarkable, for example, just how common is the colour green in Gaelic arms when compared with English and Anglo-Norman heraldry. This question will be discussed more fully below under heraldic tinctures (§05.07). Although the simple broad stripes, the "honourable ordinaries", do occur in Gaelic heraldry, they are not as common as in Anglo-Norman or English heraldry, nor in continental heraldry either. The relative rarity of the ordinaries is presumably related to the prevalence of Celtic symbols in Gaelic heraldry. It would seem that the Gaelic nobility did not bother with ordinaries, because they were anxious to display ancient symbols on their shields. Another distinctive feature of Gaelic heraldry is the use made of shields divided quarterly in order to display various charges (§22.06). For an account of heraldry in Gaelic society in both Ireland and Scotland see Roelofsma (1982) and Pye (1970).

Neither the story concerning Brutus nor the narrative in the Irish synthetic history is true, but Keating's claims indicate that heraldry was well established by the 1630s. Reference to the heroes' banners are to be found in the stories of the Fianna, see, for example, Meek 1986.

Although native elements are clearly visible in the heraldry of the Irish chieftains, there is no need to be overzealous in discovering them. Boars, stags and serpents are frequently encountered in Irish heraldry, but such animal charges are not uncommon in English and continental Euopean heraldry as well. Heraldry was not indigenous in Ireland, but rather a system of symbols that the Irish learnt from the Anglo-Normans. The Gaelic chieftains were reluctant to adopt heraldry at first, and the bulk of them failed to adopt heraldry until they had become thoroughly anglicized. Although there are native elements in Gaelic heraldry, the borrowed elements are dominant. Irish heraldry in general, and Gaelic heraldry in particular, cannot be understood without reference to the heraldry practised outside Ireland.

03.00: Heraldic terminology

As soon as heraldry emerged in western Europe, a specialist vocabulary arose to describe the various coats of arms and the things that could be seen on them and around them. Such terminology was first developed in French in France. Soon, however, heraldic vocabulary began to be devised in other languages, English, Dutch, German, Welsh, etc. Much of the heraldic terminology used in England was itself based on French, and that is still true today. It is interesting that the documents produced by English heralds were in French until the second half of the reign of Henry VIII (1509-47).

03.01: Heraldic terminology in Irish

As has been mentioned above (§§01.00-01.08), it seems that many of Gaelic chieftains began using heraldry between the thirteenth and the fifteenth centuries. At that time many of them would have spoken Irish only. Since in addition it appears that Gaelic nobles, who had adopted heraldry, themselves granted arms to their followers, it is likely that a vocabulary in Irish emerged to cater for such grants. That vocabulary does not unfortunately survive, although *armas* 'coat of arms' and *machaire* 'field' (that is, the background of the shield) are not infrequently met with in literary texts in Irish.

A heraldic terminology independent of Irish appears to survive to some degree in the Gaelic of Scotland. Edward Dwelly gives a number of Gaelic heraldic terms in his Scottish Gaelic-English dictionary, and it seems that they are indigenous coinages.

Arms and heraldic banners are described in Irish poetry from time to time, for example, in the dispute concerning the red hand of Ulster between Dermot Mac an Bhaird, Eoghan Ó Donnghaile and Niall Mac Muireadhaigh printed by Cameron in *Reliquiae Celticae*. Geoffrey Keating describes the banners of the tribes of Israel (§02.01) and he claims that the Gaels themselves based their own heraldry on the heraldry of the Israelites. Isolated quatrains are to be found in manuscripts in Irish which describe coats of arms. The following description of the coat of arms of O'Loughlin Boirne has been printed by John O'Donovan, for example:

> *A gcampa Uí Lochluinn dob fhollus a mbláthbhrat sróill,*
> *A gceann gach troda le cosnamh do láthair gleo,*
> *Seandair thorthach ar gcosnamh le mál go cóir*
> *Is anncoir gorm fá choraibh do chábla óir*

> 'On O'Loughlin's field was clear in a fair banner of satin,
> to defend in battle at the head of every encounter,

a fruiting ancient oak protected well by a warrior
and an anchor azure surrounded by twists of golden cable'.

Since that quatrain is in *ambrán* metre, it can hardly be earlier than the seventeenth century. Egan O'Rahilly describes the arms of O'Callaghan in his lament for Donal O'Callaghan (†1724). He says:

> *A armus, is é tarraingthe i n-órdhath*
> *Faolchú fhaobhrach éigneach bheodha,*
> *Ag tréigean imill na coille 'n-a combrith,*
> *'S ag dul ar seilg ar leirgibh Fódla.*

'His arms: drawn in the colour gold,
a fierce destructive vigorous wolf,
running at speed from the edge of the wood
and going off hunting upon the slopes of Fódla, that is, Ireland.'

03.02: Heraldic terminology in Modern Irish

It is clear from what has been said above that heraldry was described in Irish. It is also true that none of the Irish blazons cited to date has been in any sense precise from the technical point of view. A heraldic blazon should be sufficiently unambiguous that a heraldic artist could accurately paint the arms merely by reading the verbal description. Although occasional blazons can be found in Irish language manuscripts from the eighteenth and nineteenth centuries (§§17.05, 27.06), as far as I am aware only one Irish scholar used Irish consistently in order to describe armorial bearing, namely Dermot O'Connor, to whom reference has already been made (§01.04; see also §28.07). O'Connor's heraldic vocabulary is neither accurate nor consistent; he does seem, however, to have preserved some elements of the traditional Irish heraldic vocabulary.

Irish was not used consistently until the office of the Chief Herald of Ireland was established under the independent government. Since 1943 the Chief Herald has been issuing bilingual patents in English and Irish. Some have been in Irish only. Much of the terminology of the office of the Chief Herald can now be found in the Irish dictionaries of de Bhaldraithe and Ó Dónaill. It must be admitted that there were until the nineteen-nineties gaps and inconsistencies in the Irish terminology used by consecutive Chief Heralds. More recently an attempt has been made to remedy such imperfections in the heraldic vocabulary used for Irish language grants. Indeed the revised terminology was used in the Irish version of this book which was published in 2001.

03.03: Canting arms

The custom of relating the main charge in a coat of arms to the surname of the bearer is a very well-established practice in heraldry. Punning arms of that kind are known as "canting coats". Many examples can be found in Irish heraldry. The pun is often based on the English form of a name. Three hakes appear in the arms of Hackett (IF: 215) and three herons in the arms of Aherne (IF: 211).

Some of the puns are based on Irish. The arms of O'Sheehan (*Ó Síocháin* in Irish; cf. Irish *síocháin* 'peace') contain a reference to peace, namely a dove with an olive branch in her beak (§12.06); branches (Irish *craobhacha*) are used in the arms of Creagh (Irish *Craobhach*; see §10.10). The arms of Kennedy (Irish *Ó Cinnéide*) contain three helmets (< Irish *cinnéide*, understoood to mean 'garment for the head').

It is not infrequently impossible to say whether the canting coat is based on the English or the Irish form of the name. Three roaches can be seen in the arms of Roche (Irish *Róiste*) and a griffin in the arms of Griffin. The Irish for 'griffin' is *gríobh* and the surname Griffin is *Ó Gríofa* in Irish, where *Gríofa* is for earlier *Gríobhtha* 'griffin-like'.

04.00: The heraldic achievement

If a person is entitled to use a coat of arms he is an *armiger*. The shield itself and the surrounding items: the helmet and the crest above it, the supporters on either side, the compartment on which they stand and the motto beneath it are frequently called a *coat of arms*. Precisely speaking the shield with all its surrounding ornaments is known as an *achievement*. The term *coat of arms* refers only to the shield and the charges on it. Since the shield is the essential feature of a heraldic achievement, it is right to start with that.

04.01: The Shield

> *Agus ná feiceann tú bainte ar armus mo scéithe-se agus ar dhruim mo shleighe gur fear marbhtha céad d'aon bhéim mise, agus gur me is oighre ar Shancho Panza*
>
> 'And do you not see depicted on the arms on my shield and on the back of my lance that I am a man who slays a hundred at one blow, and I am a worthy successor to Sancho Panza'
>
> (Mahon O'Cronin according to Egan O'Rahilly)

The shield can stand by itself and theoretically the shield can be of any shape. In the early years of heraldry the long narrow-based shield was common; unfortunately such a shape had a limiting effect on the way charges could be drawn and the use of such shields was gradually replaced. The equilateral shield with pointed base is the shape of choice nowadays. That shape is the most efficient for displaying arms and because it resembles the old-fashioned smoothing-iron it is usually referred to as the "heater" or "heater shield".

In the second half of the fourteenth century a small shield, the target, became common for use in jousting. The distinctive feature of this variety of shield is that there was a notch in the upper right hand corner. This notched was used to rest the spear on in jousting. When, however, shields of this kind began to be used in heraldry, artists often put notches in both corners of the targets they drew. It was not long then until the other edges were decorated with scrolls, etc. By the time that tournaments were abandoned in the sixteenth century, the ornamentation of heraldic shields had become excessive. Contemporary heraldic artists have returned to the simple style of the early days of heraldry.

Since ecclesiastics were not, as a rule, military men, in the beginnings of heraldry they were often reluctant to use shields for their coats of arms. Instead they used ovals or cartouches. The cartouche was common in the eighteenth and nineteenth centuries as the default shape for armigers of all kinds. The arms of the city of Dublin, for example, on the frontage of the Mansion House in Dawson Street are displayed in a cartouche. On the other hand the same arms above the door appear in a shield. The arms of the Knights of St Patrick from the eighteenth and nineteenth centuries that can be seen on their stall plates in St Patrick's Cathedral, Dublin, are also in cartouches. The royal arms themselves were often displayed in a cartouche at that period; as, for example, on the fascia of the Irish Houses of Parliament in College Green, Dublin (now the Bank of Ireland).

04.02: The banner

Arms are not exclusively displayed on shields or cartouches. They can also be shown on square flags or banners. There are fine examples of heraldic banners above the choir stalls in St Patrick's Cathedral, Dublin. They are the banners of those men who were knights of the Order of St Patrick when the Church of Ireland was disestablished in 1871. Further banners can be seen displayed in St Patrick's Hall in Dublin Castle; these are the banners of the last knights of the Order before it was discontinued. A further set of heraldic banners could be seen in the Heraldic Museum in Kildare Street, Dublin. They were of the Irish chiefs whose genealogies had been confirmed (§31.05). Unfortunately, the problems with the recognition of false claimants, has led to the removal of the banners.

Corporate arms are often seen flying in the capital and elsewhere in the form of flags over the institutions to which they belong, Trinity College, for example, University College and the College of Surgeons. Such flags are in reality heraldic banners.

Heraldic banners sometimes appear as part of the heraldic achievement. The supporters, that is the figures which support the shield, are often seen holding banners. The kings of France used angels as their supporters and the angels were usually depicted holding flagstaffs from which flew versions of the French royal arms (*Azure three fleurs-de-lis Or*). The supporters of the arms of Northern Ireland are also holding heraldic banners (§24.06).

> NOTE: In recent years University College, Dublin, has for some purposes replaced the arms granted to the college in 1911 with a para-heraldic logo which violates the established conventions of heraldry. Or as one commentator has written "UCD moved away from using its coat of arms in favour of a pseudo-heraldic 'brand mark' to be employed for 'all UCD visual identity and communications uses'." This logo is certainly not a coat of arms; and it is emphatically not a "crest" as urged by the authorities of the college themselves.

04.03: The standard

*Gach lá pátrúin tigid lucht ceirde na cathrach i prosesion onórach
mórthimpeall na reigléas réamhráite go mbratachaibh agus stannardaibh*
'Every pattern day the tradespeople of the city parade in a solemn
procession round the above mentioned church with flags and with
standards' (Tadhg Ó Cianáin 1608).

Elizabeth II, the queen of the United Kingdom, has a heraldic banner, which is
often erroneoulsy referred to as "the Royal Standard". The heraldic standard by
rights is a long triangular flag, on which appear the armiger's arms, badge, motto
and crest. Standards of various kinds have been used at different times by the
major Irish noblemen. The standard of Gerald, 14th Earl of Kildare (†1611/12)
and the standard of the Earl of Ormond (1615) are depicted on Plate 4.

05.00: Tinctures

The colours found in heraldry are classified under four headings: metals, colours, stains and furs. Collectively they are known as tinctures. When describing a coat of arms naming a tincture more than once is often avoided by saying of the field, of the second, of the third, etc., (§18.03*d*).

05.01: Metals

There are two metals *Or* and *argent* (ar.), e.g. *Argent a saltire gules* (Fitzgerald, IF: 214) and *Azure three oak leaves argent* (Tobin, IF: 220). Although Or and argent are metals, they are usually represent by yellow and white respectively. Notice also that in blazon *Or* is often spelt with a capital letter in order to distinguish the word from the conjunction *or*.

05.02: Colours

Five colours are in customary use in heraldry: *gules* (red), *azure* (blue), *vert* (green), *sable* (black) and *purpure* (purple). These are abbreviated g, az. or b, vt., sa. and purp. The exact shade of the colours is not important provided the colours used are as clear and bright as possible. In heraldry in these island there is also a light blue distinct from azure. This is called *bleu céleste* and is used in particular for people and institutions connected with the Airforce or aviation in general. There are further colours that have a limited used in Continental European heraldry.

05.03: Stains

There are three stains: *sanguine*, a tint between red and brown; *murrey*, between pink and purple; *tenné*, tawny or orange. Some handbooks claim erroneously that sanguine and murrey are identical. The stains were have been very uncommon in the past, but they have been more frequent recently. A good example are the arms of Kells, County Meath: *Argent a cross of eight roundels sanguine one three three one each charged with a bezant all within a bordure Or masoned sable*. The cross of roundels is a heraldic representation of folio 33r in the Book of Kells. See also the arms of Victoria College, Belfast (§13.08).

There do not appear to be any examples of either murrey or tenné in Irish heraldry. One third of the Irish tricolour is tenné, however. If one wanted to describe the national flag in heraldic language, one would say *Party per pale of three vert argent and tenné*. Since the stains are not common, there are no generally accepted abbreviations for them.

TINCTURES

05.04: Furs

Ermine is the commonest heraldic fur, that is with ermine spots sable on argent. The spots are the tails of ermines or stoats. If the spots are argent upon a sable, the fur is referred to *ermines* or sometimes *counter-ermine*. If the background is Or and the spots are sable, the fur is *erminois*. If the background is sable and the spots Or, the fur is *pean*. Ermine is seen in the arms of O'Regan: *Or a chevron ermine between three dolphins azure* (IF: 219) and ermines in the arms of O'Broder: *Per pale gules and sable on a fess Or between three griffins heads of the same as many mullets ermines* (IF: 211). Erminois occurs in the arms of O'Quigley (§10.01).

Vair is another heraldic fur. It originated with the use of squirrel skins sewn together as a lining for cloaks, etc. In Irish vair is called *véir*, but in early grants in Irish by the Chief Herald, the fur was sometimes known as *ilchraicneach* 'of many skins'. The grey-blue backs and the white bellies of the fur were stylized and that gave rise to the appearance of vair as we know it today. An example can be seen in the arms of Fleming: *Vair a chief chequy Or and gules* (IF: 214). Unless otherwise specified the alternating sections of vair are argent and azure. The arms of Prendergast, County Tipperary, display vair with Or for argent: *Gules a saltire vair Or and azure* (BGA: 822).

05.05: Charges proper

If a charge (that is something on a shield or crest or as a supporter) is in its natural colour or colours, it is said to be *proper*. Clearly proper refers to representations of people, of animals, flowers or buildings as a rule. The accepted abbreviation for proper is *ppr*. In the early days of heraldry the term proper referred to the heraldic colour appropriate to the charge in question. Nowadays proper means that the charge or item is drawn in a naturalistic fashion.

05.06: The tincture rule

Since heraldry began as a way of distinguishing one knight in armour from another, it was necessary to keep the different shields as visible as possible. Very early in the history of heraldry a rule emerged which prohibited placing a colour on another colour, or a metal on another metal. Colours are placed on metals, and metals are placed on colours. This is known as the tincture rule and it is still applied, although there are some noticeable exceptions.

The tincture rule does not apply either with furs or with charges proper. Either may be placed on metals or colours. The stains are classified as colours. The tincture rule is not applied either when the field is divided into many parts. The rule is not applied either in the case of the chief, the bordure or the canton.

Apart from those legitimate exception, there are coats of arms which break the tincture rule. Perhaps the best known example are the arms of the Crusader kings of Jerusalem: *Argent a cross potent between four crosses Or*. A good example of a breach of the tincture can be seen in the arms of Meredith, recorded in the Office of the Ulster King of Arms: *Gules on a chevron sable between three goats heads erased as many trefoils Or* (CGH: 67).

05.07: The relative frequency of the tinctures

The French scholar, Michel Pastoureau, has shown that vert is the rarest of the heraldic colours. According to his figures in the thirteenth and fourteenth centuries vert was never more than 6% of either colours or metals on arms anywhere in western Europe. The average frequency of vert was somewhere between 2% and 3%. Pastoureau did not include Ireland in his study, but if one examines both Gaelic and Anglo-Normans arms listed by MacLysaght in IF, one sees that vert is fairly common among them. I calculate that the colour vert is to be found in two coats of arms out of every nine. That is to say that the frequency of vert in Irish heraldry reaches approximately 7%–9% of the total of colours and metals together. It would seem, therefore, that from the point of view of the use of vert Irish heraldry is unusual.

05.08: Tricking and hatching

The blazon is usually enough for the expert to visualize the arms exactly. In order to facilitate the visualization, however, often a *trick* is drawn. *Kennedy's Book of Arms* (K) is a collection of heraldic tricks. In the trick when there is more than one charge of the same kind the second and third, for example are indicated by numbers, and the various tinctures are shown by abbreviations.

There is another method to indicate tinctures in black and white, namely by a system of lines and dots known as *hatching*. It is generally agreed that the Italian, Silvester da Pietra Santa, first devised the system of hatching for his book *Tesserae Gentilitiae* (Rome 1638). Nowadays printing in colour is easier than it has ever been and thus hatching is not as common as it once was.

A. Hatching

| Argent [Ar.] | Or [Or] | Gules [Gu.] | Azure [B.] | Sable [Sa.] | Purpure [Purp.] | Vert [Vt.] |

PRATT   WINGFIELD   CARDEN

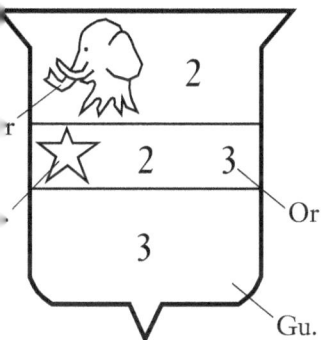 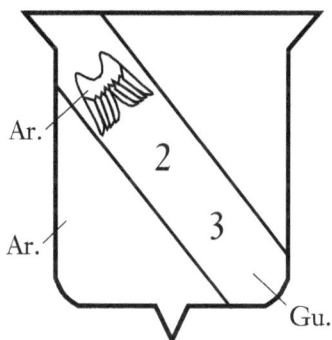 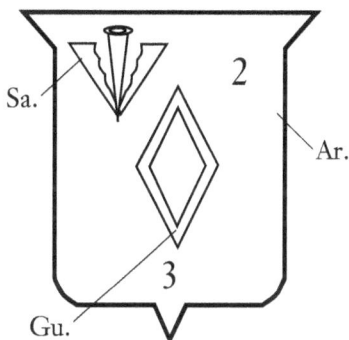

B. Tricking
(based on Kennedy)

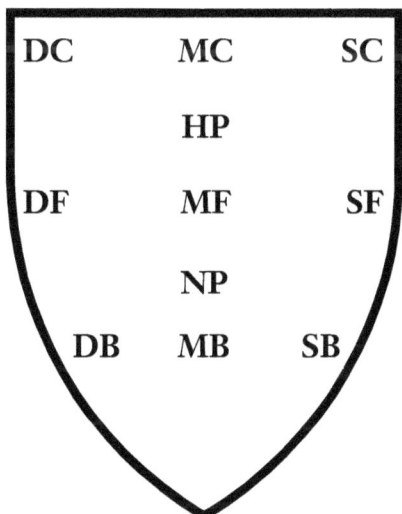

C. Divisions of the Field

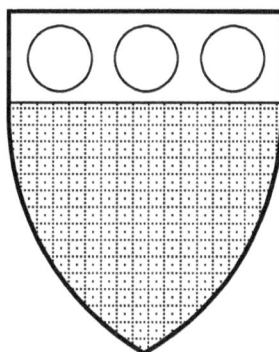

D. Diapering

Figure 2

06.00: The field

The surface of the shield on which the various charges stand is known as the *field*. Anything appearing on the field is known as a *charge*. In order to blazon a coat of arms accurately the position of the various charges must be described exactly. Three different areas are distinguished horizontally, the right side or *dexter*, the middle and the left side or *sinister*. *Dexter* and *sinister* refer to the right hand side and the left hand side of the bearer of the arms. *Dexter* will therefore appear to the viewer as being on the left, and similarly *sinister* will appear on the right.

Three horizontal positions are also distinguished, *chief*, *base* and *fess* between them. The mid position or fess is named from the fess, an honourable ordinary that goes across the shield (§07.01). If a charge is *in chief*, *in base* or *in fess*, unless otherwise specified, it is assumed to be in the middle at that height. If it is necessary to specify that it is indeed in the middle between dexter and sinister point one says that the charges is *in the chief point*, *in the fess point* or *in the base point*. When it is necessary to describe a charge that is not in the middle of any of the three heights, one says it is *in the dexter chief*, *in the sinister base*, etc.

To complete the picture it is necessary to mention two further points: the *honour point*, that is, horizontally in the middle of the shield between the chief point and the fess point; the *nombril point* between the fess point and the base point. Those two and the other nine points are indicated in Figure 2c. The abbreviations should be understood as follows: C = in chief; B = in base; F = in fess; M = middle; D = dexter; S = sinister; HP = honour point; NP = nombril point.

If we now look at the arms of Trinity College, Dublin, we see that the various charges are floating in the shield, and thus it is necessary to specify exactly where each of them is: *Azure a bible closed clasps to the dexter between in dexter chief a lion passant in sinister a chief a harp all Or and in base a castle with two towers domed each surmounted by a banner flotant to the side of the shield argent the dexter banner charged with a cross the sinister with a saltire gules.*

06.01: Simple divisions

The field may be divided in numerous ways. The most basic are those divisions that make two halves of the field. If a horizontal line divides the field, it is *party per fess* or *per fess*. If the line is vertical the field is said to be *party per pale* or *per pale*. The arms of Sealy, for example, are *Per pale Or and gules* (K: 54). If the dividing line goes from the edge of the shield in dexter chief to the edge at sinister base, the field is *party per bend* or *per bend*. *Per bend Or and argent three dexter hands erect couped at the wrist* are the arms of Adair of County Antrim, for example (BP: 18).

If two lines of division starting at the edges of the shield join in the middle like the gable end of a house, the field is said to be *party per chevron* or *per chevron*. *Per chevron argent and gules in chief two lions rampant and in base a boar passant all counterchanged* are the arms of Cassidy (IF: 212).

If the two lines of division of per chevron reach the top edge of the shield so that the field is divided into three rather than two, it is said to be *per pile reversed*. If the lines are curved, the field is said to be *per pile arched reversed* or the expression *mantelé* can be used. Division of this sort was not found in Irish heraldry in the past, but in recent years arms have been granted displaying per pile arched reversed, for example in the arms granted to Bundoran Urban District Council in June, 1983: *Per pile arched reversed vert and barry wavy of six argent and azure in the dexter a Latin cross of the second charged with an open book Or and in the sinister an ancient Irish pillar stone proper.*

If per pile reversed is the other way so that the point touches the bottom edge of the shield, the field is described simply as *per pile*. A good example can be seen in the arms of Newcastle West, County Limerick: *Per pile Or and argent in chief a boar's head erased sable and in fess two torteaux one dexter and one sinister.*

The arms of County Offaly (granted 1983) show a threefold division known as *tierced in fess*: *Tierced in fess vert argent and Or a lion rampant holding between the paws a cross patty concave all of the last, the cross within an annulet of the second on a point pointed in base sable a sprig of* Andromeda polifolia *proper.*

06.02: Fields per saltire and quarterly

There are two divisions of the field that divide it into four parts. When the division in the shape of St Andrew's cross (or *saltire*), it is said to be *party per saltire* or *per saltire*. Papworth cites the arms of Stephenson, Earl of Cork (1465), for example: *Per saltire argent and gules* (PO: 1056). The arms of Gorey, County Wexford (granted in 1613) are a good example of a field divided per saltire: *Per saltire argent gules Or and azure in chief a cross of the second in base a swan with an eel in her mouth both argent in dexter fess a lion passant guardant Or and in sinister fess a rose gules the seeds proper the sepals vert.* Notice that in that blazon one works from chief to base and then from dexter fess to sinister.

If the field is divided into quarters along the lines of an ordinary cross, it is said to be quarterly. An example of a quarterly coat can be seen in the arms of Tuite, Sonna, County Westmeath: *Quarterly argent and gules* (K: 10; BGA: 1036).

06.03: Varied fields

A varied field is one which is divided by several lines going in the same direction. As will be understood later, the stripes in the varied field must be of an even number and more often than not there are six of them.

If the field is divided vertically into six stripes of alternate metal and colour, it is said to be *paly of six*. See, for example, the arms of Murray, the Earl of Atholl in Scotland: *Paly of six Or and sable*. If there are eight stripes, the shield is said to be paly of eight, for example in the arms of Tallant: *Paly of eight Or and sable on a canton argent a griffin segreant gules* (K: 103; BGA: 996).

If the stripes are horizontal, the field is said to be *barry*. *Barry of six* is common, for example in the arms of Barry, Lord Santry (†1751): *Barry of six argent and gules* (BGA: 54). *Barry of eight* is also found, for example in the arms of Poyntz, Acton, County Armagh: *Barry of eight gules and Or* (BGA: 821).

Not infrequently the lines of barry are wavy rather than straight. This division is known as barry wavy and when argent and azure is often used heraldically to suggest water. The arms of Loughrea, for example are: *Barry wavy of eight azure and argent a cross gules debruised by a lymphad Or the sails furled and the oars being plied*.

If the lines of division are diagonal from left to right, the field is said to be bendy. Bendy of six is the commonest form of this division, for example in the arms of Tongue (Dublin): *Bendy of six argent and sable as a difference a mullet gules* (PO: 291).

06.04: Varied fields combined

Two different variations of the field can be combined to form interesting patterns. When paly and barry are combined, one gets *chequy*, that is to say a pattern of small squares of alternation tinctures. Kennedy gives the arms of Mooney as: *Chequy Or and azure* (K: 110). The arms of the town of Kinsale, County Cork are *Chequy argent and sable*.

If a charge bears only one line of alternating squares, it is said to be *compony*. If there are two such lines, it is *counter-compony*. The arms of Doyle give an example of counter-compony: *Argent three stags heads couped gules the antlers Or within a bordure counter-compony of the third and azure* (IF: 214).

When *bendy* is combined with *bendy sinister*, that is bendy from dexter base to sinister chief, the resulting pattern is known as *lozengy*. *Lozengy argent and gules*, for example, are the arms of the Grimaldi, princes of Monaco.

When *quarterly* and *per saltire* are combined, the resulting pattern is known as *gyronny of eight*. This can be seen, for example, in the arms of Crotty: *Gyronny of eight Or and vert* (BGA: 248). Perhaps arms best known in Ireland containing

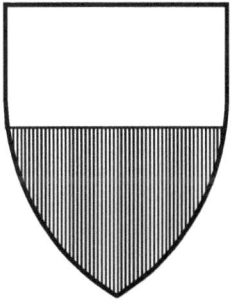

Per fess

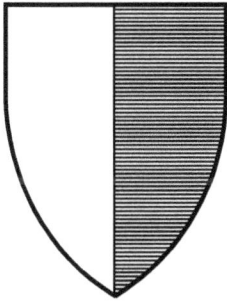

Per pale

Per bend

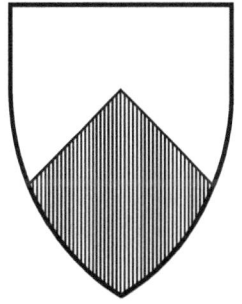

Per chevron

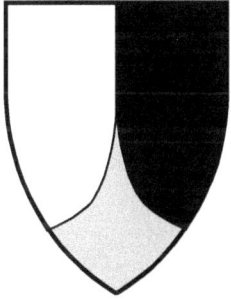

Tierced in mantle

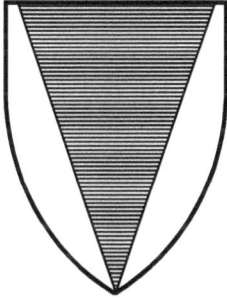

Per pile

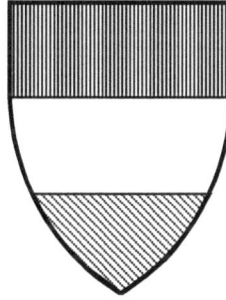

Tierced in fess

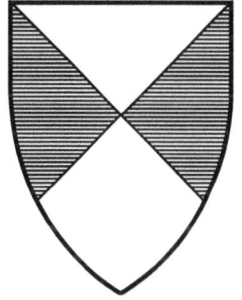

Per saltire

Per cross, Quarterly

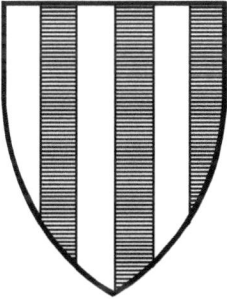

Paly of six

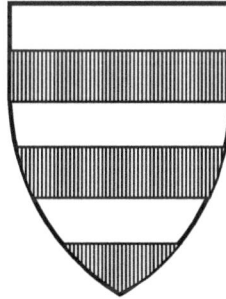

Barry of six

Bendy of six

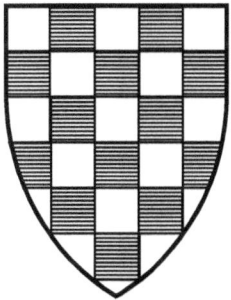

Checky

Lozengy

Gyronny of eight

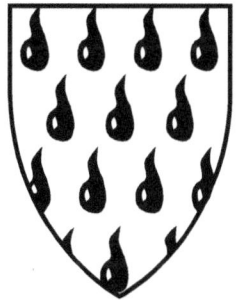

Goutté de poix

Party Fields, Varied Fields, and Powdered Fields

Figure 3

gyronny of eight are those of the Dominican Order: *Gyronny of eight argent and sable a cross flory counterchanged.*

06.05: A field semé

On occasion a pattern is formed by placing upon a field many small identical charges. The field is then said to be *semé*.

When a field is semé with particular charges a specific term is used. If a field is covered with fleurs-de-lis, for example, it is said to be *flory*. When the field is covered with crosses croslet, the field is described as *crusilly*. A good example is found in the arms of Darcy: *Azure crusilly argent three cinquefoils of the same.* A *roundel* is a disc, and a roundel Or is known as a *bezant*. When a field is semé of bezants, it is described as *bezanty*. When a field is semé of drops or *gouttes* it is described as *goutté* or *gutty*. It is customary, however, to use a different word to describe the tincture of the gouttes:

semé of gouttes argent:	goutté d'eau
semé of gouttes Or:	goutté d'or
semé of gouttes gules:	goutté de sang
semé of gouttes azure:	goutté de larmes
semé of gouttes vert:	goutté d'huile
semé of gouttes sable:	goutté de poix.

An example of goutté de poix can be seen in the arms of Higgins: *Argent goutté de poix on a fess sable three towers of the field* (IF: 216). If the gouttes are purpure, there is no specific term and one must blazon simply as *goutté purpure*.

06.06: Diaper

The decoration known as *diaper* is quite different from the patterns made when the field is varied or semé. Diaper is simply a method used to ornament a plain area of a field. Very frequently the tinctures used in diaper are simply different shades of the same tincture. Diaper can also appear in relief and figures may be added to the diaper, provided they are not heraldic charges. Diaper need not follow the tincture rule.

07.00: The ordinaries

The simple wide stripes, some of which give their names to the varied fields, are ordinaries. It is likely that they have their origin in the strong strips of wood placed across the shield to strengthen it. It is perhaps significant that arms that contain only one of the ordinaries are likely to belong to the beginnings of heraldry.

07.01: The chief, the fess and the base

The *chief* is a wide strip across the top of the shield whose upper edge is along the upper edge of the shield. *Argent a chief vert* are the arms ascribed to Meyler, County Wexford (BGA: 682). The arms of Hogan are: *Sable on a chief Or three annulets of the field* (IF: 216). From the chief derives the phrase *in chief* (see above), meaning in the upper third of the shield.

The *fess* is a broad stripe across the middle of the shield. The fess gives rise to the expression *in fess*, to which reference has already been made. The arms ascribed to de la Mazière, County Cork are *Gules a fess ermine* (BGA: 674). The arms of Jordan are *Argent a fess sable and in base a lion passant of the same* (IF: 216).

When it appears on a shield singly the ordinary is known as a fess. When more than one appear together they are known as *bars*. Two bars can be seen in the arms of Gilfoyle: *Azure two bars argent*. A fess or bar couped at both ends in known as a *humet*.

Two narrow bars occurring together are known as a *bar gemel*. The arms of Barry are *Argent three bars gemel gules*. These are canting arms. When severel bars occur together, they are known as *barrulets*.

The *base* or *terrasse* is formed by drawing a horizontal line across the lower part of the shield to form a section in a different tincture from the field. The base is becoming commoner in Irish heraldry than formerly, for example in the arms of Shannon (§16.05) and of Greystones, County Wicklow, in which latter it occurs together with two chevronels: *Per chevron argent and azure two chevronels vert between in chief as many oak branches fructed proper and in base a fish naiant of the first a terrasse of rocks also proper*.

07.02: The pale

The *pale* is a wide horizontal band from the top edge of the shield to the bottom: *Argent a pale sable* are the arms of Erskine of Scotland, for instance (BGA: 329). When there is more than one pale it is narrower than the single charge and is referred to by the term *pallet*. *Sable two pallets argent a chief Or* are the arms of Maginn (BGA: 649).

07.03: The bend and the bend sinister

The *bend* is a broad stripe from the the dexter chief to the sinister base. See, for example, the arms of Duvall: *Argent a bend gules* (K: 65) and the arms of Folliott of County Sligo: *Gules a bend argent* (K: 6).

If there are two or more bends upon a shield they are thinner than the single bend and are known as *bendlets*. See, for example the arms of Bradshaw: *Gules two bendlets Or* (K: 131).

If the bend goes from the dexter base to the sinister chief, it is a *bend sinister*. The bend sinister is not common in Irish or British heraldry, because it was erroneously believed to be a sign of illegitimacy. It is common in continental European heraldry, however.

07.04: The chevron

The *chevron* goes from one side up to the honour point and down again to the other side. If follows the line of *party per saltire*, therefore. The arms of Lecky, County Derry are a good example: *Azure a chevron Or between three mullets of the same* (K: 61).

When more than one chevron appears on the shield, each of them is thinner than the chevron by itself, and they are known as chevronnels. See, for example, the arms of Greystones (§07.01). Another example can be seen in the arms of Richard de Clare or Strongbow (†1176): *Or three chevronnels gules* (HHB: 36).

> NOTE: The so-called tomb of Strongbow in Christ Church Cathedral, Dublin, is not that of Richard de Clare, as is clear from the escutcheon of the figure on it: ... *a chief... three crosses patonce/botonny fitchy...* The knight would seem to be a FitzOsbert. The original tomb of Strongbow was destroyed when the south wall of the cathedral collapsed in 1562.

07.05: The cross and the saltire

Without doubt the *cross* is the commonest ordinary in heraldry. The most frequently occurring cross consists in two stripes, one vertical and one horizontal. There are many further varieties of cross, however, and it is therefore necessary to devote a whole chapter to them (09).

If a bend and a bend sinister are displayed together, they form a *saltire*. The most obvious example in Irish heraldry is that of the arms of Fitzgerald: *Argent a saltire gules* (§§23.01, 24.02).

Chief	Fess	Bars gemel	Base
Bend	Bend sinister	Chevron	Pile
Pile reversed	Pall	Shakefork	Saltire
Pale	Pale cortised	Pale double cortised	Pale fimbriated

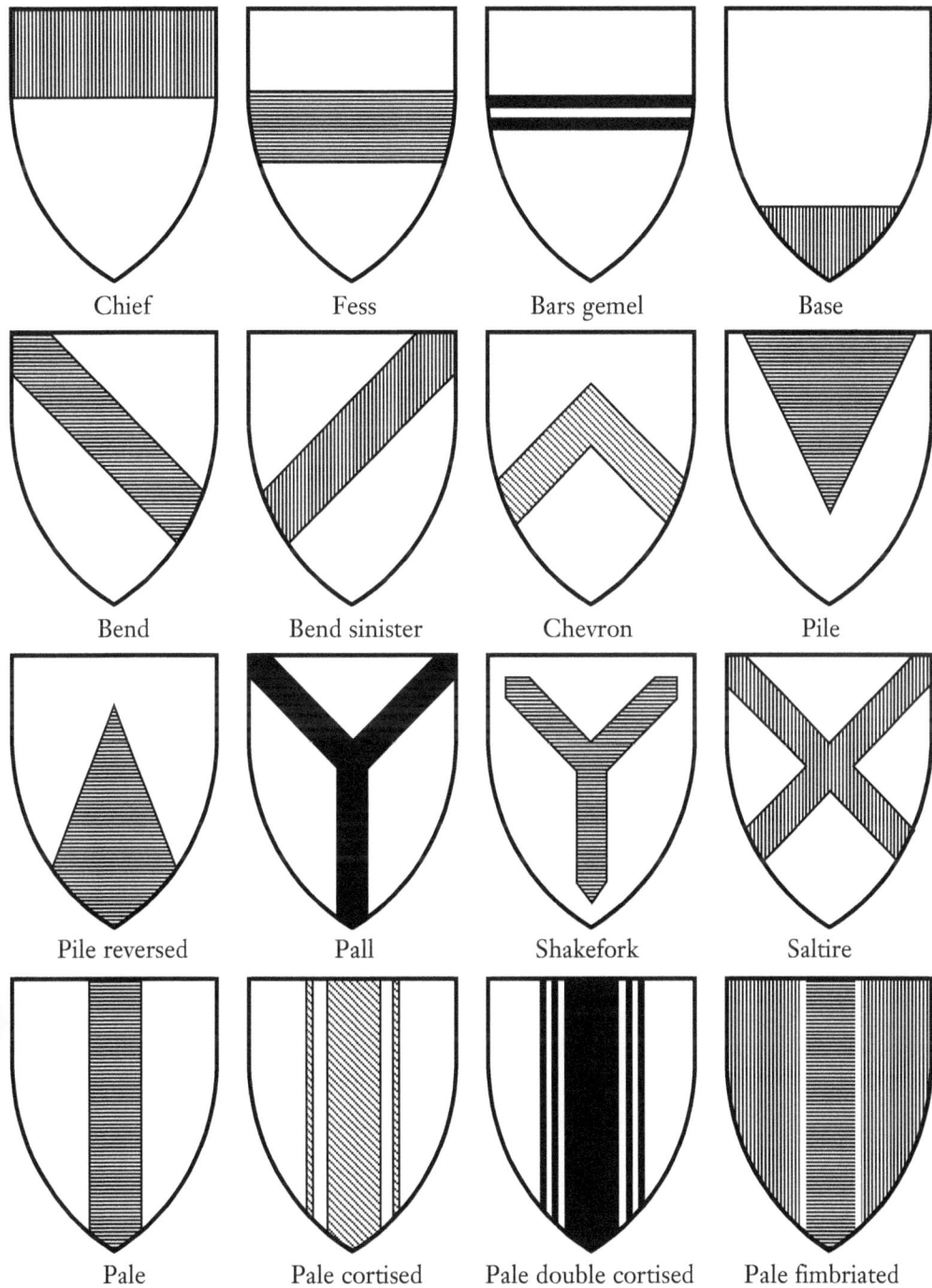

The Ordinaries

Figure 4

07.06: The pile and the pall or pairle

The *pile* is a rather unusual ordinary. As a rule it goes from top to bottom and its sharp end reaches the nombril point. On occasion it appears the other way round, with the apex in the honour point. This latter is blazoned a *pile reversed*. On other occasions the pile issues from the the dexter or sinister base or from the dexter or sinister side of the shield. There are sometimes more than one pile on a shield. Three piles issuing from the sinister base appear in the arms of Shannon Town (§16.05).

The *pall* or *pairle* is a charge which covers the shield in the shape of a letter Y. A good example can be seen in the arms of Nigeria: *Sable a pall wavy argent*. The pall wavy is a heraldic representation of the Niger and the Benue, the two principal rivers of the country.

Although the *pall* derives ultimately from the ecclesiastical garment known as the pall or *pallium*, this latter must be distinguished from the heraldic pall. The ecclesiastical *pallium* can be seen in the arms of the Archbishops of Armagh and of Dublin (§27.04). The ecclesiastical pall has edging and fringe on the lower arm; it does not reach the edge of the shield in base.

On occasion the pall appears in a form in which no limb reaches the edge of the shield and each limb ends in a point (§08). This is known as a shakefork and is seen in the arms of Cunningham of Scotland: *Argent a shakefork sable*.

07.07: Ordinaries vs varied field.

When three examples of the same ordinary appear on a shield, the field must be shown between them and on both sides. If the field does not appear on either side, the shield will a varied field. Take for example the arms: *Argent three pallets azure*. There are three pallets on the shield and four spaces, two between the pallets and two on the sides, that is to say seven separate stripes. If the tincture of the field is not visible either on the far left or right, only six stripes appear, and the shield is *paly of six*.

07.08: Ordinaries cotised

Not infrequently on a shield one sees a narrow version of an ordinary running alongside the ordinary on both sides without touching it any point. In this case the ordinary is said to be *cotised*. The cotises are usually about a quarter of the width of the ordinary itself. The *cotise* when used as a charge by itself is a narrow bar, about a quarter of the width of the fess.

The arms of Rowley, Baron Langford, Summerhill, County Meath, are *Argent on a bend cotised sable three crescents Or* (BP: 1007). The arms granted to the Ulster Bank in 1957 are: *Gules on a cross argent cotised Or a right hand couped at the*

In pale

In fess

In bend

In bend sinister

In cross

In saltire

In orle

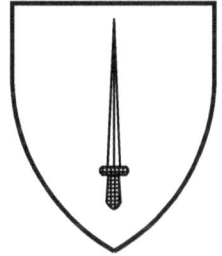

Palewise the point upwards

Palewise the point downwards

Fesswise the point sinister

Bendwise

Bend sinisterwise

In saltire

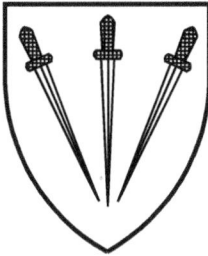

In pile

Fesswise in pale

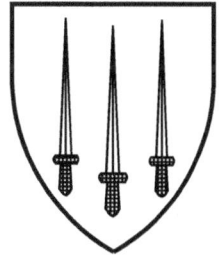

Palewise in fess

Heraldic Orientation

Figure 5

wrist of the field. The cotises in the arms of Oadby are decorated with fleurs-de-lis (§18.04b).

When the ordinary is cotised twice on both sides, it is said to be *double cotised.*

Cotises can be used on either side of charges lying in the direction of an ordinary. The arms of Whelan, for example are: *Argent four lozenges conjoined in bend azure cotised of the same on a chief gules three fleurs-de-lis of the field* (IF: 218).

07.09: Fimbriation

Since colour may not stand on colour nor metal on metal, if a charge of a certain colour is placed on a colour it must be given an outline of a metal in order to prevent the colours touching each other. The same is true when metal is placed on metal. When a charge receives a narrow outline of this sort, it is said to be *fimbriated.* Fimbriation is common with the cross, but it occurs with other charges as well. A good example is seen in the arms of Balbriggan: *Vert on a pale gules fimbriated Or between in the dexter a spindle and in the sinister a fish head to base argent in chief two industrial pipes in saltire proper and in base a water-wheel gold.*

Fimbriated lozenges can be seen in the arms of Killarney: *Purpure three lozenges conjoined in bend sinister azure fimbriated Or in dexter chief a stag springing to sinister and in sinister base two quills crossed in saltire all Or.* The arms of County Meath are per pile arched and fimbriated (§24.05).

07.10: Orientation of charges in groups

When two or more charges appear on a shield, they are not infrequently placed in the position of an ordinary. In such cases it is sufficient to blazon them as *in pale, in fess, in bend*, etc.

Assume that there are three mullets on the field. Unless otherwise stated, two will appear above and one below. Instead of that, however, they could be placed one above the other, that is, one in the chief point, one in the fess point and one in the base point. In which case they are said to be *in pale*. If they appear side by side, they are said to be *in fess*. If one of the mullets is in the dexter chief, one in the sinister base and the third in the fess point, they form a bend and are said to be *in bend*. The lozenges in the arms of Killarney mentioned above (§07.09) are *in bend sinister*.

If there were five mullets on the field, one could be at the fess point, one at the chief point, one in at the base point and to in the area of the fess to dexter and to sinister. In this case they form a cross, and naturally enough they are said to be *in cross*. One need only place two of them in the dexter and the sinister chief respectively, and another two in the dexter and sinister base, while leaving the fifth mullet in the fess point to create a saltire of mullets. In which case the mullets are said to be *in saltire*. The expression *in saltire* is also useful when describing long charges. One can say of two swords, two pastoral staffs, two arrows, etc., that they are *crossed in saltire*.

When a number of charges are places round the edge of the shield without any of them touching the edge, they are said to be *in orle*. The *orle* is a sub-ordinary which will be discussed below (§10.01).

If there are three swords on a field, with their hilts upwards and their tips in the nombril point, they resemble a pile and are said to be *in pile*. Further long charges can be in pile also.

07.11: Orientation of single charges

When a charge is placed upon an ordinary, unless otherwise stated, the charge is in an upright or vertical position. The bend and the bend sinister, however, are exceptions. If any charge is placed on either, it follows the line of the bend or bend sinister. If a charge upon a bend or bend sinister is upright, that must be mentioned in the blazon.

It does not matter on which edge either annulets or mullets are placed, because their shape remains the same. A long charge, however, a sword or arrow, for example, can either be placed erect, flat or even diagonally. In such cases the suffix *-wise* is used after the name of the ordinary to specify the orientation of the charge. If a sword is erect, for example, one says that it is *palewise*, if it lies flat, it is *fesswise* or *barwise*. If the charge lies diagonally across the shield, it is said to be *bendwise* or *bend-sinisterwise*.

The arms of MacLysaght are blazoned as follows: *Argent three spears erect in fess gules on a chief azure a lion passant guardant Or* (IF: 217).

08.00: Ornamental lines

Up till now the lines we have mentioned have all been plain except the pall or pairle (§07.06). For variety's sake heraldry takes advantage of a number of more ornate lines. The various kinds can be seen in Fig. 5.

The only difference between *indented* and *dancetty* is the number of indentations. There are only three with dancetty, whereas the line indented contains a row of teeth. A line indented can be seen in the arms of O'Shea, for example: *Per bend indented azure and Or two fleurs-de-lis counterchanged* (IF: 219). Lines dancetty can be seen in the arms of Morris of Galway: *Or a fess dancetty and in base a lion rampant of the same* (IF: 218 and §26.08).

The difference between engrailed and invected is that the curves in the line engrailed are concave, whereas in the line invected they are convex. Engrailed lines can be seen in the arms of O'Connolly of Kildare: *Argent on a saltire engrailed sable five escallops of the field* (BGA: 221). Lines invected can be seen in the arms of McDonagh of Connacht: *Per saltire invected Or and vert in chief two lions passant guardant gules in base a boar passant argent tusked, crined and unguled of the first langued of the third* (IF: 214).

Wavy lines appear in the arms of Clements, Earl of Leitrim: *Argent two bendlets wavy sable on a chief gules three bezants* (PO: 286; K: 88).

The arms of Boyle, Earl of Cork, display a line embattled: *Per bend embattled argent and gules* (BGA: 111; K: 86). The arms of Anketill, County Monaghan are: *Argent a saltire raguly vert* (BG: 17). Lines rayonny can be seen in the arms of O'Hara, Baron Tirawley: *Vert on a pale rayonny a lion rampant sable* (IF: 216; K: 29).

Donal Begley, Chief Herald of Ireland 1981–95, has an interesting coat of arms: *Azure a fess urdy and rayonny in base Or*. The fess suggest a row of little soldiers cut from a strip of paper, and is thus a reference to the armiger's surname, *Begley* < *Ó Beaglaoich* 'descendant of a little soldier'.

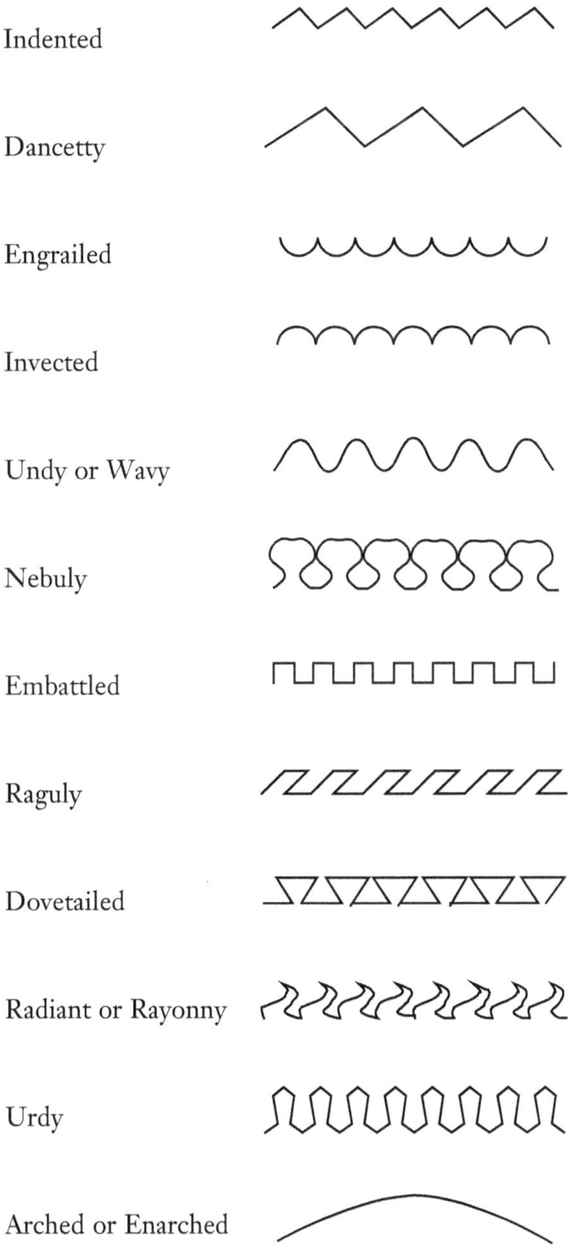

Indented

Dancetty

Engrailed

Invected

Undy or Wavy

Nebuly

Embattled

Raguly

Dovetailed

Radiant or Rayonny

Urdy

Arched or Enarched

Ornamental Lines

Figure 6

09.00: The cross

> *Amhuil iomorro agus iomchras na saighdiúireadha bratach nó armas an phrionnsa faoi a mbíd ag cogadh, mar an gcédna as cóir don mhuinntir ghlacas an tsácramuint si armas agus bratach Chríost .i. an chroch naomhtha ré a rug buaidh a gcruadhchomhrac na páisi, d'iomchar agus dul síos go dána agus cathughadh go feardha feadhmláidir an aghaidh a námhad* 'As indeed soldiers carry the banner or the arms of the prince under whom they fight, so it is right for those who receive this sacrament, to bear the arms and banner of Christ, i.e., the holy cross by which he was victorious in the fierce battle of the passion, to go down and do battle in manly and effective fashion against the enemy' (*Buaidh na Naomhchroiche* ('Victory of the Holy Cross') 5735-40).

Heraldry arose in the Christian west one generation after the First Crusade. The cross is the symbol of Christendom. Not astonishingly therefore the cross in all its different manifestations is the commonest inanimate charge to be seen in coats of arms. It has been suggested that there are altogether more than 300 different variations of the cross.

09.01: The simple cross

> *Do deachaidh aon do na bráthrib rompa acus do thaisealbh dóibh airm a mbuí in sciath ar cúl na haltóire móire acus foruaradar in sciath glégeal go gcrois deirg isin dú sin* 'One of the friars led them to the place where the shield was behind the high altar and they found a bright white shield with a red cross in that place' (*The Lorgaireacht an tSoidhigh Naomhtha* 'Quest for the Holy Grail' 553-55).

The word *cross* without qualification is to be understood as a simple fess and pale combined. The arms of Walter Burke, Earl of Ulster (†1271), for example were: *Or a cross gules* (§§23.02, 24.06). The outline of the cross can have an decorated edge, for example in the arms of Warner High Sheriff of Dublin (1813): *Ermine on a cross engrailed Or five mullets vert* (K: 10).

If the limbs of the cross are shortened so as not to reach the edges of the shield, the resulting figure is known as a *cross couped*. *Gules a cross couped argent* are the arms of the Swiss Federation, upon which was based the symbol of the International Red Cross, *a cross couped gules*.

Cross

Cross couped

Latin cross

Calvary cross

Patriarchal cross

Cross potent

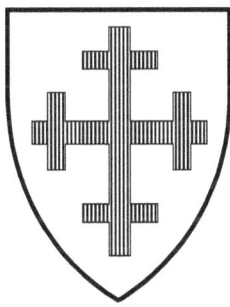

Cross crosslet

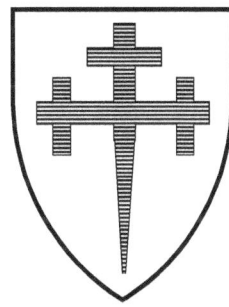

Cross crosslet fitchy ι

Cross patty

Maltese cross

Tau cross

Cross flory

Cross patonce

Cross botonny

Cross moline

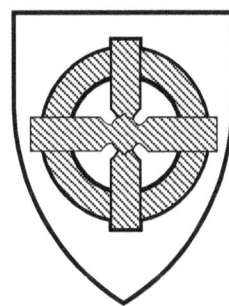

Celtic cross

The Cross

Figure 7

IRISH HERALDRY

09.02: The Latin cross, the Calvary cross and the patriarchal cross

The Latin cross has a long lower limb, for example in the arms of O'Donnell: *Or issuing from the sinister side an arm fesswise vested azure cuffed argent holding in the hand proper a Latin cross gules* (IF: 213).

If a Latin cross is placed upon steps, it is known as a *Calvary cross*. It is necessary in the blazon to specify how many steps or grieces there are, three being the usual number, for example in the arms of Martin of Dangan, County Galway: *Azure a Calvary cross of three grieces argent at the end of the dexter arm a sun in splendour Or at the end of the sinister arm a crescent decrescent of the second* (IF: 217).

If the cross has two horizontal limbs rather than one, it is known as a *patriarchal cross*. The cross of Lorraine, the symbol of the Free French during the Second World War, was a patriarchal cross. A good Irish example can be seen in the arms of Vesey, Viscount de Vesci of Abbey Leix: *Or on a cross sable a patriarchal cross of the field* (BP: 518).

09.03: The cross potent, the cross patty and the cross crosslet

If at the end of every limb of a cross couped there is a crosspiece, the figure is known as a *cross potent*. The arms of the Crusader Kingdom of Jerusalem are perhaps the most notable example (§05.06). Compare also the arms of Cross of Darton, County Armagh: *Quarterly gules and Or in the first and fourth quarters a cross potent of the the second* (BGA: 248).

If each limb of a cross couped is widens out from the centre of the cross, the result is a *cross patty*. The cross patty was the symbol of the Knights Templar. Some of the lands of Cork cathedral belonged at one time to the Knights Templar. The arms of the diocese of Cork therefore contain a cross patty: *Argent on a cross patty gules a crozier palewise enfiled with a mitre labelled Or* (EH: 212). The cross patty occurs in other contexts as well, for example, in the arms of O'Hannon: *Quarterly gules and Or on a bend sable three crosses patty argent* (IF: 215).

If each limb of the cross couped itself is crossed by a transverse piece the cross is called a *cross crosslet*. The arms of Wall are a good example: *Azure a lion rampant between three crosses crosslet all Or* (IF: 220).

If the lower limb of any cross couped ends in a point, it is said to be *fitchy*. A cross crosslet fitchy can be seen, for example in the arms of Concannon: *Argent in base a mount proper and arising therefrom an oak tree vert on its summit a hawk also proper between two crosses crosslet fitchy in fess azure* (IF: 212; K: 80).

THE CROSS

09.04: The Maltese cross and the Tau cross

If each limb of the cross patty ends in two points, the figure is known as a *Maltese cross* or a *cross of eight points*. The Maltese cross is the symbol of the Military Order of Malta (§31.04). It not infrequently appears in heraldry in that context.

If each of the three lower limbs of a cross couped are widened slightly but the upper limb is wholly missing, the figure is know as a *Tau cross* or *cross of St Antony*. An example can be seen in the arms of Drury: *Argent on a chief vert a Tau cross between two mullets Or* (K: 98).

09.05: The cross flory, the cross patonce, the cross botonny and the cross moline

If each limb of the cross ends in a fleur-de-lis it is a *cross flory*, for example in the arms of the Dominican Order (§06.04).

When the ends of each limb are splayed into three, the cross is called *patonce*. Five crosses patonce can be seen in the arms of Castlebar, County Mayo (§10.03).

If each limb of the cross ends in a trefoil it is known as a *cross botonny*. An example of a cross botonny can be seen in the arms of Kilrush, County Clare (§10.07). In the early days of heraldry a cross botonny and cross crosslet were not always distinguished (§07.04).

Another variety of cross is similar to the cross flory, but the middle point of the fleur-de-lis is missing. This is known as a *cross moline*. It takes its name from the *fer de moline*, the piece of iron attached to a millstone to provide a socket for the drive shaft. A square in the middle of a cross may be removed, in which case thre cross is described as *quarter-pierced*. An example can be seen in the arms of Daniel Molyneux, Ulster King of Arms (†1632): *Azure a cross moline Or quarter-pierced of the field in the dexter chief a fleur-de-lis of the second* (BGA: 694). That is a canting coat, punning on the name *Molyneux*.

09.06: The Celtic cross

Not astonishingly the *Celtic cross* or *wheeled cross* is common in Irish heraldry, particularly in Irish corporate heraldry. In the blazon it is always necessary to specify whether the cross is by itself or supported by a pillar. A Celtic cross without a supporting pillar can be seen in the arms of County Meath (§24.05).

09.07: Charges in the form of a cross

Various charges can be placed to form a cross. A good example of a cross with two transverse limbs can be seen in the arms of Kells (Ceanannus Mór), County Meath: (§05.03).

10.00: The subordinaries

Subordinaries are basic charges similar to but less in size than the ordinaries.

10.01: The bordure, the orle and the tressure

> *Sciath ildhealbhach bhocóideach bháindearg ar stuaidhleirg a dhroma agus líntídhe do litreachaibh órdha in imeallbhordaibh na ríghscéithe sin* 'A variegated convex shield of pink over his back and lines of golden letters on the bordure of that noble escutcheon' (*Eachtra an Mhadra Mhaoil* 68-70).

The bordure is a narrow edging that goes round the shield without any space between it and the rim of the shield. See, for example the arms of O'Flanagan: *Argent from a mount in base vert an oak tree issuing proper all within a bordure of the second* (IF: 214). The bordure may be charged with further items, for example in the arms of O'Mara: *Gules three lions passant guardant in pale each per pale Or and argent within a bordure azure charged with eight scallops of the third* (IF: 217). The bordure may also be compony or counter-compony, as for example, in the arms of Doyle (§06.04).

There is another variety of edge which goes circles the shield leaving a space between it and the rim. This is known as an *orle*. An example can be seen in the arms of O'Quigley: *Gules an orle argent over all a bend erminois* (IF: 219)

The arms of Brownlow, Lord Lurgan, can be blazoned as follows: *Per pale Or and argent a inescutcheon sable within an orle of eight martlets of the same* (BGA: 136; K: 88). These arms might possibly be blazoned: *Sable on a bordure per pale Or and argent eight martlets of the field*.

The *tressure* is a narrower variety of orle. It usually appears double and decorated with fleurs-de-lis whose heads point alternately inwards and outwards. In such cases the charge is known as a *double tressure flory counterflory*. The double tressure of this kind is a distinctive feature of Scottish heraldry.

The bordure, orle and tressure have one characteristic in common. When they occur on a field which shares the shield with another per pale, only half of the subordinary is drawn, that is to say that the bordure (or orle or tressure) stops at the line of division.

10.02: The inescutcheon

When a small shield is placed in the middle of the shield, it leaves a space between itself and the edge of the shield. Usually the space in question is wider than a bordure. An example of the inescutcheon has already been noted in the arms of Brownlow above (§10.01). An inescutcheon also appeared in the arms of Viscount Molesworth of County Dublin: *Gules an inescutcheon vair within an orle of eight crosses crosslet Or* (BP: 1212).

Bordure

Orle

Double tressure flory
counterflory

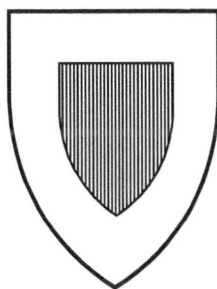

Inescutcheon

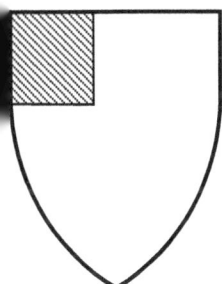

Canton

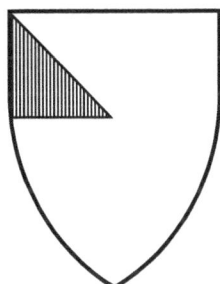

Gyron

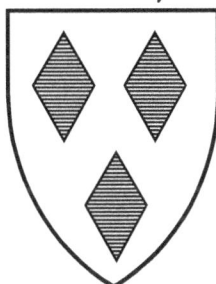

Lozenges

Mascles

Rustres

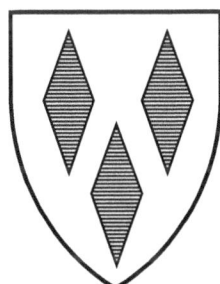

Fusil

Fret

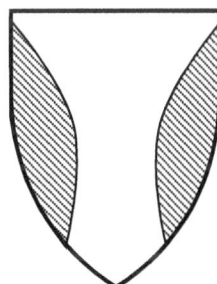

Flanches

Billet

Label

Roundels and
annulets

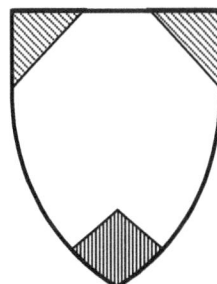

Point dexter, point
sinister, point in base

The Subordinaries

Figure 8

Perhaps the best known example of the inescutcheon in Irish heraldry is in the coat of arms of the province of Ulster (§24. 06).

10.03: The canton

The canton is a square in the dexter chief. It is smaller in size than a quarter of the shield divided quarterly. A canton may be seen in the arms of Crowe: *Argent on a mount vert an oak tree fructed proper a canton gules charged with an antique Irish crown Or* (IF: 214). A canton is also seen in the arms of O'Hagan (§17.03) and in the arms of the town of Castlebar: *Gules a saltire argent charged with five crosses patonce vert between in chief a castle and in fess two yew trees all proper on a canton Or two pikes in saltire gules.* The edge of the canton is rarely ornamented.

10.04: The gyron

If the dexter chief quarter of a shield divided quarterly is itself divided diagonally, that is, per bend, the result is a gyron. A single gyron is rare in heraldry, although a *gyron* dexter and a *gyron sinister* occur in the arms of Mortimer (§22.00), which was once used by the city of Galway (§25.04) and by Drogheda (§25.13).

10.05: The lozenge, the mascle, the rustre and the fusil

The diamond-shaped subordinary is known as the *lozenge*. This is the origin of the varied field known as *lozengy.* (§06.04). The lozenge is rarely found singly. There are three lozenges in the arms of O'Broder (§05.04). Four lozenges form a cross in the arms of Peacocke of County Clare (§09.07).

The lozenge is sometimes shown voided, that is, with the middle hollowed out, in which case it is known as a *mascle.* A good example is seen in the arms of Carden, Templemore, County Tipperary: *Argent a mascle gules between three pheons sable* (BGA: 167).

When the lozenge is pierced with a circular hole, it is known as a *rustre.* The Perys of Ireland bear *Or three rustres sable* (THBF: 185).

A narrower variety of the lozenge is known as the fusil; it occurs in the arms of MacCostello: *Or three fusils azure* (IF: 213).

10.06: The fret

If a bendlet, bendlet sinister and mascle are interwoven, the resulting figure is known as a *fret.* The arms of Blake is perhaps the best-known Irish example: *Argent a fret gules* (IF: 211).

A whole field or charge can be covered with a fret-like pattern, which is described as *fretty.* An example can be seen in the arms of Taafe: *Gules a cross fretty azure* (IF: 219; K: 88).

THE SUBORDINARIES

10.07: The flaunch

Curved sections on either side of the shield are known as *flaunches*. Flaunches usually come in pairs. The edge of the flaunch is not decorated as a rule, though they are sometimes fimbriated. A good example are the arms of Kilrush, County Clare, which were granted in 1982: *Azure two flaunches fimbriated argent in the dexter a cross botonny and in the sinister an annulet rayonne Or in base an anchor with cable palewise of the third.*

10.08: The billet

The billet is a rectangular charge that resembles a block of wood. A very good example can be seen in the arms granted to the Garda College, Templemore, County Tipperary in 1982: *Argent two bars gules the upper charged with three lozenges the lower with as many billets Or in chief a dexter hand erect couped at the wrist holding a scroll fesswise all proper.*

The field can be semé of billets, in which case it is called *billety*. The royal arms of the Netherlands are a good example: *Azure billetty a lion with a coronet Or armed and langued gules holding in his dexter paw a sword argent hilted of the second and in the sinister paw seven arrows of the fourth pointed and bound together Or.*

10.09: The label

The label is a cotise in chief with three or five points hanging from it. The label is used as a difference for the oldest son (§23.05).

10.10: The roundel

The *roundel* is a disc. Roundels of various tinctures have their own names as follows:

roundel argent	plate
roundel Or	bezant
roundel gules	torteau
roundel azure	hurt
roundel vert	pomeis
roundel sable	pellet
roundel purpure	guze
roundel tenné	orange
roundel barry wavy argent and azure	fountain.

Here are some examples in Irish heraldry:

Plates can be seen in the arms of Purcell of County Limerick: *Argent a boar passant gules tusked, unguled and crined Or langued azure on a chief of the last three plates* (BGA: 829).

Bezants appear in the arms of Creagh: *Argent a chevron gules between three sprigs of laurel vert on a chief azure as many bezants* (IF: 213).

Torteaux appear in the arms of Devereux of County Wexford: *Ermine a fess gules in chief three torteaux* (BGA: 282); and in the arms of Newcastle West (§06.01).

Three **hurts** can be seen in the arms of Staples: *Argent on a fess sable between three hurts two in chief and one in base three dragon's heads erased Or* (K: 49).

Pellets can be seen in the arms of Oliver: *Or a chevron sable between in chief two pellets and in base a salmon naiant gules* (K: 8).

10.11: The annulet.

When a roundel is voided it is called an *annulet*. There are numerous examples in Irish heraldry, for example in in the arms of O'Hogan: *Sable on a chief Or three annulets of the field* (IF: 216); and in the arms of Mangan (§15.06).

10.12: The point in base, the dexter point and the sinister point

A small point issuing from the bottom of the shield is known as a *point in base*. There is an example in the arms of County Offaly (granted 1983): *Tierced in fess vert argent and Or a lion rampant holding between the paws a cross patty concave all of the last the cross within an annulet of the second on a point in base sable a sprig of* Andromeda polifolia *proper*. Another example can be seen in the arms of Sligo Town (granted 1953): *Per pale vert and azure on the dexter a ruined antique square tower on the sinister an oak tree eradicated proper on a point Or a hare courant attached to the hind foot thereof an escallop all of the third at the centre chief point an escallop argent.*

A triangle in the position of the canton is called a *dexter point*. On the sinister side it is known as a *sinister point*. The upper edge of the dexter point and sinister point lie flush with the top of the shield, and thus are distinct from the gyron. A dexter and sinister point appear in the arms of Arklow, County Wicklow: *Argent in base water barry wavy azure and of the first an ancient ship of one mast prow to the front proper the sail unfurled and charged with a raven the wings raised sable in chief a dexter and sinister point gules the dexter charged with a potter's wheel Or and the sinister with a salmon leaping proper.*

In those arms the two points in chief are of the same colour, which mean that the shield could have been blazoned as *party per chevron enhanced*. In French such a division is known as *chaperonné*.

11: Animals

11.00: The lion

> *I maighin Maighe Ratha*
> *i lá churtha an chruadhchatha,*
> > *gá seoladh don chuire chas*
> > *budh leomhan uile a n-armas*

'On the field of Magh Rath on the day the hard battle was faught as the curly-haired band went forth their coat of arms was a lion only'

(Niall Mac Muireadhaigh)

The lion is the heraldic animal *par excellence* and by far the commonest animal charge in heraldry. The lion was always a frequent charge in the heraldry of the English colonists in Ireland and the native Irish appear to have adopted the lion in their own coats of arms.

The lion is most frequently seen *rampant*, that is to say standing in his rear right limb holding his two forelimbs fiercely in front of him. Examples can be seen in the arms of MacMurrough: *Gules a lion rampant argent* (IF: 218) and Lacy: *Or a lion rampant purpure* (IF: 217; §24.06).

The lion is most frequently shown facing to dexter. If he is looking at the spectator, however, he is said to be *guardant*, for example in the arms of O'Lalor: *Or a lion rampant guardant gules* (IF: 217; K: 35).

Frequently in Irish heraldry two lions rampant are displayed facing each other as though they were fighting. These are described as *combatant* and a good example can be seen in the arms of O'Hynes: *Per pale indented Or and gules two lions combatant counterchanged* (IF: 216). *Combatant* is sometimes rendered *combatant rampant* but the *rampant* is redundant. On occasion the two lions appear to be holding something between them, for example in the arms of O'Carroll Ely: *Sable two lions combatant Or armed and langued gules holding between them a sword erect the point upwards proper the pommel and hilt of the second* (IF: 212; K: 30). If the claws and tongue are of a different tincture from the rest of the animal, their tincture is mentioned. If the tongue is red, however, it does not have to specified.

11.01: The lion passant

> *Agus iar ngabháil sin chuige fiafraighis de cá suaitheantas budh loinn leis ina sgéith. Agus do ráidh Séarlus gurab trí leomhain ag troid le haon ridire dob fhearr leis do dhealbhadh innte gan mhoill. Agus do rinne amhlaidh gurab uime sin do hainmnigheadh Ridire na Leomhan fair isin chuing ridireacht' agus éidighthe sin*

'And taking them to himself he asked him what bearings he would like in his shield. And Séarlas said that he should like three lions fighting with a single knight to be represented without delay. And he did thus, so that he was called the Knight of the Lions in that discipline of chivalry and raiment'

(*Eachtra Ridire na Leomhan* 'Adventures of the Knight of the Lions' 308-15)

After the lion rampant the lion passant is the second most common form of the lion. His two hind limbs and his left forelimb touch the ground but his right forelimb is raised in minatory fashion; see, for example the arms of O'Toole: *Gules a lion passant argent* (IF: 220; K: 30).

If two or three lions passant are placed one above the other, they are said to be in pale (§07.10). See, for example the arms of O'Rourke: *Or two lions passant in pale sable* (IF: 219: K: 17).

The lion passant may also be guardant, as for example, in the arms of Hickey: *Azure a lion passant guardant Or on a chief ermine a bend sable* (IF: 216: K: 23).

The lion on occasion is depicted looking backwards over his shoulder. In that case he is said to be *reguardant*. The lion passant is often also reguardant, for example in the arms of MacMahon of Thomond: *Argent three lions passant reguardant in pale gules armed and langued azure* (IF: 217; K: 10).

The lion can also be sitting or *sejant*, lying or *couchant*, standing or *statant*. None of these postures is as common as rampant or passant.

11.02: The demi-lion

Sometimes only the upper part of the lion rampant is visible. The upper section of his tail is also shown raised behind this back. In such cases the beast is described as a demi-lion, for example in the arms of Terry of County Cork: *Azure a fess argent between three crosses crosslet Or on a chief of the last a demi-lion gules* (BGA: 1003; K: 50).

11.03: The lion's head

Limbs of lions are found as heraldic charges on occasion (§18.04*b*). More common is the *lion's head*. If the head appears to have been torn off at the neck, it is described as erased. An example can be seen in the crest of Morris of Galway *A lion's head erased argent goutté de sang* (IF: 218 and §26.08). The boar's head erased (§11.07) and the stag's head erased occur fairly frequently.

11.04: The leopard

In medieval heraldry the term *leopard* not infrequently referred to the lion passant. The leopard of nature also appears in heraldry, where it can be easily

Lion rampant

Lion passant

Lion passant guardant

Demi-lion

Lion's head erased

Leopard's face

eopard's face jessant-de-lis

Lynx passant

Cat-a-mountain sejant guardant

Stag trippant

Stag at gaze

Stag's head caboshed

The Lion, etc.

Figure 9

recognized by its spots. A good example is seen in the crest of Blake: *A leopard passant proper* (IF: 211). The animal in the Blake crest is sometimes said to be a *cat-a-mountain* (§11.05)

A leopard's head is also a common charge. It appears full-face and without any neck and is blazoned as a *leopard's head caboshed*. See, for example, the arms of Parsons, Viscount and Earl of Ross (extinct 1764): *Gules three leopard's heads caboshed argent* (BGA: 778).

On occasion the leopard's head caboshed appears with a fleur-de-lis emerging from its mouth and rising from the back of the creature's head. This is known as a *leopard's head jessant de lis* and in origin is probably an ornate variety of fleur-de-lis. In earlier times the fleur-de-lis was depicted with a ball in the centre, which was decorated with an animal's head. An Irish example can be seen in the arms of King-Tenison, Earl Kingston, Boyle, County Roscommon: *Gules on a bend engrailed Or three crosses crosslet fitchy sable between two leopard's heads of the second jessant de lis azure* (BP: 982; cf. K: 83).

11.05: The lynx and the cat-a-mountain

Although the lynx belongs by rights to the cat family, in heraldry it is depicted as a wolf. It often appears *cowed*, that is with the tail between the two rear limbs. A good example can be seen in the crest of Lynch of Galway: *A lynx passant azure collared Or* (IF: 217). This crest (*lynx*) puns on the armiger's surname (*Lynch*). Lynxes are the supporters of Browne, Earl of Kenmare: *Two lynxes argent goutté de poix collared plain and chained Or* (BP: 959).

The common cat of heraldry is the wild cat, known as the *cat-a-mountain*. It is depicted as a tabby cat and is most often seen in the crest, for example in the crest of Burke: *A cat-a-mountain sejant guardant proper collared and chained Or* (IF: 211; K: 81).

A domestic cat appears in the crest of Dawson-Damer, Lord Portarlington: *A tabby cat's head affronté erased at the shoulder proper in its mouth a rat sable* (BGA: 269).

11.06: The stag

Cernunnos, the horned god, was an essential part of pagan Celtic iconography. He was often depicted as a stag. It is likely that the stag in native Irish heraldry is in some sense an echo of Cernunnos. The stag is a common charge in the arms of the Munster chiefs. In the arms of MacCarthy the stag is *trippant*, that is to say, walking: *Argent a stag trippant gules attired and unguled Or* (IF: 212). The stag is *statant* in the arms of Kinnealy of Munster: *Gules a stag statant argent*.

When the stag is stationary and looking at the spectator, he is said to be *at gaze*. An example can be seen in the arms of Robinson: *Vert on a chevron engrailed between three stags at gaze Or as many trefoils slipped of the field* (K: 20).

The leaping stag in the arms of O'Doherty is blazoned as *springing*: *Argent a stag springing gules on a chief vert three mullets of the field* (IF: 213).

When a stag is depicted running at speed, he is blazoned as *courant* or *in full course*. The arms of Clonmel, County Tipperary provide a good example: *Argent on a bridge of five arches proper resting on a base azure therein three fishes naiant two and one of the first a stag in full course of the second attired Or pursued by a greyhound springing sable langued gules*.

Stag's heads erased are displayed in the arms of Doyle (§06.04). The hind and the fawn also occur in heraldry but neither is common.

> NOTE: Although the stag in the heraldry of the native Irish probably has its origins in pagan Celtic iconography, by the 16th century the stag in the arms of MacCarthy Mor were regarded as a canting coat. W. Darrell in his manuscript Irish Gatherings (1566) ascribes Gules a hart courant to MacCarthy Mor, whom he calls *Mackhartymore, erle of Clemkerne*. *Clemkerne* appears to be a corruption of *Clancarty*. The form *Mackhartymore*, however, seems to imply that the surname had been connected with the hart or stag.

11.07: The boar

Muc Dá Thó, cé mór i meas,
níor churtha ris an láimh i gcoimh-mheas;
 armas corma an torc fa mear,
 armas troda an bhos bharrgheal

[Muc Dá Thó, though he was great in estimation, is not to be compared with this hand; his arms in a gathering is a swift boar, the arms of him of the white-tipped palm]

(Eoghan Ó Donnghaile).

The boar was an important animal for the ancient Celts and there are many references to boars, to swineherds and to pork in the Gaelic tradition. The boar is very common in the heraldry of the Gaels of both Ireland and Scotland. In Ireland, after the lion, the boar is the commonest heraldic beast. It is probable that the frequent occurrence of the boar in Gaelic heraldry is a reflection of the cultic importance of the boar in Gaelic tradition.

The boar is usually depicted passant, for example in the arms of O'Malley: *Or a boar passant gules* (IF: 217). If the tusks, hoofs and bristles of the back are of a different tincture from the rest of the animal, that must be mentioned in the blazon, for example in the arms of O'Hanly: *Vert a boar passant argent armed, hoofed and bristled Or between two arrows fesswise of the second the head of that in chief pointing to dexter that in base pointing to sinister* (IF: 215).

There are two boars in the arms of O'Sullivan Beare, one passant, the other *counter-passant* or *passant to sinister* (§18.00).

Boars are sometimes depicted combatant. See, for example, the arms of MacSweeny Doe: *Azure two boars combatant Or in chief two battle-axes crossed in saltire of the last* (BGA: 647; K: 16).

Boar's heads are very common in Irish heraldry. When the head is *erased* a jagged edge can be seen behind the beast's ears; when it is *couped*, the edge is straight and clean. Boar's heads erased are depicted in the arms of MacDermot: *Argent on a chevron gules between three boar's heads erased azure armed and langued Or as many crosses crosslet of the last* (IF: 213; K: 21). Boar's heads couped can be seen in the arms of O'Moroney: *Azure a chevron Or between three boar's heads couped argent langued gules* (IF: 218).

11.08: Miscellaneous dogs

The *greyhound* is the commonest dog in Irish heraldry. A greyhound rampant is depicted in the arms of O'Fallon: *Gules a greyhound rampant argent holding betweenthe forepaws a tilting spear point to dexter all Or* (IF: 214).

The Irish wolfhound is also found in Irish heraldry, for example as the supporters of the arms of the Ulster Bank (granted 1957): *On either side an Irish wolfhound proper collared chequy [of two rows only] Or* (CCH: 392).

In the early days of heraldry the chief hunting-dog was a large-eared variety known as the *talbot*. The breed survives in heraldry, but is not otherwise known. An example can be seen in the arms Wolsely, baronet, of Mount Wolsely, County Carlow: *Argent a talbot passant gules a crescent as difference* (K: 118). A talbot can be seen also in the canting crest of Talbot (K: 90).

11.09: The wolf and the fox

> *Agus atá suaitheantas iongantach ele fair bheós .i. sgiath deilgthi dealbh-áluinn gona horlár óir órloisgthi ina fhírmheadhón agus dealbh faolchon aigmhéile urbhadhaighe ar lár an orláir órdha sin* 'And he has another remarkable coat of arms still, namely a beautiful wrought shield with its field Or gold-burnished in its middle and the form of a fierce destructive wolf in the centre of that golden field'

> (Sir Uilliam's arms according to the author of *Eachtra Uilliam*).

The wolf is fairly common in Irish heraldry. The wolf is passant in the arms of O'Flynn: *Gules a wolf passant argent in chief three bezants* (IF: 214), but rampant in the arms of MacQuillan: *Gules a wolf rampant a chief Or* (IF: 219).

The fox is attested in Irish heraldry, in the arms of O'Donoghue for example: *Vert two foxes combatant argent on a chief of the last an eagle volant sable* (IF: 214). A fox's head is depicted in the crest of MacGarry: *A fox's head couped gules holding in its mouth a snake proper* (IF: 215).

11.10: The horse

> *Trí fiain-tuirc i bhforaois fuair,*
> *Ruire a' marcaíocht ar eich óig,*
> *León léimeach ar uaithne fód –*
> *Armas na gCrualaíoch anallód*
>
> ['Three wild boars in a chilly forest, a hero riding on a young steed, a lion springing on a green sward was the arms of the Crowleys in days gone by']
> (Pádraig Ó Crualaoi).

A horse passant is depicted in the arms of O'Halloran: *Gules a horse passant argent saddled and and bridled proper on a chief of the second three martlets azure* (IF: 215). A horse's head can be seen in the arms of Marsh of County Laois: *Gules a horse's head couped Or between in chief two trefoils and in base three fleurs-de-lis all argent* (BGA: 661; cf. K: 100). Narcissus Marsh, Church of Ireland archbishop of Dublin, bore a variant of those arms (§26.01). A horse in the rampant posture is described as *forcené*.

A winged horse is known as a *pegasus*. An example can be seen in the arms of O'Quin of Annaly: *Vert a pegasus wings elevated argent a chief Or* (IF: 219).

11.11: The antelope

The heraldic *antelope* is quite unlike the natural animal of that name. It resembles a goat but its horns are serrated and it has the hooves of a stag. It is sometimes known as an *ibex*. The heraldic antelope can be seen in the fourth quarter of the arms of McGrath: *Argent an antelope trippant sable attired Or* (IF: 215; K: 16; §22.06).

11.12: The elephant

The *elephant* is more common in Irish heraldry than one might expect. The crest of O'Concannon, for example is *An elephant sable tusked Or* (IF: 212; cf. K: 80). An elephant is the sinister supporter of Alexander, Earl of Caledon, Tyrone (BP: 285).

Elephant's heads are depicted in the arms of Saunders: *Argent a chevron sable between three elephant's heads erased of the same on a chief gules a sword erect point upwards argent hilted gules pomelled Or between two bezants* (cf. K: 121).

11.13: The monkey

A monkey can be seen in the crest of Fitzgerald, Duke of Leinster: *A monkey statant proper environed around the middle with a plain collar and chained Or* (BP: 1043).

There is an interesting tale attached to the monkey. It is said that when John, son of Thomas Fitzgerald, first Earl of Kildare (†1316) was a baby, a fire broke out in Woodstock Castle, near Athy, County Kildare. In the confusion he was forgotten and when the servants returning to his chamber to fetch him, found the place destroyed and no sign of the child. At that point an unusual noise was heard coming from one of the towers. Looking up those present saw a monkey, that was normally chained, with the infant safe in its embrace. When he grew up the earl adopted the monkey as his crest to commemorate the incident.

11.14: Other animals

Many further animals can be seen in Irish heraldry, for example, the bear, the bull, the cow, the goat, the sheep, the hare, the squirrel and the hedgehog. There is not space here to give an example of every one. Notice, however, that the sinister supporter of Moore, Viscount Mount Cashel, County Tipperary is *A rhinoceros proper collared and chained Or* (BP: 1244). The dexter supporter of Robinson, baron Rosmead, County Westmeath is a *kangaroo reguardant* (§11.06). That is a reference to the time the first baron spent as Governor of New South Wales (1872-79).

Boar passant

Boar's head erased

Boar's head couped

Greyhound courant

Wolf-hound erect

Talbot passant

Horse forcené

Pegasus passant

Antelope passant

Other animals

Figure 10

12: Birds

12.00: The eagle

> *Leomhan is fíolar fola,*
> *deacair cosc na cianfhoghla,*
>   *i mbánbhrat síodamhail sróill –*
>   *eagal tromghoin a thionóil.*

'A lion and a hunting eagle, difficult it is to stop his plundering from afar — in white silky satin—there is fear of the severe wounding by his muster' (*anon* describing O'Doherty's banner).

The eagle is very common in continental European heraldry. It is found fairly frequently in Irish heraldry also. The eagle is most often shown *displayed*, that is facing forwards with the wings spread on eithe side. See, for example the arms of Boylan: *Argent an eagle displayed sable armed Or* (IF: 211). A double-headed eagle is depicted in the arms of Browne: *Or a double-headed eagle sable* (IF 211). The arms of the late Mícheál de Brún, archbishop of Galway, namely a version of those arms demidiating the arms of three dioceses can be seen on the west wall of Galway Cathedral.

Eagle's heads are to be seen in the arms of O'Casey: *Argent a chevron between three eagle's heads erased gules* (IF: 212).

12.01: The vol

Two eagle's wings joined at the shoulder but without any other part of the bird are known as a *vol*. The arms of Viscount Powerscourt contained three: *Argent on a bend gules three vols of the field* (BGA: 1123; K: 88). These are canting arms, since viscount's surname is Wingfield.

12.02: The martlet

Since the swallow is not seen landing or perched, it was believed in former times that she had no feet. The swallow without feet is the second most popular bird in heraldry, and she is known as a *martlet*. See, for example the arms of O'Gormley: *Or three martlets two and one gules* (IF: 215).

12.03: The falcon

The falcon is a powerful bird of prey and is well attested in heraldry. A good example can be seen in the arms of O'Madden: *Sable a falcon volant seizing a mallard argent* (IF: 217; and cf. K: 65). The falcon is often depicted as ready for falconry with bells on its feet. In such cases it is described as *belled*. A good example can be seen in the crest of O'Meagher: *A falcon argent belled Or* (IF: 217; K: 24).

Eagle displayed

Two-headed eagle

Wings inverted

Three martlets

Raven

Pelican vulning herself

Ostrich

Phoenix

Cornish chough

The Eagle and other Birds

Figure 11

12.04: The raven

The raven was the emblem of the Vikings and it is used in contemporary Irish heraldry for towns, etc. that had strong connections with the Norsemen. See, for example, the arms of Wicklow town: *Azure on a mount in base vert a fire beacon fired proper on a chief wavy Or a demi-raven displayed sable*. Compare also the arms of County Dublin (§24.09), which are no longer in use.

12.05: The pelican

At one time it was generally believed that the pelican wounded herself in order to feed her young on her own blood. Although the origin of this belief is uncertain, it gave rise to the use of the use of the pelican a symbol of Christ and of the Eucharist. The pelican is often therefore shown vulning herself, for example in the crest of O'Cullane (Collins) and O'Meara (IF: 213, 217). The latter is blazoned: *A pelican vulning herself proper*. When the pelican is depicted in her nest feeding her yound with her blood, she is said to be *in her piety*, for example in the crest of Aherne (IF: 211).

12.06: The dove

The dove is the symbol of peace and is found as the chief charge in the arms of O'Sheehan: *Azure on a mount in base vert a dove argent holding in its beak an olive branch proper* (IF: 219). These are canting arms, since the Irish name *Ó Síocháin* 'O'Sheehan' is similar to the Irish word *síocháin* 'peace'.

12.07: The ostrich

The ostrich possesses remarkable digestive powers, a fact that seems to have influenced its depiction in heraldry. The ostrich is usually shown with a horseshoe or old key in its beak or some similar item of ironmongery. The arms of MacMahon of Oriel: *Argent an ostrich sable hold in its beak a horseshoe Or* (IF: 217; K: 17).

The heraldic plume consist of three or more ostrich feathers, for example in the crest of Butler: *Out of a ducal coronet Or a plume of five ostrich feathers argent and rising therefrom a falcon of the last* (IF: 211; K 43). See the standard of Thomas Butler in Plate 4.

12.08: The phoenix

The phoenix is a fabulous bird. It was believed that there was only ever one bird and that he used to burn himself on a pyre every 500 year in order that he might rise rejuvenated from the ashes. In heraldry the phoenix is depicted as an eagle rising from flames of fire. He has long feathers rising from the top of his head on occasion. An Irish example of the heraldic phoenix can be seen in the arms of

Tullamore, County Offaly: *Azure rising from a mount in base vert a phoenix in a flaming pyre all proper in the honour point a Bridget's cross between two crosses crosslet Or.*

12.09: The chough

The *chough* (*Pyrrhocorax pyrrhocorax*) is a member of the crow family, but is a handsome bird with its curved red beak and red legs. A good example can be seen in the arms of O'Kirwan: Argent a chevron sable between three choughs proper (IF: 217: K: 12). These are canting arms, since the Irish surname *Ó Ciarubháin*, earlier *Ó Ciardhubháin*, anglicized *O'Kirwan, Kirwan* means 'descendant of the small black one'.

12.10: The robin redbreast

The robin is associated with the O'Sullivans, and a robin appears in the crest of O'Sullivan and of O'Sullivan Beare. The former is blazoned as follows: *On a ducal coronet Or a robin redbreast holding in the beak a sprig of olive all proper* (IF: 219; K: 16).

13: Fish, reptiles, and insects

13.00: Fish

Fish are frequently encountered in heraldry. If a fish is swimming horizontally, it is said to be *naiant*. If it is swimming vertically with its head upwards, it is *haurient* If its head is downwards it is said to be *urinant*.

13.01: The salmon

Sometimes the blazon merely mentions a fish, without being more specific; e.g. the arms of Clonmel to which reference has already been made (§11.06). More frequently, however, the *salmon* is mentioned by name. The salmon was always the most important fish in Gaelic tradition; the salmon of wisdom is mentioned in the Finn cycle for example. Moreover in Irish bardic poetry chieftains are often likened to salmon with either of the terms *maighre* 'salmon' and *eo* 'salmon'. Until fairly recently the salmon appeared on Irish coinage.

A salmon appears in the arms of O'Neill, for example: *Argent two lions combatant holding between them a dexter hand couped at the wrist in chief three mullets wavy all gules in base waves of the sea and a salmon naiant therein all proper* (IF: 218; cf. §01.02; K: 23).

The salmon occurs in Irish corporate heraldry also, for example in the arms of Fermoy, County Cork (granted 1985): *Per chevron azure and barry wavy of six argent and sable a chevron grady ensigned with a Latin cross Or in chief two salmon leaping respecting each other of the second.*

13.02: The roach

Roaches can be seen in the canting arms of Roche: *Gules three roaches naiant in pale argent* (IF: 219; K: 32).

13.03: The escallop

The escallop is the shellfish (mollusc) most commonly encountered in heraldry, for example in the arms of O'Connolly of Kildare (§08.00). An escallop is depicted twice in the arms of Sligo town (§10.12), where it is a canting reference to the name of the town: *Sligeach* 'Sligo' < *slige* 'a shell'.

13.04: The whale and the dolphin

Although neither the whale nor the dolphin is a fish, in heraldry they are both numbered among the fishes. A whale appears in the arms of O'Cahill of Munster: *Argent a whale spouting in the sea proper* (IF: 212; cf. K: 16).

Three dolphins are depicted in the arms of O'Regan: *Or a chevron ermine between three dolphins azure* (IF: 219).

Two salmon naiant

Two salmon hauriant

Two salmon urinant

Three escallops

Dolphin

Serpent erect wavy

Rod of Aesculapius

Caduceus

Lizard erect

Fish and Reptiles

Figure 12

13.05: The serpent

Although there were never any snakes in Ireland, the serpent is very common in Irish heraldry. A serpent can be seen by itself or wound round a sword in the following arms: O'Dea (IF: 213), O'Donovan (IF: 214), MacEgan (IF: 214), O'Gallagher (IF: 215), O'Hea (IF: 216), O'Mahony (IF: 217), O'Quin of Thomond (IF: 219) and O'Sullivan (IF: 219). The serpent was a familiar of Cernunnos, the horned god of the ancient Celts, and indeed in Celtic iconography the serpent is horned. This suggests that the serpent is really a hypostasis of the god himself. It is also apparent from storytelling in Irish that the serpent or serpentine monster (*ollphéist*) was an essential element in the Gaelic tradition. It is likely, therefore, that the frequent presence of the serpent in Irish heraldry is an attenuated survival of Celtic mythology.

The serpent is Irish heraldry is often embowed or it appears wound round a sword. The arms of O'Dea, for example, are emblazoned as follows: *Argent a dexter hand couped at the wrist proper cuffed indented azure lying fesswise holding a sword in pale also proper in chief two serpents embowed vert* (IF: 213). A serpent erect is to be seen in the arms of the town of Naas, Co. Kildare (§25.12).

13.06: The rod of Aesculapius and the caduceus

The snake moults from time to time. The ancient Greeks believed that when it did so, it was rejuvenating itself. To the Greeks, therefore, the serpent was a sign of immortality and was thus associated with the art of the physician. The *rod* (or *staff*) *of Aesculapius* depicts a serpent wound round a rod. It is found in heraldry as a sign of doctors, hospitals and other medical institutions. A good example can be seen in the arms of the Midwestern Health Board (granted 1975): *Per saltire gules and azure in chief a staff of Aesculapius Or in base a castle double-towered between the towers and obtuse spire surmounted by a cross flory argent in fess two antique crowns of the third.*

The rod of Aesculapius must be distinguished from the *caduceus*, that is, the rod of Mercury or Hermes, the messenger of the gods.

> *Ro éirig Mercuir mac Maia ingine Athlaint ... ocus ro ghabastar a chathbarr órecair ilbhrechtnaighthi ima cheann ocus ro ghabastar a fleisc ceannchaim cumachtaich ina láim .i. cadruca ainm na fleisce sin* 'Mercury the son of Maia daughter of Atlanta rose up...and he put his golden ornamented variegated helmet on his head and took his mighty staff with its curved top in his hand, i.e., caduceus is the name of that staff' (*Togail na Tebe* 'The Destruction of Thebes' 585-90).

There are two snakes entwind round the caduceus and there are small wings at its top. Since Mercury is the messenger, the caduceus is used in heraldry for the arms of newspaper companies, etc. I know of no Irish example, but the Times Publishing Company in Britain has the arms: *Argent eight barrulets sable overall a caduceus in pale Or* (CCH: 386).

13.07: The lizard

There is only one indigenous reptile in Ireland: the common *lizard* (*Zootoca vivipara*). Nonetheless the lizard, or evett, is quite common in Irish heraldry. It may well be that the heraldic lizard is in origin another representation of the cultic serpent. The Christian church was unhappy with the pagan snake and thus replaced it sometimes with the lizard.

The arms of O'Corrigan are blazoned as follows: *Or a chevron between in chief two trefoils slipped and in base a lizard passant all vert* (IF: 213). The arms of MacCotter (IF: 213) are *Azure three evetts in pale proper*. There is a story to explain the lizard in the crest of O'Flaherty (§19.06).

13.08: The bee and the ant

Insects are not particularly common in heraldry, but the *bee* and the *ant* are both found as charges on occasion. The bee is a symbol of assiduity and can be seen, for example, in the arms of Victoria College, Belfast: *Per pale sanguine and sable on the dexter a harp Or and on the sinister an open book proper edged and bound gold on a chief vair a pale azure charged with a bee argent* (CCH: 398). A beehive with bees flying around it can be seen in the crest of Fitzmaurice, Marquis of Lansdowne (§19.05).

An *ant gules* appears in the arms of Ballymena Academy: *Argent a humet azure between in chief two dexter hands [couped at the wrist] and in base an ant gules* (CCH: 44).

14.00: Heraldic monsters

The *pegasus* (§11.10) and the heraldic *antelope* (§11.11) are fabulous beasts and they could be included here. There are many further heraldic monsters.

14.01: The dragon

The dragon is one of the most basic heraldic monsters. It has four legs and the wings of a bat. Some commentators suggest that the crocodile was the animal that suggested the dragon to people. It is also probable that the serpent of Genesis and Revelation inspired the idea of the dragon. In Irish heraldry on the other hand it is more than likely that the dragon is yet a further hypostasis of the cultic snake.

A dragon occurs in the crest of Fitzpatrick: *A dragon reguardant vert surmounted of a lion guardant sable dexter paw resting on the dragon's head* (IF: 214).

A *Chinese dragon* is the dexter supporter of Hart, baronet, Kilmoriarty, County Armagh (BP: 837) and the sinister supporter of Gough, Viscount Limerick (§23.08).

14.02: The wyvern

The *wyvern* has the head, body wings and forelimbs of the dragon, and his scaly tail coils round and upward. The wyvern is thus a two-legged dragon. It can be seen in the arms of MacGillycuddy: *Gules a wyvern Or* (IF: 215) and in the badge of Old Wesley RFC.

14.03: The cockatrice

If the head, comb and wattle of a cock is placed on the wyvern's body, the resulting creature is a *cockatrice*. It was believed that the cockatrice was hatched from a cock's egg by a serpent on a dunghill. That belief contains a grain of truth, apparently. On occasion a hen may suffer from hormonal imbalance and grow the comb and wattle of a male bird. She may also start crowing like a cock, but is nonetheless still capable of laying eggs. When our ancestors saw such a hybrid bird, they did not understand the cause, but rather ascribed the phenomenon to the Devil. It would seem that such an understanding gave rise to be superstition that a monster would emerge from the egg of such a demonic creature.

Two cockatrices vert the wings elevated and endorsed the tails nowed the combs and wattles gules are the supporters of Nugent, Earl of Westmeath (BP: 1793).

14.04: The griffin or gryphon

Another imaginary creature found in heraldry is the *griffin* or *gryphon*. It has the body, tail and hind limbs of a lion but the forelimbs, thorax and head of an eagle.

Dragon

Wyvern

Cockatrice

Griffin or gryphon

Male griffin

Enfield

Unicorn

Mermaid

Sea-horse

Heraldic monsters

Figure 13

It has ears as well. When the griffin is in the rampant posture, it is said to be *segreant*. A griffin occurs in the canting arms of O'Griffy or Griffin: *Sable a griffin segreant Or langued and armed gules* (IF: 215). A griffin passant appears in the the the arms of Hanratty: *Azure a griffin passant the wings elevated Or* (IF: 216). Griffins combatant are depicted in the arms of Trehy or Troy: *Azure two griffins segreant combatant Or* (IF: 220).

Griffin's heads occur in the arms of O'Broder (§05.04) and in the arms of Ryan or Mulrian: *Gules three griffin's heads erased argent* (IF: 219).

14.05: The male griffin

There is a subspecies of griffin known as the *male griffin*. The male griffin lacks wings but its body is covered in spikes. The most notable Irish example, perhaps, is the sinister supporter of the Marquis of Ormond: *A male griffin argent beaked rayed collared and chained Or* (BP: 1336).

14.06: The enfield

Another fabulous beast that appears in Irish heraldry only in the crest of O'Kelly of Uí Maine is the *enfield*: *On a ducal coronet Or an enfield vert* (IF: 216; K: 15). The enfield has the head of a fox, the chest and forelimbs of an eagle, and the body and tail of a wolf. It is said that the enfield was the beast that emerged from the sea at the battle of Clontarf (1014) to protect the corpse of O'Kelly against the Danes. The enfield was in all probability the ancient badge of the O'Kellys and in origin was a water animal that lived in one of the loughs of eastern Connacht. The enfield was therefore similar in kind to the water beasts that were believed to inhabit many of the lakes of Ireland and Scotland. The name *enfield* itself (?via the stage *alphyn*) is probably a corruption of Irish *onchú, onchainn* 'fabulous creature' (Williams 1989).

Although supporters are not usually mentioned in connection with Farrell or O'Farrell in Ireland, some members of the family on the Continent bore supporters. Two otters proper are the supporters ascribed by Rietstap to Farrell and O'Farrell in his *Armorial Général*. Those beasts may well have been enfields originally.

14.07: The unicorn

The *unicorn* was an important animal in the middle ages and many virtues were ascribed to it. The heraldic unicorn has an antelope's body, the head of a horse with a single long twisted horn, the tail of a lion, the limbs of a stag and cloven hoofs. Two unicorns appear in the arms of O'Neilan: *Sable two unicorns passant in pale argent horned and hoofed Or* (IF: 218). A unicorn also occurs in the arms of

Gerard Slevin, Chief Herald of Ireland (1953-82): *Sable a unicorn forcené argent in chief two crosses crosses fitchy Or the whole within a bordure ermine.*

The unicorn is the national animal of Scotland and appears as a supporter in the royal arms of the British monarch. Unicorn Pursuivant is also one of the officers of arms in the court of Lord Lyon King of Arms.

14.08: The mermaid

The mermaid with her looking-glass and comb is fairly common in Irish heraldry, for example in the arms of MacAuliffe: *Argent three mermaids with combs and mirrors in fess azure between as many mullets of the last* (IF: 211).

14.09: The sea-horse

The sea-horse is a horse as to the upper part of his body although he has duck's feet rather than hoofs. The lower part of his body is that of a fish with a coiled tail. The crest of the City of Belfast is: *A sea-horse gorged with a mural crown proper* (CCH: 54).

15.00: Human figures

The human being in real life can sometimes be the ugliest and most vicious monster. It is probably best nonetheless to put human beings in a class by themselves

15.01: Naked human figures and the wild man

The arms of O'Donnellan are blazoned as follows: *Argent an oak tree eradicated proper on the sinister side a slave sable chained to the stem gules* (IF: 213; K: 34). The wretched black slave in those arms is depicted naked. O'Coffey of County Cork has the crest: *A man riding on a dolphin proper*; he is depicted naked also (IF: 212; K: 72). It is likely that the naked man riding a dolphin is an echo of ancient Celtic mythology.

The wild man appears quite commonly in heraldry. He is not depicted entirely naked for he wears a wreath of leaves about the waist and the temples as a rule. A good example can be seen in the dexter supporter of MacDonnell, Earl of Antrim: *A savage wreathed about the temples and loins with ivy all proper* (BP: 60).

15.02: Clothed figures

Clothed figures are well attested in heraldry. For example the arms of O'Loughlin are: *Gules a man in complete armour facing the sinister shooting an arrow from a bow all proper* (IF: 217; K: 16). A knight is depicted in the arms of MacGuire: *Vert a white horse fully caparisoned thereon a knight in complete armour on his helmet a plume of ostrich feathers his dexter hand brandishing a sword all proper* (IF: 215; K: 30).

Clothed human figures are common as supporters on either side of the shield, for example in the arms of the City of Dublin (§25.01).

15.03: Christ, the Blessed Virgin Mary and the saints

Since corporate arms may well be depicted in mosaics on the floor and on other small and unimportnt items like notices and pamphlets, for example, it is probably better not to depict Christ or God the Father in such arms. Such figures do on occasion occur in heraldry, nonetheless. The arms of the diocese of Waterford is a good example (§27.05).

St Patrick is depicted in the crest of the now defunct arms of County Antrim: *A demi figure representing St Patrick in a habit vert trimmed with gold the nimbus Or holding in the dexter hand a slip of shamrcok and supporting over the sinister shoulder a shepherd's crook proper* (CCH: 34). The saint is also shown in the obsolete arms of East Down Rural District Council (§16.06).

The Blessed Virgin Mary, St John the Baptist and St Jarlath can be seen in the arms of the diocese of Tuam (§27.05).

HUMAN FIGURES

15.04: The human head

As well as complete human figures portions of the human body are often seen in heraldry. The head is perhaps the commonest portion. A *blackamoor's head* is depicted in the crest of O'Conroy of County Offaly: *A blackamoor's head in profile couped at the shoulders sable and bound round the temples with a ribbon argent* (IF: 212; K: 18).

The crest of O'More is particularly gruesome: *A dexter hand lying fesswise couped at the wrist holding a sword in pale pierced through three gory heads all proper* (IF: 218; K: 19).

An entire human skeleton can be seen in the arms of the City of Londonderry (§25.05).

15.05: The human hand

Without doubt the "red hand" of Ulster is the commonest dexter hand in Irish heraldry. Technically speaking the red hand is *a dexter hand appaumé couped at the wrist gules*. The origin of the red hand is not known, but it is associated with various Ulster faimilies. A poetic dispute survives from the sixteenth century in which Síol Rudhraighe and the descendants of Niall of the Nine Hostages argue who has the exclusive right to use the red hand as a badge. It is noteworthy that the red hand is found in many Ulster arms, those of O'Neill, MacCartan, O'Donnelly, MacDonlevy and Magennis, for example. It is apparent that the red hand was an essential element in the pagan iconography of the Gaelic Irish.

The red hand of Ulster is very common in the corporate heraldry of Ulster. The most obvious example is in the arms of the Province itself (§24.05), but it is found in the arms of many further institutions. The arms of Castlereagh Rural District, County Down, are blazoned as follows: *Quarterly argent and Or in the first quarter a dexter hand appaumé gules in the second and the third quarters a cogwheel azure in the fourth quarter an eagle displayed on a chief vert a rural crown Or* (CCH: 98).

James I initiated the hereditary title of baronet in 1611 in order to provide money for the plantation of Ulster. It is for that reason that baronets (unless they are baronets of Nova Scotia) bear a red hand on a small inescutcheon in their personal arms. Curiously the red hand of the baronet is not a dexter but a sinister hand, but this has been the case since the inception of the honour.

15.06: The arm and the cubit arm

The forearm or *cubit arm* is not as common as the hand, but there are several examples nonetheless. The arms of O'Donovan, for example are blazoned: *Argent issuing from the sinister side of the shield a cubit dexter arm vested gules cuffed of the first the hand grasping a scian in pale the blade entwined with a serpent all proper* (IF: 214; K: 28).

The *arm* is the whole arm from shoulder to fingers. The dexter arm is the more common. See, for example, the arms of O'Gowan or Smith, of Ballygowan, County Down: *Argent two naked arms in fess one issuing from the dexter fess point the other from the sinister grasping a torch erect and inflamed issuant from the dexter base a similar arm grasping a sword in pale all proper* (BGA: 941; K: 58).

Arms and cubit arms are common in Irish crests. Most frequently the arm is in armour and holds a sword or dagger (§01.01).

15.07: The human heart

A representation of the human heart is quite common in Irish heraldry. A good example can be seen in the arms of Crean: *Argent a wolf rampant sable between three human hearts gules* (IF: 213; K: 69). Those are canting arms since *Crean* is from Irish *Ó Croidheáin* and *croí, croidhe* is the Irish for 'heart'. Hearts were used in the arms of John Henry Newman also (§26.04).

16: Plants

16.00 Trees

Trees are so common in the heraldry of the native Irish, that they are in all probability are survivals of the iconography of the ancient Celts. We know that the pagan Gaels showed great reverence to certain trees and that they used to name people after trees, e.g. *Mac Dara* 'son of the oak tree', *Mac Cuilinn* 'son of the holly', *Nath Í* 'grandson of the yew', etc. If trees belonged originally to pagan Celtic cults, it is perhaps not astonishing that they are to be seen at a later period in Gaelic heraldry.

The *oak tree* is the commonest tree in Irish heraldry and when the species of a tree is mentioned, it is shown as an oak tree. If a tree is still growing, it is depicted on a shield as issuing from a mount in the base of the shield. A good example can be seen in the arms of O'Connor Faley (§30.01).

A tree is sometimes depicted as having been torn out of the earth with its roots visible. In such cases it is said to be *eradicated*. Compare, for example, the arms of O'Connor Don: *Argent an oak tree eradicated vert* (IF: 212; K: 17). An eradicated holly tree can be seen in the arms of O'Dowling: *Argent a holly tree eradicated proper on a chief azure a lion passant between two trefoils slipped Or* (IF: 214: K: 81).

Two yew trees appear in the arms of Castlebar, County Mayo (§10.03). That is a reference to the name of the county, that is, *Mayo < Maigh Eo* 'plain of the yew trees'.

16.01: The hurst

A hurst of oak trees is shown in the arms of O'Callaghan, rather than a single tree: *Argent a mount in base vert on the dexter side a hurst of oak trees issuant therefrom a wolf passant towards the sinister all proper* (IF: 212; K: 17). Egan O'Rahilly mentions those arms in his lament for Donal O'Callaghan (§03.01). Remarkably the arms of O'Callaghan ar very similar to the arms a German family called Busch: *Azure a mount in base vert a lion passant Or emerging on the sinister side from a hurst of the second* (THBF: 316).

16.02: Branches and leaves

Branches are a common charge in heraldry, in the arms of Creagh, for example (§10.10). Branches of elder (Irish *trom*) are depicted in the arms of Trim (Irish *Baile Átha Troim*), County Meath: *Or a bend wavy debruised by with a castle between three elder branches all proper*.

Single leaves also appear in Irish heraldry. The arms of Tobin, for example, display oak leaves: *Azure three oak leaves argent* (IF: 220; K: 10). Nettle leaves appear in the arms of O'Clery: *Or three nettle leaves vert* (IF: 212).

16.03: The cinquefoil, the quatrefoil, and the trefoil

There are in heraldry stylized leaves or plants that are named according to the number of their leaves: *trefoil, quatrefoil, cinquefoil,* etc. The arms of Darcy, mentioned above (§06.05) are a good example of the cinquefoil. Blood of Ireland bore four quatrefoils: *Quarterly argent and azure four quatrefoils counterchanged* (BGA: 92).

The trefoil is sometimes described as slipped, that is, with a stalk below. In such cases the charge is effectively the Irish shamrock and it common in Irish heraldry. The shamrock has been long associated with St Patrick and the teaching of the doctrine of the Holy Trinity, but that may rather be an attempt to ascribe a Christian meaning to a pagan symbol. In origin the shamrock may simply be a version of the triquetra, an ancient sun symbol. It is also worth mentioning that the shamrock (*Kleeblatt*) is the badge of Hanover in Germany.

The trefoil slipped is common in Irish personal heraldry, for example in the arms of O'Sheridan: *Or a lion rampant vert between three trefoils slipped of the same* (IF: 219; K: 28). It is most frequently seen, however, in Irish corporate heraldry, for example in the arms of 1) the National University and 2) Unversity College, Dublin:

1) The National University (granted 1913): *Vert a harp Or stringed with seven strings argent in chief a mullet of five points of the second charged with a trefoil slipped of the field.*

(2) University College, Dublin (granted 1912): *Vert a harp Or stringed argent on a chief of the second a pale azure charged with three castles flammant proper between two trefoils slipped of the field.*

16.04: The rose

The heraldic rose is a stylized flower of five petals. Sepals vert can be seen as a rule between each pair of petals and seeds in the middle of the flower. In such cases in blazon the tincture of the rose is mentioned first—gules and argent are the commonest—and then the sepals and seeds are blazoned as *barbed and seeded* of the appropriate tinctures, most often proper. If the rose is stalked, it is blazoned as *slipped.*

The rose is often associated with England and is in this context sometimes encountered in Irish heraldry, for example in the arms of Athlone: *Gules a lion passant guardant Or on a chief of the same two roses of the field slipped vert.*

Roses appear in the heraldry of the native Irish also, for example in the arms of O'Dineen: *Azure two swords crossed in saltire the points upward argent pommelled and hilted Or between four roses of the same* (IF: 213).

Tree on a mount

Tree eradicated

Three trefoils

Three trefoils slipped

Three quatrefoils

Three cinqfoils

Rose

Three fleur-de-lis

Pomegranate

Trees and Plants

Figure 14

16.05: The fleur-de-lis

> *Acus ro innis fós an ainmhidhi ngalair acus in dá phlúr da lísa at-chonnairc*
> *isin eclais amhail ro ráidhsiom remhainn* 'And he spoke also of the sick
> animal and the two fleurs-de-lis he had seen in the church as we have
> recounted' (*Lorgaireacht an tSoidhigh Naomhtha* 'Quest for the Holy
> Grail' 2574-76).

The *fleur-de-lis* is usually taken to be a lily, but the stylized heradlic fleur-de-lis
is closer in appearance to the iris. Although the fleur-de-lis is associated
particularly with the kings of France, the reason for the link is not certain. The
most likely explanation is that an alternative form *fleur-de-luce* was taken as a pun
on the name *Louis* of so many French kings. Since kings of England and then of
Great Britain claimed France until 1800, the fleur-de-lis appeared on the
English and then British royal arms until then. The Tudors bore quarterly arms
with three fleurs-de-lis in the first quarter and fourth quarter and the three lions
passant guardant in the second and third. Those arms appeared at one time in
the arms of the City of Galway (§25.04d). The arms of Waterford were also
based on a version of these arms (§25.10).

The fleur-de-lis is fairly common in heraldry quite apart from the French
connection. There are several examples of the charge in Irish personal heraldry,
the arms of O'Shea for example (§8.00) and of Sarsfield: *Per pale argent and gules*
a fleur-de-lis counterchanged (IF: 219; K: 48).

Two fleurs-de-lis appear in the arms of Letterkenny (granted 1982): *Vert a*
bishop's staff erect Or between two salmon opposite each other urinant proper on a chief
arched of the second a cross crosslet fitchy gules between two fleurs-de-lis of the field.

The fleur-de-lis is sometimes used to decorate other charges. When a charge
ends in a fleur-de-lis, it is blazoned as *flory*. A good example is to be seen in the
arms of the town of Shannon: *Azure three piles in bend issuing from the sinister base*
Or flory at the point argent in base a terrasse of the same masoned sable. Those arms
are a clever heraldic representation of three jet planes with their slipstreams
taking off from Shannon airport. The fleur-de-lis also appears on the double
tressure flory counter flory (§10.01) and on the leopard's face jessant de lis
(§11.04).

16.06: Flax and varieties of grain

The flax flower (*Linum usitatissimum*) is common in Ulster arms, for example in
the rather pedestrian arms of County Down granted in 1967: *Vert on a fess Or*
fretty gules a fish naiant argent in chief three garbs Or and in base on water barry wavy
of four argent and azure a lymphad sail furled pennon and flags flying all Or two flax

flowers slipped and leaved proper (CCH: 138). It is perhaps a mercy that those arms are now obsolete.

Ears and stalks of various varieties of corn are common in heraldry. Barley stalks, for example, appear in the arms of East Down Rural District Council (granted 1966): *Per chevron vert and Or a chevron wavy party per chevron wavy argent and gules in chief a salmon naiant proper between in chief three stalks of barley conjoined Or and two weaver's shuttles in saltire of the same and in base a demi-man in the form of St Patrick habited and nimbed Or supporting over his shoulder a shepherd's crook* (CCHL 146).

16.07: Fruit

Grapes appear in the arms of D'Olier, Huguenots who settled in Ireland at the end of the seventeenth century: *Or on a chevron gules between three bunches of grapes sable a crescent of the first surmounted by a bezant all within a border azure semé of fleurs-de-lis of the first.* (AF: 396).

The La Touche family were also Huguenots who had a residence in Marlay House, County Dublin among other places. There was pomegranate in their arms: *Argent a pomegranate slipped in pale proper on a chief gules two mullets of the field* (BGA: 587; K: 29).

16.08: Further flowers

There are narcissi in the arms of Lambart, Earl of Cavan: *Gules three narcissus flowers pierced argent* (BP: 324; K:92).

Bog rosemary (*Andromeda polifolia*) can be seen in the arms of County Offaly (§06.01). The flower is very rare in Ireland except in the Midlands.

17.00: Further charges

Most of the traditional inanimate charges in heradlry are immediately recognizable. Some on the other hand may be unfamiliar and they may also have unfamiliar names. Here we list only the mostly commonly encountered of such charges.

17.01: Anchor

An anchor is depicted in the arms of Kilrush, County Clare (§10.07) and in the arms of Godwin Swift, the uncle of Jonathan Swift (§26.02).

17.02: Bow and arrow

Many arms display an arrow or arrows. A good example is the coat of arms ascribed to O'Hanly (§11.07).

A bow and quiver of arrows can be seen in the arms of O'Moloney: *Azure on the dexter side a quiver of three arrows on the sinister a bow erect all Or* (IF: 218).

17.03: Shoe

A shoe proper occurs in the first quarter of the arms of O'Hagan: *Argent a shoe proper on a canton per chevron gules and ermine three covered cups Or* (IF: 215; cf. K: 98). In the ceremony of installing a Gaelic chieftain his most prominent follower put a shoe on his foot. When O'Neill was made king in Tullyhogue, the chieftain of the O'Hagans put the shoe on him.

17.04: The bugle horn

Three hunting horns appear in the arms of Bellingham of Castlebellingham, County Louth: *Argent three hunting horns sable stringed and garnished Or* (BGA: 69; K: 111). The *garnishes* are the rings round the horn.

17.05: Castles and towers

Castles are common in Irish heraldry. Unless otherwise stated the castle has two towers and a crenellated wall beteween. The best-known example perhaps is the coat of arms of the City of Dublin (§25.01). The castle in the arms of Tralee has two towers and the blazon specifies that there are three arched gates into it as well.

Single towers are often encountered in heraldry as well. A good example can be seen in the arms of O'Higgins (§06.05).

The tower in the arms of Plunkett has three turrets: (IF: 218; K: 86). A tower of three turrets appears also in the arms of O'Kelly of Uí Maine and of O'Shaughnessey (IF: 216; K: 15 and IF 219; K: 15).

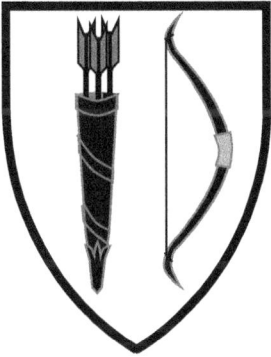

Quiver and bow

Shoe

Castle

Three towers

Three water bougets

Three covered cups

Three fleams

Keys crossed in saltire

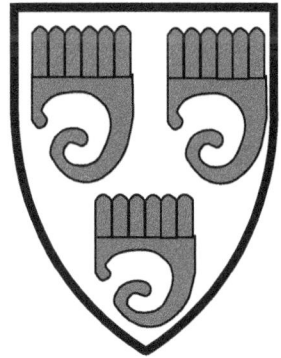

Three clarions

Miscellaneous Charges 1

Figure 15

17.06: Water bouget

The *water bouget* is a stylized representation of an ancient vessel for water. It resembles two leather botttles suspended from a tranverse bar; the latter was placed over the shoulder in order to carry water from place to place: An example can be seen in the arms of Lightburne of Ireland: *Azure a water bouget Or on a chief argent three bendlets sable* (PO: 346).

17.07: Cups and covered cups

The commonest kind of cup in heraldry is the *covered cup*, that is, a goblet with a cover. Without doubt the best-known Irish example is to be seen in the arms of the Butlers (§23.03). There are three covered cups in the arms of Fagan as well: *Per saltire gules and ermine three covered cups in fess Or* (IF: 214; K: 59) and in the arms of O'Hagan (§17.03; and *cf.* §30.02).

Gaelic cups without a cover are depicted in the arms of O'Coffey of County Cork: *Vert a fess ermine between three Irish cups Or* (IF: 212; K: 72).

17.08: Swords

Since the sword is one of the commonest charges in Irish heraldry, we have a wealth of examples. The arms of O'Dowd, for example, are blazoned as follows: *Vert a saltire Or in chief two swords in saltire points upwards the dexter surmounted of the sinister argent pommels and hilts of the second* (IF:214; K: 30). The sword in the arms of O'Davoren is dripping blood: *Argent a sword erect in pale distilling drops of blood proper pommel and hilt Or* (IF: 213; K: 22).

As well as the ordinary swords mentioned above, Irish heraldry offers examples of more unusual swords. A sword with wavy blade is depicted in the arms of O'Finnegan, and in the crests of MacGorman and MacKeown, for example (IF: 214; 215, 217). A *scimitar* is depicted in the crest of O'Hegarty, O'Kennedy and Wall (IF: 216, 220). A *claíomh solais* or 'sword of light' appears in the crest of O'Hart, though it is blazoned as a *sword flammant proper* (IF: 216). A *flaming sword azure* is depicted in the crest of O'Flanagan (IF: 214).

The dagger resembles the sword but its blade is shorter. Many examples can be seen in Irish personal heraldry, for example in the arms of O'Hartagan, O'Kearney, O'Mullan of Connacht and O'Riordan (IF: 216, 218, 219) and in assorted crests.

17.09: Harp

Since the harp is the symbol of Ireland, it is often seen in Irish corporate heraldry. The harp is the main charge in the arms of University College, Dublin (§16.03) and a harp with a crown over it is depicted in the arms of Dublin University granted in 1862: *Quarterly azure and ermine, first a bible open proper clasped Or, third a castle argent two towers fired proper, in fess point a harp surmounted by a royal crown Or.*

The harp is also sometimes seen in personal heraldry, for example in the arms of O'Mulvihill: *Per fess argent and gules in chief two lions combatant azure holding between them a dexter hand couped at the wrist gules beneath them a salmon naiant proper in base an Irish harp Or stringed of the first between two pole-axes proper the blades outwards* (IF: 218).

17.10: Helmet

Although the helmet is usually employed in heraldry only as one of the exterior ornaments of the shield, there are Irish examples of the helmet as a charge on the shield itself. A notable example can be seen in the arms of O'Kennedy: *Sable three helmets in profile proper* (IF: 216 and §26.07). These are canting arms, because the name O'Kennedy in Irish is *Ó Cinnéidigh*, which was understood as deriving from *cinn* 'head' and *éide* 'dress, garment'.

17.11: Crowns and coronets

The British royal crown is common in the official heraldry of Ireland before independence, in the arms of the University of Dublin, for example (§17:09). Moreover coronets of rank appear over the arms of peers. The duke's coronet is decorated with strawberry leaves, whereas the marquis has a coronet of alternate pearls and leaves. There is usually a cap of red satin lined with ermine inside the royal crown and the peer's helmet. This is known as a cap of *maintenance*. The cap of maintenance appears in the crest of Darcy: *On a cap of maintenance gules lined ermine a black bull armed Or* (IF: 213; K: 75).

Two varieties of crown are still common in Irish heraldry. The first is the *ancient crown*, that is, a rim of gold on which stand five tall triangular points. Three ancient crowns appear in the arms of Munster, for example (§24.03) and a single ancient crown is depicted in the arms of Crowe (§10.03).

The second kind of crown or coronet is known as the *ducal coronet*. It resembles the duke's coronet which has eight leaves. The ducal coronet has only six. The ducal coronet is usually depicted without cap of maintenance and it appears mostly in crests, for example in the crest of O'Farrell: *On a ducal coronet Or a greyhound springing sable* (IF: 214; K: 24).

There are yet two more crowns that are particularly common in civic heraldry in Northern Ireland. The first of those is in the shape of a ring consisting of an embattled wall. It is known as a mural crown. It is most commonly seen above the shield, though it does on occassion occur as a charge on the shield itself. A good example can be seen in the arms of the Association of Municipal Authorities of Northern Ireland, which was granted in 1954:

Quarterly gules and Or in the first quarter a mullet of six points argent charged with a dexter hand couped at the wrist of the first in the fourth quarter a mural crown also argent (CCH: 272). A mural crown appears also in the arms of Belfast (§25.02) and in personal heraldry in the arms of Gough (§23.08).

The second variety is the *rural crown*, which consists of alternate ears of corn and sprigs of oak. An example can be seen in the arms of Castlereagh (§15.06).

17.12: Horseshoe

The horseshoe is depicted in heraldry with the curve above and the ends facing downward. Kennedy gives an example in the arms of Ferrier which would be blazoned as follows: *Argent on a bend cotised sable three horseshoes of the first* (K: 32). Those are canting arms because *Ferrer* is a variant of *farrier* 'a blacksmith'. As has been mentioned above (§12.07), a horseshoe is often shown in the beak of the ostrich.

17.13: Fleam

The *fleam* is a surgical instrument resembling a razor with a curved blade. It is most commonly seen in the arms of surgeons and of surgical institutions. Sir John W. Moore (b. 1845) was a professor in the Royal College of Surgeons, Dublin. The arms granted to him were: *Azure on a chief dancetty Or a fleam between two mullets all gules* (AF: 981).

17.14: Key

Keys are frequently encountered in heraldry, particularly in ecclesiastical heraldry. A notable example is that of the crossed keys that appear behind the coat of arms of the Pope, and which symbolize the spiritual power claimed by the Pontiff in heaven and on earth (§27.07). When keys are blazoned, their orientation must be mentioned and whether the wards are above or below, for example, in the arms of the Diocese of Down: *Azure two keys in saltire the wards upward Or suppressed by a lamb passant argent* (BGA: 297).

17.15: Clarion or Sufflue

The *clarion* is a musical instrument shaped like Pan pipes or a harmonica but with a handle to hold the device. Some commentators appear to have believed that the clarion was a rest on which the lance was rested during a tournament. That was certainly not true, but it has meant the the clarion is also sometimes known as a *rest*. The arms of Granville, Lord Lansdowne (created 1712; extinct 1734): *Gules three clarions Or* (BGA: 420).

Cap of maintenance

Three ducal coronets

Mural crown

Rural crown

Three crescents

Three crescents
increscent

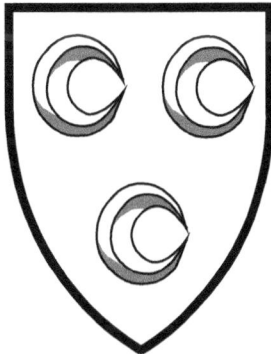

Three crescents
decrescent

Lunel

Sun in splendour

Miscellaneous Charges 2

Figure 16

17.16: Grenade

There is no difference between the grenade and the bomb, but if fire appears to be coming from three places rather than one, it is blazoned as fired in three places. Both Burke and Kennedy cite the arms of Ball: *Argent a chevron between three grenades sable fired proper* (BGA: 44; K: 107). Those are canting arms, since the grenade is also known occasionally as a *fire-ball*.

17.17: Sun and moon

A representation of the sun is common in the heraldry of the native Irish. The sun, depicted with a human face encircled by rays, is known as *sun in splendour*. A notable example is seen in the arms of MacBrady: *Sable in sinister base a dexter hand couped at the wrist proper pointing to the sun in splendour Or in the dexter chief* (IF: 211; K: 18). The sun here is probably a distant echo of the iconography of the ancients. Figures known as *Sol Invictus*, that is, a human face with rays all around is well attested in classical antiquity. Compare also the person known as *Oghma Grianaineach* 'Oghma with the face of the sun' who is numbered among Tuatha Dé Danann.

The *crescent* is the commonest representation of the moon in heraldry. Strictly speaking it is not a moon at all since the horns are upwards. Three crescents occur in the arms of Lally: *Argent three eagles displayed two and one gules each holding in its beak a laurel sprig proper between as many crescents two and one azure* (IF: 217). Three crescents are also depicted in the arms of Macgovern: *Azure a lion passant Or in chief thre crescents of the same* (IF: 215; cf K: 38).

If the horns of the crescent are to dexter like the moon itself when it is waxing, the charge is known as *a crescent increscent*. If the horns are to sinister it is a *crescent decrescent*. A crescent increscent occurs in the arms of MacDonnell of County Clare and Connacht: *Azure an ancient galley sails set and flags flying argent between in chief a Calvary cross of three grieces Or between in the dexter a crescent increscent of the second and in the sinister a dexter hand couped at the wrist appaumé proper and in base a salmon naiant of the second* (IF: 213; K: 16). Both crescent decrescent and sun in splendour appear in the arms of Martin of Galway (§09.02).

The crescent is very common in Spanish heraldry where it is a symbol of the reconquest of Spain from the Moors. The heraldic *lunel* consists of four crescents forming a cross with the horns of each crescent touching one of the horns of its neighbour. A good example appears in the arms of Éamonn de Valera (§26.06).

FURTHER CHARGES

17.18: Fasces

The *fasces* is depicted as a bundle of rods with an axe in the middle. The fasces was carrieds before the lictors (magistrates) of ancient Rome. The fasces also became the symbol of the Italian Fascists.

The fasces appears in the crest of Andrew Porter, baronet, Master of the Rolls in Ireland: *On a fasces fessways a cherub all proper* (BP: 1401). A fasces appears in the crest of Lord Killannin (§26.08) and in the arms granted to Charles J. Haughey in 1966 (§26.09).

17.19: Books

A book is almost *de rigueur* in arms newly granted to a school or college. The book, however, is a well established charge in heraldry. The Conroys had always been historians and scribes and not astonishingly the arms of Conroy contains a book: *Azure an ancient book open proper indexed and edged Or a chief embattled of the last* (IF: 212; and cf. K: 40).

17.20: Ships

The commonest sea-going vessel in heraldry is known as the *lymphad*. This is an anglicized spelling for the Scottish Gaelic *luing fada* 'long ship'. Unless otherwise specified in the blazon, the lymphad has only one mast. A lymphad can be seen in the third quarter of the arms of McDonnell of the Glens of Antrim: *Argent a lymphad sails furled sable* (IF: 213). A lymphad occurs in the arms of O'Driscoll, but it has three masts and is blazoned as "an ancient galley" (IF: 167 and 214). A rowing boat without mast or sail appears in the arms of O'Flaherty (IF: 214) and MacHugh of Galway (IF: 216).

Unless otherwise specified a ship or boat sails to dexter. The ship in the arms of Arklow sails towards the spectator (§10.12). The patent granting the arms, however, does not specify the direction of the ship.

17.21: Millrind

The millrind is that piece of iron in the middle of the millstone into which the rotating shaft fitted. The shape of the millrind can be seen at the end of the cross moline. Four millrinds appear in the arms of Earl Winterton, Gort, County Galway: *Ermines on a cross argent quarterpierced of the field four millrinds sable* (BP: 1829).

17.22: Maunch

The heraldic maunch is a representation of a lady's sleeve of the twelfth century, from which hangs a long lappet from the cuff. Three maunches appear in the arms of Maunsell of County Limerick: *Argent a chevron sable between as many maunches of the same* (BGA: 670). Those are canting arms, punning on the similarity between the surname *Maunsell* and the name of the charge, *maunch*.

17.23: Woolsack

The woolsack resembles a cushion. There are three in the arms of Redmond: *Gules a castle with two towers argent between three woolsacks Or* (IF: 219).

17.24: Mullets, stars and estoiles

The *mullet* in heraldry usually has five straight points. Although its resembles a star, the mullet in origin was probably a spur rowel (cf. the French word *molette* 'spur rowel').

The mullet of five points is frequently encountered in Irish heraldry, for example in the following arms: MacAuliffe, O'Doherty, O'Doran, O'Malone, O'Monaghan and O'More (IF: 211-18).

A star can also have six points, as in the arms of Moran: *Sable three stars of six point rayed Or* (IF: 218). The stars in the arms of MacKeown have eight points: *Argent two lions combatant sable holding between them a dexter hand appaumé couped at the wrist gules in chief four stars of eight points in base in waves of the sea a salmon naiant all proper* (IF: 217).

Since the mullet was in origin part of a spur, it is sometimes encountered in heraldry pierced through the middle with a round hole. In such cases it is known as a *spur rowel*. The crest of La Touche was a spur rowel. The La Touche family owned Marlay House in Rathfarnham, County Dublin, and the crest of a spur rowel can be seen carved into the stone over the door of the house there.

When a star has six wavy points, it is known as an *estoile*. The estoile is common in Irish heraldry. An example is the coat of arms of MacShanly: *Azure a lion passant Or in chief three estoiles of the same* (IF: 219). An estoile of eight points is depicted in the arms of O'Duggan: *Azure a crescent decrescent between nine estoiles of eight points Or* (IF: 214).

17.25: The broad arrow and the pheon

The *broad arrow* is a stylized arrow head with one barb on either side. The point faces upward unless otherwise stated. An example appears in the arms of Walsh of Iverk: *Argent a chevron gules between three broad arrows sable* (IF 220; K: 8).

If the inner edge of the barbs is engrailed the charge is known as a *pheon*: The arms of MacColgan contain three pheons: *Azure a lion rampant Or between three pheons the points downwards* (IF: 212).

Three mullets

Three spur rowels

Three estoiles

Three bugle-horns

Three fire-balls

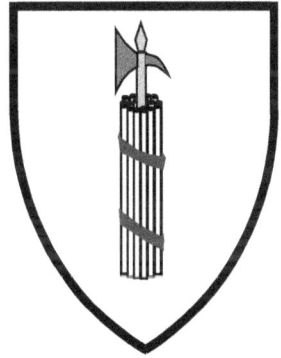

Fasces

Open book indexed

Lymphad

Rowing boat

Miscellaneous Charges 3

Figure 17

17.26: Catherine wheel

This, the symbol of St Catherine, who was martyred in Alexandria in the fourth century, is a wheel of six or eight spokes with a number of curved blades round its circumference. According to Burke the arms of William Scott, (†1661), High Sheriff of Queen's County were: *Argent a crescent sable between thre Catherine wheels of the same the whole within a bordure engrailed gules* (BGA: 907).

17.27: Clouds

Clouds are not common in heraldry, although examples are occasionally encountered, for example in the arms of Leeson, Earls of Miltown: *Gules a chief argent on the lower part a cloud the rays of the sun issuing therefrom proper* (BP: 1202).

17.28: The shield

The *inescutcheon* has been mentioned above when discussing the subordinaries (§10.02). A shield, smaller than that, is often encountered, for example in the contemporary arms of the City of Galway (§25.04*d*). Baronets display the red hand of Ulster on a small shield.

Sometimes more than one shield appear together in a coat of arms, for example in the arms of Hay of Tacumshane and Ballinkeele, County Wexford, which were confirmed in the visitation of 1618: *Argent three shields gules* (BGA: 472). The Hays of Wexford were, it seems, a branch of the well-known Scottish family.

17.29: Spears and lances

Two kinds of spear are found in Irish heraldry, the ancient Gaelic spear and the jousting lance. The first of these is a wooden shaft with a spearhead at the end. The jousting lance is more ornate. Little can be seen of the shaft, since much of it is covered by the handguard. The spear can be seen in the arms of MacLysaght (§07.11; K: 83). A jousting lance appears in the arms of O'Fallon (§11.08).

The spearhead by itself occurs in the arms of Macnamara, for example: *Gules a lion rampant argent in chief two spearheads Or* (IF: 218).

17.30: The weaver's shuttle

The weavers's shuttle is common in the corporate heraldry of Ulster by reason of the importance of linen manufacturing in the history of the province. A good example can be seen in the arms of Dungannon Urban District Council: *Or a castle proper in chief a dexter hand gules on a chief sable a shuttle fesswise of the field* (CCH: 140).

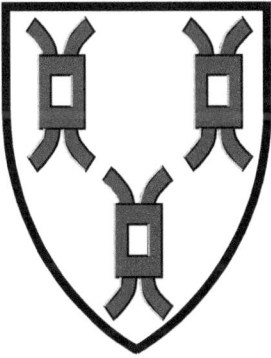

Three mill-rinds

Maunch

Three woolsacks

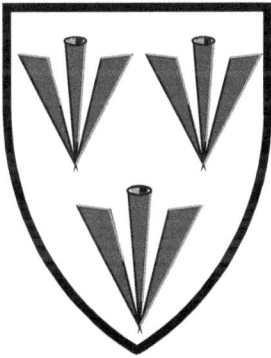

Three broad arrows
points downwards

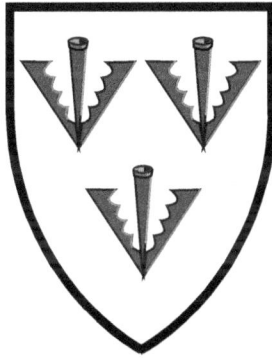

Three pheons points
downwards

Three Catherine wheels

Three spears

Three lances

Battle-axe

Miscellaneous Charges 4

Figure 18

17.31: The fire-beacon

The *fire-beacon* is an iron basket on a stand with flames coming out of it. Since fire-beacons were used on the coast in former times and a means of communication, they are mostly seen in the arms of maritime towns. A fine example is seen in the arms of Wicklow Town (§12.04).

When arms were granted to County Dublin in 1944, the patent claimed the crest (that lacked a helmet beneath) was a fire-beacon. In fact the crest did not contain a fire-beacon, but rather flames of fire by themselves.

17.32: The pole-axe

There are numerous examples of *pole-axes* in Gaelic personal heraldry. In the fourth quarter of the arms os MacSheehy, for example, one finds: *Azure three pole-axes palewise in fess Or* (IF: 219). Compare also the arms of O'Mulvihil (§17.09).

17.33: Modern artefacts

Although it is perhaps not always in the best heraldic taste, modern artefacts appear in heraldry on occasion. Irish heraldry is not so given to such contemporary charges as is, for example, the corporate heraldry of England, there are notable examples in Ireland nonetheless. In the arms of Balbriggan, County Dublin (§07.09), for example, the following items are depicted: a spindle, a water wheel and two industrial pipes crossed in saltire. In the arms of St Killian's Community School, Bray, granted in 1989, one sees *a representation of the binary system as a scientific sign,* that is to say a charge taken from computing. It would seem then that almost anything can be made into a heraldic charge.

18: Blazon

Blazon is the name given to the accurate description of a coat of arms. Blazon uses the specialized heraldic vocabulary and it follows certain conventions in such a way that the reader should be able to draw the arms without reference to any visual respresentation of them. Before discussing the basic rules of blazon, however, we must pay attention to two important aspects thereof, namely *counterchanging* and charges *throughout*.

18.00: Counterchanging

Counterchanging is a common occurrence in heraldry. Although counterchanging is simple in theory, in practice it can lead to apparently complicated results. Assume, for example, that the field is *per pale Or and azure*. If a fess is placed on that field so that the portion lying on the half of the shield that is *Or* is itself *azure*, and the other half on the *azure* half is *Or*, then we have an example of counterchanging and the result are the arms of Cusack (IF: 165 and 213).

Another example can be seen in the arms of Barret of County Cork: *Barry of ten per pale argent and gules counterchanged* (IF: 211). Charges counterchanged can be seen in the arms of O'Scanlan of Munster: *Per fess engrailed argent and azure three lions rampant counterchanged* (IF: 219). Compare also the arms of O'Shea (§08.00).

The arms of Sarsfield (§16.05) depict a single charge counterchanged, that is, one half of one tincture and the other of another. A fess and two boars counterchanged appear in the arms of O'Sullivan Beare: *Per pale argent and sable a fess between in chief a boar passant in base another counter-passant all counterchanged armed hoofed and bristled Or* (IF: 184 and 219; K: 26).

18.01: Charges throughout

When a charge that normally reaches the edge of the shield fails to reach the edge, it is said to be couped. In the same way when a charge reaches the edge of the shield when it usually does not, it is said to be *throughout*. If, for example, the four corners of a lozenge meet the four edges of the shield, it is a *lozenge throughout*. Similarly if the four arms of a cross patty reach the edges of the shield, as for example in the royal arms of Denmark and of Sweden, it is blazoned as a *cross patty throughout*.

A shield *per chevron throughout* is very similar to a shield *per pile reversed throughout* (§06.01), except that the division of the shield in *per chevron throughout* begins at a higher level than *per pile reversed throughout*.

18.02: The order of blazon

When blazoning a coat of arms the following order is followed:

(a) the field is mentioned first, that is, whether it is plain or divided and what tincture or tinctures are involved;

(b) the main charge or charges, i.e, ordinary, animal or animals, &c. are mentioned next;

(c) charges around the main charge are then specified;

(d) charges on the main charge are given thereafter;

(e) differences, if any, are blazoned (§§23.04-23.05);

(f) anything which is overall are mentioned last, e.g. bordure, canton or inescutcheon.

Assume that there is no mark of difference in the arms, but that there is a major charge, a chief with minor charges on it, a bordure and a canton, they are mentioned in that order, e.g. *Or a lion passant sable on a chief azure three estoiles of the field the whole within a bordure ermine overall a canton gules charged with a harp also of the field.*

18.03: Some further features of blazon

There are some further features of blazon listed below, though not necessarily in order of importance:

(a) It is the custom of the Office of the Chief Herald of Ireland to use punctuation in blazon. The English kings of arms however avoid punctuation marks, lest a change in punctuation might alter the nature of the blazon. It follows therefore that blazons should be as unambiguous as possible. Punctuation marks are not used in blazons in this book.

(b) In order to distinguish the heraldic tincture *Or* from the conjunction *or*, the former is spelt with a capital *O*.

(c) It is advisable not to mention a tincture more than once. In order to avoid repetition one can say, *of the field, of the first, of the second,* &c.

(d) When a tincture is mentioned it refers to every thing mentioned previously that has not had a tincture ascribed to it. Thus, for example, in the blazon *Argent a bend between two lions rampant all within a bordure gules,* the bend, the lions and the bordure are all gules.

(e) Rather than write the tinctures out in full, one can make use of abbreviations (§§05.01, 05.02, 05.05).

(f) It is not necessary to mention a number more than once. If three bars are mentioned and then three mullets, for example, one can say in the second case *as many mullets.*

(*g*) When the field is quarterly, that is mentioned first, but the tinctures of the quarters are not mentioned until each one is blazoned separately.

(*h*) In fields per saltire and gyronny of eight, etc. the blazon works from the top to the bottom and from the dexter to the sinister side.

18.04: Sample blazons

The following five blazons have no connection with Ireland. I cite them simply to indicate how complicated arms are to be described. Since they have been quoted from other works, punctuation is used in them.

(*a*) *Per fess azure and Or a pale per fess Or and sable in base between in chief two representations of the astronomical sign of Aries Or a ram's head caboshed argent armed Or* (V. J. S. Doddrell, HWW: 128).

(*b*) *Gules, on a bend cotised flory counter-flory Or, a lion's gamb erased bendwise of the field, between two torteaux, that in chief charged with two keys in saltire, wards upwards and outwards, argent, and that in base with a pierced cinquefoil ermine* (Oadby UDC, CCH: 290).

(*c*) *Argent, three piles in point sable, the centre pile charged with a saltorel flory Or* (for Laing of Colington) *impaled with Or, a double-headed eagle displayed ermine, beaked and membered gules; over all, on a fess azure, three chess pawns Or* (for Bouwer) (Mrs H. M. Laing of Collington (*née* Bouwer) AWW: 230).

(*d*) *Quarterly: I and IV, sable a sheep, and in chief a mullet of six points Or* (for Berger): *II and III, gules, a greyhound passant reguardant argent menaced by three arrows Or in bend-sinister heads downwards, and in chief a crescent argent* (for Carrière) (Jacques Berger-Carrière AWW: 96).

(*e*) *Per fess nebuly chequy azure and or, each of the last charged with a goutte of the first, and sable, in base five estoiles four and one of the second, all within a bordure argent charged with eight crosses couped gules* (Borough of Wandsworth, AH: 228).

19.00: The crest, etc.

So far we have discussed in detail only the shield and what can be placed upon it. It is now time to say something about the external ornaments of the shield, that is to say those things which together with the shield itself make up the heraldic achievement. We should start with those items which appear above the shield, the wreath, the mantling and the crest.

19.01: The crest

The crest in origin was an ornament with which the helmet was decorated. The simplest form of crest was practised in the twelfth and thirteenth centuries, namely a fan-shaped plate which was attached to the top of the helmet. This item was apparently designed to deflect blows or at least to lessen their impact. On occasion the plate itself was decorated with a figure or charge of some kind. A further step in the development of the crest occurred, when the outline of the plate was cut to resemble the outline of the charge. To begin with the shapes so produced were in two dimensions only. By the late thirteenth century or the early fourteenth however the three-dimensional crest began to appear. That was in effect the fully developed crest, which was made of either wood or leather. Such an ornamentation on the top of the shield must have been rather awkward, and it is very unlikely that it was every actually worn in battle. It was probably used almost entirely for tournaments and other ceremonial occasions. When one speaks about the crest in modern heraldry, one is talking about the fully developed crest and the other items connected with it, that is, the wreath and the mantling.

19.02: The helmet

The helmet has two functions in heraldry. In the first place it provides a place for the crest. In the second place it indicates the status of the armiger. In contemporary Irish heraldry people are not distinguished by rank (although men and women are kept separate for the most part by the fact that females do not usually have helmets in their arms), since the newly created armiger in Ireland is simply provided with the helmet of an esquire, that is, a plain closed helmet of steel facing to dexter. Within those criteria it is for the heraldic artist to determine both the size and the variety of helmet used. Under British rule, however, a knight, peer or baronet employed an open helment facing forward.

There are disadvantages pertaining to the direction in which the helmet faces. One used to find sideways crests on helmets that faced forward, and crests that faced forward on helmets facing to dexter. The cat-a-mountain passant in the crest of Blake, for example, looks fine on a helmet which points to dexter. If the same crest appears on a baronet's helmet, which faces forward, the cat and the helmet are facing different directions, and the cat resembles nothing so much as a dog travelling in a car with his head out of the window. In order to avoid such mismatches modern heraldic artists usually turn the crest slightly, and the helmet if possible, so that the two orientations are not completely at variance with each other.

In the eighteenth and nineteenth centuries the helmet was often depicted as though it were a human head, that is, with a narrow neck and rounded head. Such a helmet could never have fitted over the head of a knight, however, since every part of the helmet should be broader than the broadest part of a man's head. Modern heraldic artists base their helmets on the helmets of the middle ages.

19.03: The wreath

The crest was fixed to the helmet with bolts or cords, and since that in itself was rather unsightly, various methods were employed to disguise the join. One such method was the *contoise* or scarf, a love token from a noble lady, which was placed between the helmet and the crest. Then the scarf was curled round the helmet until *ca* 1250 it formed a wreath. In modern heraldry the wreath appears as a entwined ribbon. As a rule it is of two tinctures. Unless otherwise stated those are the tinctures of the shield, namely the chief metal and the chief colour of the arms; or, in the case of quarterly arms, the chief metal and colour of the first quarter. The first section of the wreath on the dexter side is of the metal.

On occasion a cap of maintenance appears in place of the wreath, or a ducal coronet takes the place of a wreath (§17.11).

19.04: The mantling or lambrequin

A protective cloth hangs from the helmet. This is the *mantling* or *lambrequin*, which in origin was a small cape attached to the back of the helmet and which fell upon the knight's shoulder to protect him from the heat of the sun. The edge of the mantling is usually depicted as scalloped or gapped. It is said that such indentations reflect the cuts and tears of the lambrequin received by the knight on the field of battle.

During the sixteenth and seventeenth centuries the mantling was usually shown as red with silver lining. Nowadays, unless otherwise specified the colours of the mantling are identical with the main tinctures of the shield itself. They are identical with the tinctures of the wreath (§19.03).

The heraldic mantling can be depicted in an infinite number of ways. The heraldic artist has complete freedom the draw the mantling as he wished. As a result one can say that the taste of the artist and the practice of his day are best expressed in the lambrequin.

19.05: Indifferent crests

As noticed above, the crest was originally a two-dimensional figure, but in its fully developed form it was a shape in three dimensions made from leather or wood. When heraldry departed from the field of battle and from the tournament, absurd crests began to be granted which could never have stood upon any actual helmet. Irish examples of such improbable crests include, for example: *A sun in splendour arising from clouds the whole proper* (Blackwood, Baron Dufferin); *An ermine spot* (Tabuteau, Portarlington); *A demi-eagle displayed argent gazing upon the sun in splendour* (Wingfield, Viscount Powerscourt); *A demi-lion gules holding in its paws the sun Or* (Leeson, Earl Milltown).

Fitzmaurice, Marquis Lansdowne has two crests. The first is *a beehive beset by bees volant* (BP: 1013). Brooke-Little says of that crest:

> One of the crests of Lord Landsdowne is a beehive beset by bees volant. When it became necessary to make a crest for the 5th marquess to place over his stall at Windsor, as he was a Knight of the Garter, the wood carver gave up the unequal struggle of keeping bees in suspended animation, and so left them out. New grantees should heed the moral of this tale, which is: if you want any of your family to become Knights of the Garter, choose a crest which can be modelled in the round. (CGH: 196 fn.).

19.06: The crest and Gaelic symbolism

The Gaelic nobility did not adopt heraldry until the crest was fully developed. They were able therefore to display aspects of native symbolism in their crests.

The robin redbreast is associated with the O'Sullivans and one finds references in Irish storytelling to *spideog chróndearg de mhuintir Shúilleabháin* 'the scarlet redbreast of the O'Sullivans'. It is therefore not astonishing that the robin redbreast appears in the O'Sullivan crest (§12.10). The cat-a-mountain is the symbol of the Keanes and the animal appears in their crest: *A cat-a-mountain rampant proper* (IF: 216). It is probable that the crest in this case is canting one, since the name Keane is from Irish *Ó Catháin*, of which the first syllable contains the Irish word *cat* 'cat'. The Burkes and the Blakes of Connacht are of Anglo-Norman origin. They adopted the cat-a-mountain for their crests, presumably in imitation of the Gaels.

The enfield is seen in the crest of O'Kelly of Uí Maine. As has been mentioned above (§14.06), the enfield is the family beast and it is not without significance that it occurs in the crest.

The crest of O'Flaherty is a *lizard passant vert*. It is said that one of the ancestors of the O'Flahertys, Amalgaid Earclasach, was fleeing from his enemies.

He came to an isolated spot and because he was exhausted, he lay down to rest and fell asleep. When his enemies were about to come upon him, a lizard ran up and down his face to wake him. Amalgaid seized his chance and escaped from his enemies. The tradition of the O'Flahertys is that the crest has its origin in that incident. Indeed the very epithet of Amalgaid is *Earclasach*, which contains the element *earc* 'lizard' (R. O'Flaherty, *Chorographical Description of Iar Connaught*, edited by J. Hardiman, 363 fn.). It is probable, however, that the story was an attempt to rationalize the origin of association of the lizard with the family. It is more likely that the lizard is a manifestation of some reptilian monster, which was associated with the family in pre-Christian times.

The red hand of Ulster is exceptional among Gaelic symbols, because it appears in the arms themselves, both in the arms of O'Neil and of Magennis. One should remember, however, that the red hand is more suitable for the shield than for a crest. Nor should it be forgotten that the O'Neils were among the first of the Gaelic nobility to adopt heraldry.

Many animals and fabulous creatures appear in the crests of the Gaelic nobility, the mermaid of the O'Byrnes, for example, and the hound of the O'Farrells. These creatures in all probability were associated with the relevant family in the pre-heraldic period and were placed in their crests when they eventually adopted heraldry.

19.07: The crest and heraldic errors

In England and Ireland the eighteenth and nineteenth centuries were a period in which heraldry degenerated somewhat. One result was that the crest often took over the function of arms on the shield, and was used by itself instead of the arms. This practice was wholly at variance with the essential nature of heraldry. In the middle ages, the shield was used to distinguish knights. The crest was to begin with a decoration which could be altered at the whim of the armiger. In the eighteenth and nineteenth centuries, however, the crest largely usurped the position of the armorial bearings themselves. One of the most regrettable results was that the word *crest* came to be not only for the crest, but for the arms themselves. This is still widespread and is wholly mistaken. *Crest* and *arms* are not synonymous and to call a coat of arms a crest is a sign of ignorance.

Not only did the word *crest* come to be applied to the coat of arms, but it was often displayed on a rigid horizontal wreath above the shield. Instead of being depicted over the helmet on a properly curved wreath, the crest appeared immediately over the arms. This is another regrettable and unheraldic practice which should at all times be discouraged. Edward MacLysaght was the first Chief Herald of Ireland, and he really ought to have known better. In his work

Irish Families, however he depicts all the crests of arms over a rigid horizontal wreath rather than correctly over a helmet; see IF: 159-85.

19.08: Crests in corporate heraldry

In Ireland today when a person is granted arms, he receives a crest with both helmet and wreath. Crests are not granted, however, to towns and other corporations. Dublin County Council was an exception. When MacLysaght granted them arms in 1944 the arms contained a crest. Although it was part of the grant, the crest did not appear over a helmet, but rather on a wreath directly over the shield (§17.31). It should also be pointed out that the arms of County Dublin are now mercifully obsolete, having been replaced by the arms of three new county authorities.

To be fair to MacLysaght the practice of granting corporate arms without a helmet was well established in Ireland before he became Chief Herald. In 1890, for example, a crest without a helmet was granted to the City of Belfast, about which Fox-Davies remarks:

> In Ireland no helmet at all was painted upon the patent granting arms to the city of Belfast, in spite of the fact that a crest was included in the grant, and the late Ulster King of Arms [Sir Bernard Burke] informed me he would not allow a helmet to any impersonal arms. (CGH: 244).

It seems that Burke believed that it would be incorrect to grant a crest on a helmet to a corporation, since a corporation has no head. This is false logic, however. If the corporation is not entitled to a helmet for want of a head, one might also argue that it is also not entitled to arms, since it does not possess a neck from which it can suspend a shield. For the purposes of heraldry the corporation is effectively a legal person and should therefore be granted both shield, crest and helmet. If the corporation is not considered to be a legal person as far as heraldry is concerned, then it should not use arms, since arms by right belong only to knights in armour.

The City of Dublin is an exceptional case, since a helmet does not appear over its arms. The heraldic achievement of the City of Dublin displays neither helmet nor crest, but only a beaver hat (§25.01). A similar hat can be seen over the arms of the City of Norwich in England.

20.00: Supporters

Since the beginning of heraldry nobles throughout western Europe used their coats of arms on one side of their seals. The spare space between the edge of the seal and the shield was often filled with other figures, human beings or animals. Gradually those figures became an essential part of the nobleman's heraldic achievement and were known as *supporters*.

20.01: Supporters in personal heraldry

Animals resembling wyverns for example can be seen on either side of the shield on the heraldic seal of Hugh O'Neill (§01.02). Supporters were not in general use in England or Ireland until the reign of Henry VI (1422-1461). In neither country did the use of supporters extend beyond the monarch, peers and during their lifetime knights. The commonest supporters were human figures, animals and heraldic monsters.

In Scotland the custom is for minor barons and clan chiefs to have supporters. It seems that in imitation of the Scottish practice during the nineteenth century chiefs of the name in Ireland began to display supporters to their arms. Fox-Davies writes:

> Whilst the official laws in Ireland are, and have apparently always been, the same as in England, there is no doubt that the heads of the different septs assert a claim to the right to use supporters. On this point Sir Bernard Burke, Ulster King of Arms, wrote: 'No registry of supporters to an Irish chieftain appears in Ulster's Office, in right of his chieftaincy only, and without the honour of peerage, nor does any authority to bear them exist'. But nevertheless 'The O'Donovan' uses dexter, a lion guardant, and sinister, a griffin; 'The O'Gorman' uses, dexter, a lion, and sinister, a horse; 'The O'Reilly' uses two lions or. 'The O'Connor Don', however, is in the unique position of bearing supporters by unquestionable right, inasmuch as the late Queen Victoria, on the occasion of her last visit to Dublin, issued her Royal Warrant conferring the right upon him. The supporters granted to him were 'two lions rampant gules, each gorged with an antique crown, and charged on the shoulder with an Irish harp or' (CGH: 319).

When the functions of the Office of Ulster King of Arms were transferred in independent Ireland to the Office of the Chief Herald, the practice began of allowing supporters to chiefs of the name (IH: vi). The custom was discontinued however. Donal Begley, Chief Herald of Ireland (1982-1995) used to say that he would not allow supporters to chiefs of the name, because there was an express prohibition on titles of nobility in the Irish Constitution (§29.07).

The Chief Herald of Ireland does not grant supporters to any armiger as a rule, although there are notable exception, e.g. Lord Killannin, for example (§26.08) and Mícheál Mac Aogáin, Bailiff of the Order of Malta.

20.02: Supporters in corporate heraldry

In England, Scotland, and Northern Ireland, supporters are granted to certain corporations, if they are of very high status, or if they have been incorporated by royal charter. It is customary therefore for the following to be granted supporters: counties, county boroughs, boroughs, cities, universities and institutions with *Royal* in their title.

The supporters granted to local authorities in Northern Ireland are sometimes of great interest. Two badgers or brocks, for example, were granted to County Fermanagh, a reference to the Brookes of Brookeborough. The supporters of Larne, County Antrim are two swans. This is presumably a reference to the story of the Children of Lir, in which Fionnuala and her brothers were changed into swans and spent three hundred unhappy years on the Straits of Moyle, close to the town of Larne.

Under the British administration the English practice as regards supporters was also in force in Ireland, although not always. The cities of Dublin (§25.01) and Waterford (§25.08), for example, both have supporters but no supporters were granted to the cities of Cork, Limerick or Derry.

In Ireland under British rule no supporters were granted to universities and third level colleges. This was unlike the practice in England. None of the following Irish institutions therefore was granted supporters: Dublin University (1862); The Royal University of Ireland (1880); Queen's College, Cork (1889); University College, Dublin (1912); the National University of Ireland (1913).

In present-day Ireland the practice of the Chief Herald appears to be somewhat uncertain as far as supporters for corporations is concerned. As a rule institutions are granted only a shield and a motto, but there are notable exceptions. Gerard Slevin granted arms to the Insurance Institute of Ireland in April 1974 which included *two phoenixes proper* as supporters.

20.03: The compartment

When there are supporters in the achievement, as a rule they stand on a small grassy hillock. This is known as the compartment.

Although the compartment is usual in contemporary heraldry, it was not always so. Instead of a compartment the supporters were made to stand on a scroll for the express purpose—known humorously as a *gas-bracket*. Otherwise they were made to perch dangerously on the motto-scroll itself, or they were allowed to hover in mid air without anything beneath them.

The shape and nature of the compartment is sometimes specified in modern grants. As a rule, however, the compartment is not part of the grant and it is left entirely to the artist to draw it as he or she wishes.

Although it is not mentioned in the blazon the supporters of the arms of County Antrim stand upon a representation of the Giants' Causeway. This is not part of the grant and on occasion they appear on the customary grassy knoll.

21.00: The motto

The motto is a phrase or war cry appearing on a scroll below the arms. The motto is not an essential part of the achievement in England. In Ireland, if there was a motto, it was shown. Nowadays in Ireland both individuals and corporations are granted a motto and it is accepted as an integral part of the arms. In Ireland and England the motto is displayed beneath the shield. In Scotland it appears above the arms. The writing over the shield are often known as a war cry, in order to distinguish it from the motto beneath. Nicholas Narbon, Ulster King of Arms, refers to the motto as *word* or *ponse* in a grant of his from 1576. In Scotland *slughorne* or *slogan* is the term often used for the war cry, which is from *sluagh-ghairm* 'army cry, war cry' in Scottish Gaelic.

It seems that a number of Irish mottoes were originally war cries. When Edward Poynings was Lord Deputy in Ireland he attempted to ban two war cries. The Irish parliament, which met in Drogheda in 1494-95 passed an act forbidding the words *Cromabo* 'Long live Cromadh' and *Butlerabo* 'Long live Butler' (*Analecta Hibernica* 10 (1940) 94), the war cries respectively of the Leinster Geraldines and the Butlers of Ormond. *Cromabo* < Irish *Cromadh abú* 'Long live Cromadh' is a reference to the castle of Cromadh in County Limerick, which was granted by the king to Maurice Fitzgerald, second baron O'Faly in 1216. At the end of the fifteenth century Ireland was much disturbed by faction fighting between the followers of the Earl of Kildare and the Earl of Ormond. The act to ban the war cries was an attempt to lessen civil disturbance in Ireland.

21.01: Historic mottoes in Irish

Numerous mottoes in the personal history of Ireland are in Irish. One might cite the following: *Ar ndúthchas* 'Our inheritance' (O'Doherty); *Buadh nó bás* 'Victory or death' (O'Hagan); *Ciall agus neart* 'Wisdom and strength' (O'Connell); *Clann na dtua abú* 'Long live the kindred of axes' (MacSweeny); *Coileán uasal* 'A noble whelp' (Woulfe—a pun on the name); *Conn can an* 'wisdom without fault' (O'Concannon—a pun on the name); *Do bheirim daoibh an chraobh* 'I give you the palm' (Creagh—a pun on the name); *Fear garbh is maith* 'A harsh man is good' (Magarry—a pun on the name); *Láidir is ó lear righ* 'Mighty the descendent of the sea king (O'Leary— a pun on the name; a ship appears in the arms); *Lámh dhearg Éirionn* 'The red hand of Ireland' (O'Neill).

21.02: Personal mottoes in other languages

Although mottoes in Irish were common among the native Irish, Latin mottoes were much commoner. That is still true with respect to personal heraldry in Ireland. After Latin the commonest language for mottoes is English. Among the other languages French appears widely. Here are some mottoes that are or were used in Ireland:

Boutez en avant 'Push forward' (Barry); *Tout d'en haut* 'All from above' (Bellew); *Suivez raison* 'Follow reason' (Browne, Marquis of Sligo); *Loyal en tout* 'Loyal in all things' (Browne, Earl of Kenmare); *Comme je trouve* 'As I find' (Butler, Marquis of Ormond); *Liberté tout entière* 'Complete liberty' (Butler of Lanesborough); *En Dieu est ma foi* 'My faith is in God' (Cheever, County Meath); *Toujours propice* 'Always propitious' (Dawson); *Ung roy, ung foy ung loy* 'One king, one faith, one law' (Burke); *J'aime mon Dieu, mon roy et mon pais* 'I love my God, my king and my country' (O'Kirwan); *Qui pance [Que pensez?]* (St Lawrence); *Prest d'accomplir* 'Ready to accomplish' (Talbot, County Roscommon); and *Sans tache* 'Without stain' (Preston, Viscount Gormanstown). There is a hidden pun in the motto of Bellew above, where the name is understood as 'Below'. A more obvious pun is seen in the two mottoes *Mon Dieu est ma roche* 'God is my rock' (Roche) and *Dieu pour la tranche, qui contre?* 'God for the trench, who is against?' (Trench).

Very occasionally in Irish personal heraldry mottoes occur in languages other than Latin, Irish or English. Calvert, Lord Baltimore had a remarkably sexist motto in Italian: *Fatti maschi parole femine* 'Deeds are masculine, words feminine'. The arms in current use by the American state of Maryland are those of Lord Baltimore and his motto is still the official motto of the state.

The motto of Comerford is a hunting cry, *So ho ho heane*, and it is not clear exactly what the expression means.

21.03: Mottoes in corporate heraldry

When arms without crests began to be granted to corporations in Ireland, often two mottoes were attached to the arms in order to render the arms less stark. As a result of this practice University College, Dublin has two mottoes *Ad astra* 'To the stars' above the shield and *Comhthrom Féinne* 'Fair play' beneath it. Similarly the National University of Ireland has *Veritati* 'For the truth' over the shield and *Fír fer* 'The truth of men' below it.

Notice that both those institutions have one motto in Latin. Under British rule Latin was the default motto language for corporations, e.g. *In portu quies* 'Peace in port' (Londonderry Port and Harbour Commissioners); *Nomine reginae statio fidisssima classi* 'In the name of the Queen a most reliable harbour for the fleet' (Queenstown [Cóbh], County Cork); *Oboedentia civium urbis felicitas* 'The obedience of the citizens is the prosperity of the city' (City of Dublin); *Pro tanto quid retribuamus* 'Let us return a little for so much' (City of Belfast); *Statio bene fida carinis* 'A very reliable harbour for ships' (City of Cork). English was also used, of course, e.g. *We will endeavour* (Royal Irish Academy); agus *Where Findbarr taught let Munster learn* (Queeen's College, Cork).

Since the Office of the Chief Herald was established, mottoes in Irish have become fashionable, for example: *Áineas Éireann* 'The delight of Ireland' (Kells, County Meath); *Ar aghaidh* 'Forward' (Castlebar, County Mayo); *As dúchas dóchas* 'Hope from our heritage' (Newcastle West, County Limerick); *Gníomhach idir carraig is cruacha* 'Active between rock and hills' (Greystones, County Wicklow); *Is fearr comhairle ná combrac* 'Counsel is better than conflict' (Carrickmacross, County Monaghan); *Is treise tuatha ná tiarna* 'Peoples are mightier than a lord' (Balbriggan); *Maoin na mara ár muinighin* 'The wealth of the sea is our hope' (Arklow, County Wicklow); *Mo radharc thar sál sínim* 'I spread my sight over the salt sea' (Wicklow); etc.

A motto in Greek was granted to Londonderry High School in 1957: Ὡς ἀεί ἐνώπιον τοῦ Θεοῦ 'As though always in the presence of God'.

21.04: Corporate Mottoes in Northern Ireland

Northern Ireland, being under British jurisdiction, has been a separate heraldic entity from the rest of the country since 1943. I know of only three mottoes in Irish that have been granted to Northern institutions after that date. They are all local authorities and in every case the motto is merely the Irish name of the place in question: *Beannchor* (Bangor, 1951); *Feor magh eanagh* [?*Féar maith eanaigh* 'good grass of a marsh'] (County Fermanagh, 1954) and *Cuil Rathain* (Coleraine, 1951).

21.05: Further insignia

If an armiger is a member of an order of chivalry, he places his personal insignia round the shield, that is, the collar and badge of the order.

The arms of the Lord Mayor of Dublin in his capacity as lord mayor are the same as those of the city. As well as the beaver hat to which reference has already been made, there are further items outside the shield on the achievement of the City, namely a sword and a civic mace crossed in saltire and around the shield the collar of the Lord Mayor (§25.01).

22: The arms of women and the marshalling of arms

22.00: Women's arms in the early period

Heraldry emerged in the first half of the twelfth century, but no arms appear to have been borne by a woman until a generation thereafter. The first attested arms used by a woman were those of Rohaise de Clare (†1156), the niece of Gilbert, first Earl of Pembroke. Like her cousin, Strongbow, her arms were three chevronels (§07.04). By the years 1220-1230 many noblewomen had adopted arms, and by the end of the century arms were in use by women among the gentry, particularly in England and in France.

Almost invariably it was married women who adopted arms. Single women did not bother with arms in the early period at any rate. When women did bear arms they were the arms of their husbands or of their fathers, and on occasion their maternal arms.

Somewhat later a practice arose that women placed their arms on a lozenge rather than on a shield. In the earliest period, however, as can be seen from seals and tombs, women's arms appeared almost always on shields. The arms of Anne, Countess of Cambridge (†1411) can be seen on the base of a stone font in Trim cathedral. Her arms appear on a shield and the arms are those of her son, Richard Duke of York, dimidiated with the arms of her father, Roger Mortimer, Earl of March (†1385). If the various tinctures are assumed from other sources Anne's arms may be blazoned as follows: *Quarterly 1 and 4 Azure three fleurs-de-lis Or* (France modern); *2 and 3 Gules three lions passant in pale Or* (England) *and overall a label of three points dimidiating Quarterly 1 and 4 barry of six Or and azure on a chief of the first two pallets between a dexter gyron and a sinister gyron all of the second and overall an inescutcheon argent* (Mortimer); *2 and 3 Or a cross gules* (Burke).

22.01: The arms of unmarried women

The practice of placing a woman's arms upon a lozenge first arose in England, and continental Europe was not long in following suit. It seems that since women did not participate in either battles or tournaments, they could not in truth display their arms upon a shield. On the other hand it should be remembered that men on occasion bore their arms of lozenges during the middle ages. At all events the practice of placing women's arms on lozenges became fixed over time and to day single women place their arms exclusively on lozenges.

As a rule woman surmount the lozenge of their arms with a ribon tied in a bow. This is known as a *love-knot*. Understandably women do not display the military elements borne by males, the helmet, lambrequin, etc. Since the motto is in essence a war cry, woman do not usually display a motto. On the other hand if a woman is a peer in her own right she does display her coronet and supporters, even if she is married. She will also display her personal insignia (of orders of chivalry, etc.) in her achievement, if she has any.

The rule that women bear their coats of arms in lozenges, does not apply to queens regnant. Female monarchs in their own right are military commanders in their capacity of heads of state, and therefore they are entitled to all military parphernalia, the shield included. Queen Victoria as queen, always bore arms on a shield. Elizabeth II bears her coat of arms on a shield as does the Queen of Denmark and as did the Queen Beatrix of the Netherlands.

The lozenge as a shape can be rather restricting for the heraldic artist, who must often distort the arms a little in order to get them to fit in the available space. In places in continental Europe the cartouche, that is, an oval shape, is sometimes preferred for the arms of a woman.

22.02: The arms of married women

> *Agus timpchioll na haimsire sin adúbhradar go bhfaicfidís cia hé an taobh ar ar chóir armas na mban do chur, ar an ttaobh ndeas nó ar an ttaobh cclé* 'And around that time they would determine on which side women should wear their arms on the dexter or sinister side'
>
> (*Párliament na mBan* ['The Parliament of Women'] 664-66).

An unmarried woman bears her father's arms, or her own arms, if she is a new grantee, in a lozenge. When a woman marries an armigerous man, she bears a shield with her own arms on the sinister side and her husband's arms on the dexter. These are known as *arms of alliance*. Some commentators believe that the husband should substitute the arms of alliance for his own arms, and some do so. There is no real reason for such a practice, however. His paternal arms should be enough for the man; it is for the wife only to bear the arms of alliance.

When her husband dies, the widow continues to bear the arms of alliance, but she does so on a lozenge, to indicate that she is a widow and on her own (§30.01).

Arms of alliance have another function, for bishops, lords mayor, etc. The man who functions in the office impales his own arms on the sinister side with the arms of his office on the dexter, as though he were a woman married to the office. An example of this practice can be seen in the arms of Narcissus Marsh as archbishop (§26.01). If a married woman has the office of lord mayor, for example, it is not certain what practice should be followed. It seems that the best solution is for her to impale her own arms with those of her husband, and then impale the arms of alliance with the arms of the office.

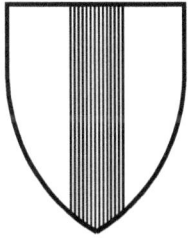

Mr Pale

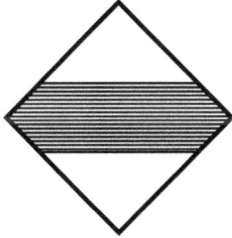

Miss Fess (not a
heraldic heiress)

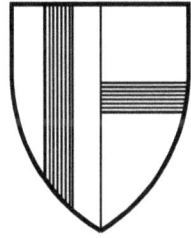

The arms of
alliance

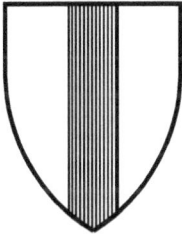

Son of Mr Pale and Mrs Pale
(née Miss Fess)

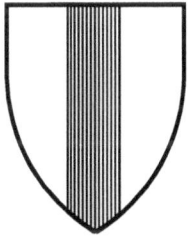

Mr Pale

Miss Bend-Fess (heraldic
heiress)

The arms of alliance
(with inescutcheon
of pretence)

Marshalling of Arms

Son or Mr Pale and Mrs Pale
(née Miss Bend-Fess)

Figure 19

22.03: Dimidiation instead of impalement

Although the modern practice is to impale the two coats of arms to obtain the arms of alliance, the custom existed at one time of dimidiating rather than impaling. This meant that half of the woman's arms appeared on the sinister side and half of the husband's arms on the dexter. A good example of dimidiated arms can be seen in the arms of Youghal, County Cork. Thomas de Clare, a younger son of Richard, Earl of Hereford, came to Ireland in 1272. He married Juliana, daughter and heiress of Maurice FitzMaurice Fitzgerald, Lord Inchiquin and Youghal, and by right of his wife he gained possession of the town of Youghal. As a result of that marriage the Provosts of Youghal used to bear on their seal of office *Or three chevronnels gules* (de Clare) dimidiating the arms of Fitzgerald, *Argent a saltire gules in chief a label of three points* (THBF: 467).

Those arms make clear the disadvantages that pertain to dimidiation. Since only one half of each arms is displayed, they are both distorted. It is not clear from the arms of Youghal whether there are chevronnels or bendlets sinister on the dexter side. The arms of Connacht incidentally are dimidiated, in which the dexter half of an eagle can be seen up against a human shoulder and arm. Those are not arms of alliance, it seems, even though two coats of arms have been conjoined (§24.04).

22.04: The arms of alliance of the heraldic heiress

When a man marries a woman who is a heraldic heiress, he impales her arms with his as long as her father is alive. When her father dies, however, he places her arms on an inescutcheon on his own arms. This is known as an *inescutcheon of pretence*. By heraldic heiress is meant the daughter of an armiger who has no sons. In the early period a heraldic heiress was the woman on whose husband the property and title of an armiger would devolve after his death. In feudal times the husband of the heiress had claim by right of his wife to the possessions and titles of his father-in-law after the latter's demise.

22.05: The descendants of an heiress and quartering

If the heraldic heiress and her husband have children, they have the right to quarter the paternal and the maternal arms. If the children's mother is not a heraldic heiress, they inherit only the paternal arms. Sons will bear the arms of the father with a difference, if their mother is not a heraldic heiress. If she is a heraldic heiress they will bear the paternal and maternal arms quartered, together with the relevant difference. A daughter will bear the arms in a lozenge without a difference, irrespective of whether she has sisters or not.

If it is necessary to quarter arms already quarterly with another coat of arms that itself is quarterly, the practice in England and in Ireland is to quarter once only. Say, for example, that Mr Pale marries Miss Bend-Fess, who bears quartered arms (her mother having been Miss Bend before she married), then their children and descendants will bear Pale in the first and fourth quarter, Fess in the second quarter and Bend in the third.

Although the first armiger in any family will always have a single coat in his arms, with the passage of time it is likely that the head of the family will marry a heraldic heiress. If this continues for a sufficiently long time, there will be more and more quarterings in the arms. In former times it was the custom for members of such a family to place in their arms as many quarterings as possible. When blazoning it might be necessary, for example, to say *Quarterly of twenty*, or *Quarterly of fifty*, etc., as the case might be. These days, however, multiple quarterings of this kind are regarded as indicative of somewhat degenerate heraldry and are discouraged. A large number of quartering give the arms the appearance of a patchwork quilt. Nowadays simplicity is preferred and it is not usual for a coat of arms to have more than four quarters.

22.06: Gaelic quartering

In English heraldry quartering is usually a means to indicate that there have been heraldic heiresses among the armiger's antecedents. In the Gaelic world, on the other hand, both in Ireland and Scotland, quartering had a different function. In Irish and Scottish heraldry quartering is simply a means to display clearly a variety of symbols taken from Gaelic iconography. Quartered arms are in such cases unitary coats with more than one section.

The arms of MacGrath give a good example of Gaelic quartering. The arms are blazoned as follows: Quarterly *1st Argent three lions passant in pale gules; 2nd Or a dexter hand lying fessways couped at the wrist proper holding a cross patté fitchy azure; 3rd Gules a dexter hand lying fessways couped at the wrist proper hold a battle-axe Or; 4th Argent an antelope passant sable armed Or* (IF: 215). Those are a single coat of arms, not four coats marshalled together.

Among arms that show Gaelic quartering one might include the following; O'Connor Faley (IF: 212); MacDonnell of the Glens (IF: 213); MacEgan (IF: 214); O'Mahony (IF: 217); Naghten (IF: 218); O'Riordan (IF: 219) and MacSheehy (IF: 219). For Gaelic quartering in Scotland, see R.F. Pye (1970), 51-8.

> NOTE: It seems that the Spaniards were the first to introduce quartering into heraldry. Both kinds of quartering survive in contemporary Spanish heraldry, that is, 1) to marshall various arms; 2) to display numerous charges in a single coat — as is the case with Gaelic quartering. The arms of de Valera (§26.06) are an example of the second kind of quartering.

22.07: Heraldic equality for women

Some modern commentators believe that the time has come to abolish the customary distinctions made in heraldry between men and women. If that were done, they argue, it would not be a new development, but a return to an earlier stage in the practice of heraldry. In the earliest days of heraldry knights and noblewomen displayed their arms in identical ways.

From the sixteenth century onwards, women have been refused shields, helmets and crests since they are not, or were not, soldiers. In which case there is a fundamental illogicality in the modern practice of heraldry, since there are many women who have commissions in the armed forces. All the same, such female officers may not use shield or helmet until they marry. On the other hand shield and the other military paraphernalia are granted to men who have never come anywhere near to the field of battle or the life of a soldier. Even if a man is a complete pacifist, if he has arms he displays them on a shield with a helmet above.

If women were made equal to men in heraldry, there would needs be certain basic changes. The system of differencing would no longer be a matter solely for sons (§23.04), but would involve daughters as well. The label would then not be the mark of difference for an oldest son, but for the oldest child. The notion of a heraldic heiress would also have to be abandoned. If either the son or the daughter of an armiger were an only child, he or she would be a heraldic heir/heiress. The spouse of the heir/heiress would be entitled to bear the arms or the daughter of the armiger in an inescutcheon in his or her own arms. If a woman were armigerous, when her husband was not entitled to arms, her children should be entitled to bear their mother's arms, on the condition that they used their mother's surname rather than the surname of their father.

The implications of heraldic equality for women would be revolutionary, but it must be admitted that the days of the superior position of men in society are long gone. We are accustomed to female prime ministers and female presidents. It does not therefore seem very sensible for heraldic authorities to attempt to maintain all the ancient traditions.

23.00: Differencing

Heraldry had its origins in the need to distinguish one knight from another, and arms are still used as personal marks. Theoretically then only one man at any time should use the same arms. Early on in the history of heraldry a method had to be devised to distinguish the arms of brothers, for example. Several methods have been used to that end, for example changing the tincture of the field, or scattering small charges on it or by ornamenting the outline of the main charge. Any method used to distinguish one coat of arms from another is known as a *difference*.

23.01: The Fitzgeralds

A good example of the change of tincture as a difference can be seen in the arms of the Fitzgeralds. Maurice Fitzgerald was the ancestor of the Irish Geraldines. His arms appear to have been *Argent a saltire gules*. Those are still in use by the Fitzgeralds of Leinster.

Maurice (†1356) son of Thomas Fitzgerald was the first Earl of Desmond. His arms were *Ermine a saltire gules*. The earldom of Desmond has been extinct since 1601 but the saltire gules on ermine is still in use by several members of the family of the Fitzgeralds of Munster.

Maurice son of Thomas was a grandson of Maurice (†1261) son of John son of Thomas Fitzgerald. Maurice son of John had a son Gilbert, and from him descend the Fitzgibbons of Kilmallock. The Fitzgibbons use a differenced version of the arms of the Munster Geraldines: *Ermine a saltire gules on a chief argent three annulets of the second* (IF: 214).

23.02: The Burkes

Walter Burke was the second son of Richard Burke (†1242), the Lord of Connacht. Walter married Maude, heiress of Hugh Lacy, Earl of Ulster, and when his father-in-law died in 1241, he himself became Earl of Ulster by right of his wife. That Ulster branch of the Burkes died out in the fourteenth century, however, with Elizabeth, daughter and heiress of William Burke, who married Lionel, Duke of Clarence (†1368), the second son of Edward III.

Walter Burke's arms were *Or a cross gules*. Although the Burkes of Ulster died out, the red cross on Or survives in the arms of the province of Ulster (§24.06). The cadet branch of the Burkes survived, that is to say the descendants of William (†1270), Richard's third son, and indeed they flourished. It was they who became Earls of Clanrickard later on. The Burkes of Connacht bore and indeed bear as arms *Or a cross gules and in dexter chief a lion sable*. Walter's and William's mother was a Lacy and a lion purpure on a field Or was the arms of the Lacys. (§24.06). It is likely that the lion which the Burkes of Connacht placed in their arms as a difference came from the Lacy arms. If so, the tincture of the lion was changed.

23.03: The Butlers

The arms of the Butlers provide some further good examples of differencing in arms. The senior branch always bore *Or a chief indented azure*. From the sixteenth century onwards, however, the Earls of Ormond have quartered that with the arms of the Chief Butler of Ireland: *Gules three covered cups Or*.

In the fourteenth century Thomas Butler, a younger son of the Chief Butler, differenced his father's arms with a bend gules overall: *Or a chief indented azure overall a bend gules*. Thomas went with his brother Edward, the sixth Chief Butler, to the shrine of St James of Compostela. On his return to take note of his pilgrimage Thomas placed three scallops *Or on the bend: Or a chief indented azure on a bend overall three scallops of the field*. Thomas was made Baron Dunboyne in 1324.

In 1660 the main branch of the Butlers of Dunboyne became extinct and a cadet branch of the family acquired the title. The arms they used were: *Or a chief indented azure three scallops bendwise counterchanged*.

The second son of Pierce Butler, the eighth Earl of Ormond, was was Viscount Mountgarret in 1550. The Mountgarrets bear as arms (quartered with Rawson): *Or a chief indented azure a crescent as difference*.

Or a chief indented azure a crescent as difference is also the blazon of the arms of the Earl of Carrick, that is, the head of another branch of the Butlers. They descend from the second son of the sixth Chief Butler of Ireland and the crescent of difference is argent and is placed on the chief itself.

For a full account of the heraldry of the Butlers in Ireland see T. Butler (1980/81 and 1991).

23.04: Marks of cadency

Heraldry is not a dead art but a living system. If methods of differencing were once necessary, they are still. A coat of arms does not belong to a group, but to a single individual. By rights neither brothers nor father and son should use the same arms. Strictly speaking every armiger should add something to his arms to ensure that he alone bears that version of the arms. Two systems of differencing are practised these days in these islands, the Anglo-Irish sytem and the Scottish one. Since these systems difference the arms of members and cadet branches of the same kindred, they are known as systems of *cadency* and the differences themselves are called *marks of cadency*.

DIFFERENCING

23.05: The Anglo-Irish system

This system developed in England in the fifteenth and sixteenth centuries. In order to distinguish a son's arms from those of his father, each son places a specific charge upon his shield. These are the mars that are used:

the first son	label
the second son	crescent
the third son	mullet
the fourth son	martlet
the fifth son	annulet
the sixth son	fleur-de-lis

Sons of sons can place their own marks of cadency on the marks of their fathers. A crescent on a label, for example, is the mark of cadency for the second son of the oldest son and a mullet on a label for the third son of the oldest son. It is not customary for the oldest son of the oldest son to place a label on the label, however. Instead he places a label of five points in place of his father's label of three points. A label on a crescent is borne by the first son of a second son and a crescent on a crescent is borne by the second son of the second son. Charles Stuart Parnell, for example, bore a crescent on a crescent (§26.05). Notice the following points also:

(1) Daughters do not use marks of cadency. They do use their father's marks of cadency if he has them.
(2) An armiger may use any tincture he wishes for his mark or marks of cadency and the tincture rule does not apply for such marks. Lest the marks of cadency be mistaken for ordinary charges, it is a good idea to place metal on metal or colour on colour; it is also wise to ensure that the cadency marks are smaller than the charges themselves.
(3) Marks of cadency are usually placed in the honour point or in the mid chief point. The mid fess point is suitable for quartered arms.

Although the system above has the appearance of perfection, it does not take long to realize that there is a snag in it. When the head of a family dies, his heir, the oldest son, removes the label from his arms. The sons of the oldest son (whose father is now the head of the family) now take the labels from their own arms. The heir now bears a simple label of three points and his two younger brothers bear the crescent and the mullet of the second and third sons. That means that there is no difference now between the sons of the oldest brother (now head of house) and the arms of their paternal uncles.

Fox-Davies points out that it is usually not long until the senior member of the family marries a heraldic heiress. He can then quarter her arms with his own, and that quartering itself can function as a difference.

Substantive revisions are recommended to the system from time to time, though none of them has been adopted to date. The problem is that differencing is effectively dead in both England and Ireland. Marks of cadency are used these days only to distinguish junior branches of the family. Little attempt is made these days to difference distinct armigers within the same branch of the family.

23.06: The Scottish system

The clan system in Scotland means that there is a limited number of surnames only in the country. Somebody with the surname Campbell, for example, is probably related to the other Campbells in Scotland. It is apparent therefore that a system of differencing is necessary to distinguish the arms of the various branches of the family from one another. Such a system in fact exist which was perfected during the nineteenth century. It more closely resembles the ancient system of differencing than the Anglo-Irish system of small charges used as cadency marks.

In the Scottish system the first, second and third sons in the first generation place their arms in bordures of differing tinctures. The relevant bordure becomes permanent in subsequent generations who ornament the edges of the bordures with engrailed, invected or indented lines. The eldest son in any generation does not adopt any permanent difference for his arms, but junior sons of the oldest son do ornament the edges of the main charge.

The great advantage of the Scottish system is that it works effectively and distinguishes the arms of everybody in the family tree. The disadvantage of it, however, is that each differenced coat of arms becomes a separate coat of arms, and accordingly it is necessary for every armiger to register his arms separately in the court of the Lyon King of Arms (§29.01).

23.07: Illegitimacy

In former times high-ranking bastard sons were common throughout Europe and every illegitimate son differenced his father's arms as he wished to form his own coat. In England and in Ireland until the eighteenth century the *baton sinister* (that is, a narrow bend sinister couped) was the customary mark of illegitimacy. Take, for example, the arms of the FitzRoys, dukes of Grafton. They descend from Henry FitzRoy (born 1663), natural son of Charles II by Barbara Villiers. Henry died in 1690 of wounds sustained in the capture of Cork for William of Orange. The dukes of Grafton bore the royal arms of the Stuarts debruised by *a baton sinister gobony of six argent and azure*.

Differencing: The Anglo-Irish System

Marks of Cadency

The first son		The fourth son	
The second son		The fifth son	
The third son		The sixth son	

Stage I

The Head of the Family

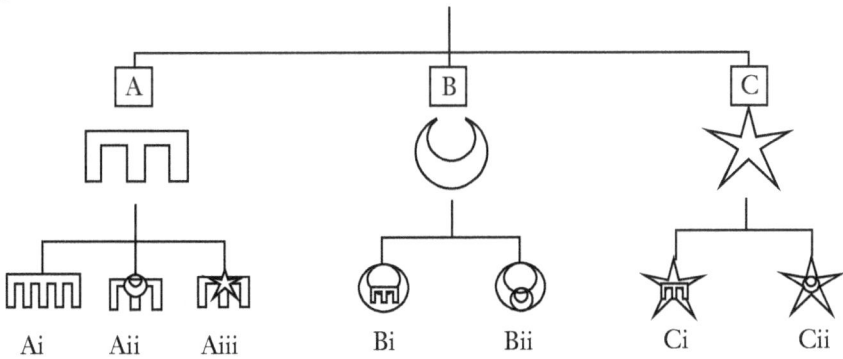

Stage I

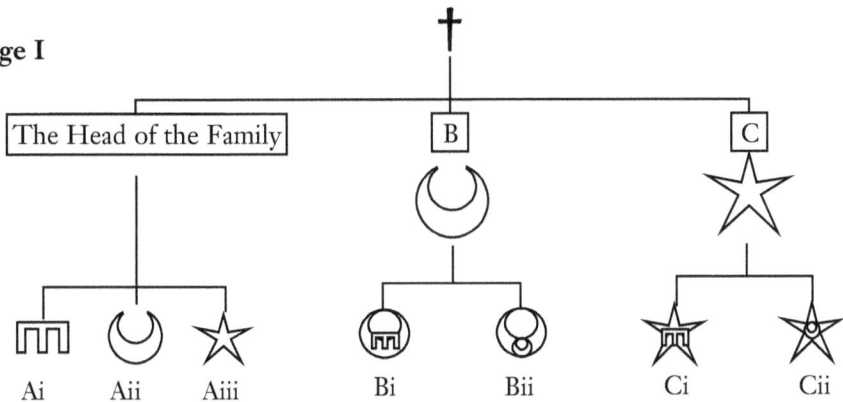

Figure 20

Another example of the royal arms borne by the descendants of a royal bastard are those of FitzClarence, earls of Munster. They descend from George (†1842), the oldest illegitimate son of William IV. The arms of the earls of Munster are those of the Hanoverian Kings (that is, quarterly 1 and 4 England; 2 Scotland; 3 Ireland; with Hanover in an inescutcheon) debruised by a *baton sinister azure charged with three anchors Or*.

The baton sinister is a narrow bend sinister couped. The bend sinister is called *barre* in French. As a result of confusion of the two terms *bend sinister* and *barre*, the solecism *bar sinister* has arisen in English as a term for illegitimacy.

In English and Irish heraldry since the end of the eighteenth century, the usual indication of illegitimacy has been the bordure wavy. Since, however, an illegitimate son had no official status nor even the surname of his father, he was legally bound to apply to the relevant authorities to obtain a completely new grant. Alternatively he could apply for a Royal Licence, or more recently in Ireland, a Government Licence to use his father's surname and his father's arms with a difference (e.g. a *bordure wavy*).

23.08: Augmentation

Augmentation or *augmentation of honour* refers to marks of difference bestowed by a monarch on an armiger to demonstrate the royal favour towards him. It would seem that the arms of Munster (*Azure three ancient crowns Or*) first came to Ireland as an augmentation (§24.03).

Arthur Wellesley was born in Dublin in 1769. He was made Duke of Wellington after his victory over Napoleon in 1814. The augmentation he received was the Union Flag on an inescutcheon at the honour point.

Augmentation has in the past been the occasion for indifferent heraldry. One of the very worst examples of augmentation can be seen in the arms of Viscount Gough of Gujerat and Limerick (created 1849). These arms exemplify three of the least satisfactory heraldic features of the period: 1) too many charges in the arms of which augmentations provide the bulk; 2) words upon the shield itself; 3) landscape instead of symbolism. The questionable taste of the Gough arms is such, that I quote the blazon here as an egregious example of heraldic excess:

Arms: *Quarterly, 1st and 4th, gules on a mount vert a lion passant-guardant Or supporting with its dexter paw the Union flag flowing to the sinister proper and over the same in chief the words CHINA, INDIA in letters of gold 2nd and 3rd azure on a fess argent between three boar's heads couped Or a lion passant gules in the centre chief point pendant from a riband argent fimbriated azure a representation of the badge of the Spanish Order of Charles III proper and on a chief a representation of the east wall of*

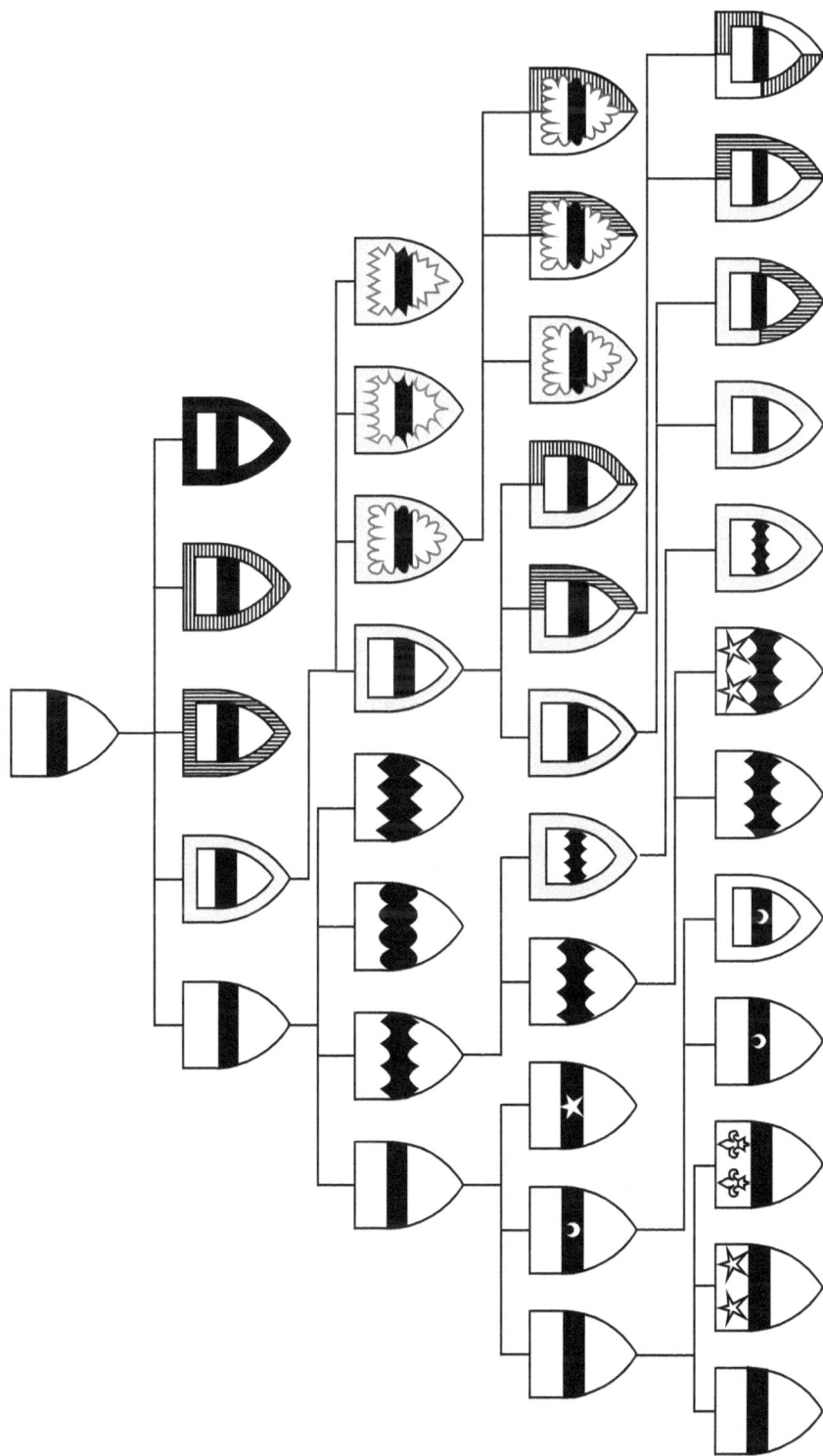

Differencing: The Scottish System
(The "Stodart" system)

Figure 21

the fortress of Tarifa with a breach between two turrets the dexter turret surmounted by the British flag flying all proper.

Crests: *1 (centre) A boar's head, couped Or 2 (dexter) On a mural crown argent a lion passant guardant Or, holding in the dexter paw two flag-staves in bend sinister proper, one the Union flag of Great Britain and Ireland surmounting the other, the staff thereof broken with a triangular banner flowing therefrom to represent a Chinese flag having thereon a dragon and in an escroll above the word CHINA 3 (sinister) A dexter arm embowed in facings of the 87th Regiment (gules faced vert) the hand grasping the colour of the said regiment displayed and a representation of a French eagle reversed and depressed the staff broken proper in an escroll above the word BAROSSA.*

Supporters: *Dexter a lion regardant Or gorged with an eastern crown gules with chain reflexed over the back gold the rim of the crown inscribed PUNJAB in letters also goldsinister a Chinese dragon Or gorged with a mural crown sable inscribed with the word CHINA and chained gold.*

Mottoes: *Over the centre (family) crest "Faugh a Ballagh"; Over the first crest "China" and over the third crest "Barossa" under the arms "Goojerat"* (BP: 755).

24.00: The arms of Ireland and of the Provinces

Coats of arms in origin were personal possessions developed in order to distinguish knights and noblemen from one another. It was not long, however, before the lord's arms came to be used as the arms of his territory. It is for that reason that one can speak of the lion of Scotland or the fleur-de-lis of France, though those two symbols belong by rights to the sovereign rather than the country. In the following paragraphs a very brief account is given of the arms ascribed to Ireland and to her provinces. It will be seen that many of those arms began as personal armorial bearings.

24.01: The harp: the arms of Ireland and of the province of Leinster

The arms *d'azur à la harpe d'or* 'Azure a harp Or' are the earliest arms associated with Ireland. They are ascribed to *le roi d'Irlande* 'the king of Ireland' in the Wijnbergen Armorial, a roll of arms written in France at the end of the thirteenth century which is now preserved in the Netherlands. It would seem that the king in question is Brian Ború or one of his descendants. Brian has always been associated with a harp and a harp is preserved in Trinity College, Dublin, which is known as the Harp of Brian Ború, although it probably dates from the fifteenth century. It is said that Brian received the harp from the Pope. Since heraldry was yet to appear when Brian died (†1014), there could have been little practice of arms when the Wijnbergen Armorial was written. It is likely therefore that the use of the harp as the symbol of Ireland originated in foreign sources outside Ireland.

The harp was not widely used as the arms and flag of Ireland until the reign of Henry VIII. Before that time the arms of Ireland were *Azure three ancient crowns Or* (§24.03). James I (James VI of Scotland) first placed the harp of Ireland in the royal arms, where it has remained ever since. The Irish harp displeased the Earl of Northampton (†1630), when it appeared in the royal arms for the first time. "The best reason that I can observe for the bearing thereof," he said, "that it resembles that country [that is, Ireland] in being such an instrument that it requires more cost to keep it in tune than it is worth."

The golden harp on a blue field are the arms of the President of Ireland. Those arms were officially adopted on 24 May 1945. The harp can also be seen on Irish euro coins and on official government papers and publications.

The coat of arms of the province of Leinster nowadays is: *Vert a harp Or stringed argent*. Those arms are only the arms of Ireland with a change in the tincture of the field. It is not known when this change occurred to give the arms of Leinster, although an example of the harp as the arms of Leinster is found as early as 1647. The arms of Leinster have been used officially as the Irish naval jack since June 1945.

There is some evidence that a different coat of arms was used for Leinster in the early seventeenth century: *Azure three crescents Or*. It is not known what is the origin of these arms but it should be noted that two crescents occur in the arms of Kavanagh, the descendants of Dermot MacMurrough and kings of Leinster.

Argent a lion rampant gules are the arms ascribed to the province of Leinster in the Devereux Roll, an English armorial of the fifteenth century. These arms may have some connection with the arms of Talbot discussed at §01.16 above. One should also remember that *Gules a lion rampant argent* are arms sometimes ascribed to MacMurrough, the Leinster chieftain (§24.10).

24.02: The arms of Ireland: the red saltire

During the period of British rule in Ireland in the eighteenth and nineteenth centuries, the arms most commonly used for Ireland were: *Argent a saltire gules*. Those arms were often referred to as the Cross of St Patrick, by analogy with the silver saltire on a blue background of Scotland, known as the Cross of St Andrew. The red saltire appeared in the insignia of the Order of St Patrick (§31.04) and it was added to the Union Flag in 1800. The red saltire also appears in arms granted during the nineteenth and early twentieth century, e.g. the Royal Irish Academy, the College of Surgeons, the Royal Dublin Society and Queen's University, Belfast.

There is some evidence that the red saltire was in use as the flag of Ireland as early as the beginning of the seventeenth century. It can be seen, for example, in the seal of Trinity College, Dublin, which was struck in 1612. The origin of the red saltire is uncertain, although it may simply be the arms of the Leinster Fitzgeralds (§23.01). The Geraldines were the masters of Ireland in the period 1475-1520 and they remained important thereafter. It is also possible that the red saltire is connected with the red ribbons which the Irish wore on St Patrick's day as early as the early seventeenth century.

24.03: The three crowns: the arms of Ireland and of Munster

The arms of Ireland before the adoption of the harp in the time of Henry VIII were *Azure three ancient crowns Or*. When Henry V died in 1413, the arms with three crowns were carried at his funeral as the arms of Ireland. Three crowns one above the other appear on Irish silver coins at the end of the fifteenth century.

Azure three crowns Or were the arms ascribed unhistorically to St Edmund, king of East Anglia. The medieval kings of England had great devotion to St Edmund. When Richard II gave his favourite Robert de Vere, Earl of Oxford the title of Duke of Ireland, he granted him the augmentation: *Azure three crowns Or within a bordure argent*. De Vere quartered that in the first and fourth quarters with his own paternal arms in the second and third quarters, *Quarterly gules and*

Or in dexter chief a mullet argent. It seems that the so-called arms of St Edmund were the basis of the augmentation granted to de Vere. The arms of St Edmund were incidentally also the origin of the arms of the University of Oxford.

It is likely, although one cannot be certain, that the arms of Ireland consisting of three crowns derive from de Vere's augmentation. Thereafter the arms became confined to the province of Munster. At the beginning of the seventeenth century, however, a different coat of arms was being used for Munster: *Gules an arm fesswise holding a sword erect all proper.* Those are in fact the ancient arms of the O'Briens of Thomond. They also, apparently, form one half of the arms of Connacht (§24.04).

Yet another arms are ascribed to Munster in a continental European armorial from the middle ages: *A golden stag on field argent* (§24.08).

24.04: The arms of Connacht

The present-day arms of Connacht are: *Per pale argent and gules on the dexter side an eagle displayed dimidiated sable on the sinister joined therewith in a sleeve argent a left arm embowed argent holding a sword erect all proper.* The first attested example of those arms as the arms of Connacht dates from 1647. There is evidence, however, to suggest that the arms of Connacht are in origin the arms of Ireland which later became confined to the western province. Various sources ascribe to Ireland: *Per pale Or and gules on the dexter side an eagle displayed dimidiated [sable] and on the sinister a human hand holding a dagger pomelled and hilted Or.* The German herald, Conrad Grünenberg (1483) gives as the arms of Ireland a shield per pale, *on the dexter side an eagle dimidiated and on the sinister an arm in armour with a sword in the hand issuing from sinister.*

The dimidiated arms with the eagle and the human arm are in all probability the generalized arms of the monastery of St James, that is the Irish monastery in Regensburg, Bavaria, which was founded *c.* 1067. Nowadays the arm is depicted upside down in the monastery's arms, but it is clearly one and the same as the arms of Ireland/Connacht. Since the monastery was an Irish foundation on German soil, there are two elements in the arms: 1) the arms of the empire: *Or a double-headed eagle displayed sable*, and 2) the arms of Ireland: *A human hand holding a sword erect*. As has been pointed out above (§24.03), those were the arms of Munster at one time, but in origin were only the arms ascribed to Brian Ború, '*imperator Scottorum*'. As such they stood for all Ireland.

There is some evidence from the seventeenth century that quite a different coat was ascribed to Connacht: *Argent an oak tree eradicated vert.* Those are the arms of O'Connor Don, who is a descendant of Rory O'Connor, king of Connacht and the last high king of Ireland.

24.05: The arms of Meath

In the seventeenth century the following arms were ascribe to the ancient province of Meath: *Azure a king seated on a throne both Or* or alternatively: *Azure a king seated upon a throne his dexter hand extended the sinister hand holding a sceptre all proper.* Those arms are themselves a coat ascribed in the sixteenth century to Ireland itself. In the arms ascribed to Ireland the field is sable, the sceptre is called a lily and the king holds it in his dexter hand. The king in these arms are presumably a reference with the king to the sovereignty of Ireland and to the high king of Tara.

The Chief Herald of Ireland granted arms to County Meath in 1988: *Per pile arched vert and azure fimbriated argent at the fess point an antique crown Or in chief in the dexter a spiral in the sinister a Celtic cross and in base a salmon naiant all of the third the whole within a bordure gold.* The vert and the bordure Or are the sporting colours of County Meath. The crown is a reference to Tara, seat of the high kings. The salmon swimming in the base azure refers to the Boyne and the salmon of wisdom. The spiral is an allusion to the carved patterns of Newgrange while the Celtic cross refers to the high crosses of Kells. Those last two charges therefore allude to the pagan and the Christian past of County Meath.

24.06: The arms of Ulster

The arms of the province of Ulster today are: *Gules a red cross on an inescutcheon argent a dexter hand couped of the second.* The first reference to these arms dates from the beginning of the eighteenth century. They are a combination of the red cross of the Burkes, earls of Ulster, with the red hand of the O'Neills.

Two other coats of arms are attributed to the province of Ulster. The first of those is *Or a dexter hand couped gules*, though the hand is sometimes a sinister hand. No example of that coat can be found before the beginning of the seventeenth century and it is apparent that it is only the arms of O'Neill (§01.02). The second arms ascribed to Ulster is less certain: *Or a two-tailed lion rampant gules* is a version from the beginning of the eighteenth century. This is similar to the arms of Ireland itself according to a Spanish source from the sixteenth century: *Or a lion rampant sable.* Since the tincture of the lion is either gules or sable, it is possible that the lions was of a colour between the two originally. In all probability therefore the arms are in origin those of Lacy: *Or a lion rampant purpure* (IF: 217). The Lacys were earls of Ulster before the title was inherited by the Burkes (§23.02). It would seem that those arms were originally used as the arms of Ulster and their use was then extended to the whole of Ireland.

When Ireland was partitioned as a result of the Government of Ireland Act of 1921, Ulster King of Arms created arms for the government of Northern

Ireland: *Argent a cross gules, overall on a six-pointed star of the field ensigned by an Imperial crown proper a dexter hand couped at the wrist of the second.* It should be noted that the cross of St George formed the basis of the arms, rather than the red cross on gold of the Burkes. Instead of the inescutcheon a six-pointed star alludes to the six counties of Northern Ireland surmounted by an imperial crown. The supporters granted to Northern Ireland were: *Dexter a lion gules armed langued and collared or, supporting a flagstaff proper, therefrom flowing to the sinister a banner azure, charged with a harp or, stringed argent, surmounted by an imperial crown proper; Sinister an Irish elk proper, collared or supporting a like staff, therefrom flowing to the dexter a banner Or charged with a cross gules.* The arms of the Burkes can be seen on the banner held by the elk, the dexter supporter.

24.07: The arms of the Republic of Ireland

Ulster King of Arms devised arms in 1921 for the southern state as well, but today those arms are assumed to be the arms of the Republic of Ireland. They are in fact the arms of the four historic provinces quaretered together: 1 *Vert a harp Or stringed argent* (Leinster); 2 *Per pale argent and zzure in the first an eagle dimidiated and displayed sable in the second issuant from the partition an arm embowed and vested the hand holding a sword erect all argent* (Connacht): 3 *Or a cross gules on an inescutcheon argent a dexter hand couped at the hand gules* (Ulster); 4 *Azure three ancient crowns Or* (Munster).

24.08: The crest of Ireland

Bernard Burke, Ulster King of Arms, mentions the ancient arms of Ireland: *Sable a king sitting on a throne his legs crossed holding in his dexter hand a lily all Or*, and he says that there was a crest over the arms: *A tower of three turrets Or from the portal therefrom a hart springing argent attired and unguled Or* (BGA: 530). Those arms have been discussed above under the arms of Meath (§24.05). It was customary to use the stag crest over the arms of Ireland, that is, *a harp Or on a field azure*. It also seems that the stag leaping from the door of the tower was in origin another coat of arms ascribed to Ireland. Among the arms ascribed to Ireland Burke cites a representation of a banner in Additional Manuscript 4814 folio 8, in the British Museum (now the British Library): *Gules a house tripple-chimneyed smoke issuant Or, a stag in the port of the first* (BGA: 530). Hayes-McCoy cites another example of those arms of Ireland, as follows: "a red shield with a silver castle from the gate of which a hart, in his natural colour but with horns of gold, is seen issuing" (HIF: 21; cf. PO: 365). In several continental armorials a variant of those arms are ascribed to the king of Ireland as early as the fourteenth century: *Azure a stag gules issuant from a gate argent.*

The Uffenbach Roll, a German armorial from *ca* 1440 gives the arms of the four provinces of Ireland. It is not clear to which province the various arms are ascribed. It appears, however, that the arms ascribed to Munster are: *Argent a stag Or* [*sic!*] These are effectively the arms of MacCarthy of Desmond (§11.06). It is also probable that the arms (and later crest) of a hart springing from the portal of a castle is related to the MacCarthy arms. The presence of the triple-turreted tower, however, is perplexing. Possibly the arms were in origin dimidiated in form, with a castle on one side and a stag on the other, and that the combined arms was mistaken for a stag or hart springing from the portal of a tower.

24.09: The arms of the counties of Ireland
Reference has already been made to the crest granted to County Dublin (§17.31). The arms themselves were *Or a raven sable standing on a hurdle sable.* The raven refers to the Norsemen and the hurdle (*cliath*) to the name of the city, Dublin (*Dublin*) from which the county took its name. These arms are now obsolete, since the area covered by the erstwhile County of Dublin has been replaced by three more recent local authorities, Fingal, South Dublin and Dun Laoghaire-Rathdown.

Like County Dublin, County Meath (§24.05) and County Offaly (§06.01), many of the counties of Ireland have received arms from the Chief Herald of Ireland since 1943. It is clear from a manuscript in the Genealogical Office (GO 60), however, that three counties of Ireland had been granted arms as early as *ca* 1665, namely County Kilkenny, County Tipperary and County Carlow. The arms in question are all very similar and they were probably granted in the same period. They are discussed in the next section.

24.10: The arms of Counties Kilkenny, Carlow and Tipperary
Manuscript GO 60 in the Genealogical Office blazons the arms of County Kilkenny as follows: *Ermine a fess party per pale dexter sable three garbs argent sinister quarterly 1st and 4th argent 2nd and 3rd gules a fret Or.* The arms containing the garbs on a sable field are sometimes ascribed to the Mac-Murroughs of Leinster (PO: 896). It is not apparent who are what is intended by the quarterly field on the sinister side.

The arms of County Tipperary in the same document are blazoned as follows: *Ermine a fesse quarterly 1 and 4 Or a chief indented azure 2 and 3 gules three covered cups gold.* The arms which appear on the fess are simply the arms of the Butlers of Ormond (§23.03), who had long had connections with the county.

The same document blazons the arms of County Carlow as follows: *Ermine on a fess per pale argent and gules on the dexter a lion rampant gules and on the sinister two lions passant guardant Or*. Burke mentions two versions of the arms ascribed to the MacMurroughs of Leinster: 1) *Gules a lion rampant argent* (cf. IF: 218); 2) *Argent a lion rampant gules holding in his paws a pole-axe of the same* (BGA: 645). It seems that a version of those arms can be seen in the dexter portion of the Carlow arms. Is is probable also that the lions passant guardant on the sinister side refer to Prince John, *Dominus Hiberniae* 'Lord of Ireland', who became king of England in 1199. We know from John's seal, which he used when he came to Ireland in 1185, that his arms contained two lions passant guardant.

25.00: Arms of towns and cities in Ireland

Soon after it was accepted that a country or district could have a coat of arms, towns and cities also acquired arms. In Ireland the arms of towns frequently carry elements of personal heraldry. Civic arms of this kind are also used in a personal context. The arms of the city of Dublin, for example, were used as the arms of the Lord Mayor of the city. If the Lord Mayor himself is armigerous, he impales his own arms on the sinister side (§22.02). If he has no arms, he bears the arms of the city by themselves during his term of office.

An account is given below of the arms of some of the most important towns in Ireland.

25.01: The arms of Dublin

Several coats of arms have been ascribed to Dublin. Papworth cites the following: *Gules a castle with towers argent* (PO: 365), although he cites no source. *Azure three castles flammant proper* are the arms currently in use. Daniel Molyneux, Ulster King of Arms, confirmed those arms during the visitation of 1607. It seems they had been in use for a long time before that date.

The citizens of Dublin first elected a mayor in 1229 and they adopted a common seal in the same year. A castle of three turrets appeared on one side of the seal and a ship with sails unfurled on the other. It is probable that the arms cited by Papworth were based on that seal. It is also apparent that the castle is a reference to the centre of the Norman town. If the single castle was replaced by three to give the arms of 1607, it is not difficult to explain the change. Three charges are usually more elegant on a shield than one by itself and three is the default number of charges in most arms. Compare, for example, the three fleurs-de-lis of France, the three lions passant guardant of England, the three crowns of Munster or the three ships of Waterford.

The flames arising from the castles are harder to explain. I know of no other example of castles flammant in the heraldry of these islands. In the seal of 1229 four human figures can be seen on the turrets of the castle, that is, an archer with a crossbow on both sides and two soldiers blowing war trumpets on the middle turret. It is possible that the flames of the arms of 1607 are based on those human figures. With the passage of time the soldiers on the ramparts became indistinct and were taken for flames issuing from the crenelated wall. It has also been less probably suggested that the flames represent the determination which the citizens have always shown to defend their native city.

When Molyneux confirmed the arms of Dublin for the lord mayor, aldermen and citizens of the city, he mentioned both the supporters and the motto. The supporters were blazoned as follows: *On the dexter side a female figure proper, namely a representation of Law robed gules lined Or in the dexter hand a sword erect and in the sinister a branch of olive both proper on the sinister side a female figure proper namely a representation of Justice robed gules lined Or in the dexter hand a branch of olive and in the sinister hand scales both proper.* There is some evidence that different supporters were in use in the fifteenth century, that is, a goose and a domestic cock.

Molyneux cites the motto *Oboedentia civium urbis felicitas* 'The obedience of the citizens is the prosperity of the city'. A different motto was also in use at one time: *Vigilance and valour.*

Molyneux mentions arms, supporters and motto only. The arms of Dublin, however, are often displayed with other insignia, namely a beaver hat over the shield, a mace and sword crossed in saltire behind it and the Lord Mayor's collar around the shield. The beaver hat and the mace and sword may have formed part of the arms as early as the fifteenth century.

25.02: The arms of Belfast

The arms of Belfast are blazoned as follows: *Party per fess argent and azure in chief a pile vair and on a canton gules a bell argent in base a ship with sails set argent on waves of the sea proper.* Crest: *On a wreath of the colours a sea-horse gorged with a mural crown proper.* Supporters: *Dexter a wolf proper ducally gorged and chained Or; sinister a sea-horse gorged with a mural crown proper.* Motto: *Pro tanto quid retribuamus* 'What shall we give in return for so much?'

Those arms were granted in 1890 by Sir John Bernard Burke, Ulster King of Arms, they are, however, identical with the arms used by the corporation of Belfast on a seal of 1640. At that time they were not the arms of the town but the personal arms of Henry le Squire, a follower of Edward Chichester, and sovereign of Belfast in the years 1635-36 and in 1639. The bell is a canting reference to the English name of the town, *Belfast*, although in reality the name is Irish *Béal Feirste* 'the mouth of the sandbank'.

On the seal of 1640 the crest stands on a helmet. As has been mentioned above (§19.08), Ulster King of Arms did not grant a helmet to Belfast, because the city had no head.

The motto is based on the Vulgate text of Psalm 115.12: *Quid retribuam Domino, pro omnibus quae tribuit mihi?* 'What shall I give in return to the Lord, for everything he has granted me?'

25.03: The arms of Cork

The arms of Cork are officially blazoned: *Or on waves of the sea a ship three masts in full sail proper between two towers gules upon rocks also proper each tower surmounted by a flag argent charged with a saltire of the third.* Motto: *Statio bene fida carinis* 'a safe harbour for ships' (based on *nunc tantum sinus et statio male fida carinis* from the Aeneid II 23). Although the arms were matriculated by the Chief Herald in 1949, the towers and the ship occurred on the seal of the city as early as the seventeenth century.

It is difficult not to believe that there is some connection between the arms of Cork and the arms of Bristol in England. The arms of Bristol depict a ship emerging from a castle on waves of the sea. There is some evidence for the existence of the Cork arms in Tudor times, when a bird appears in the rigging of the ship.

It seems that Spanish sailors were accustomed on Good Friday to suspend an image of Judas from the rigging of their ships and to burn the image thereafter. It is possible, therefore, that the bird in the rigging was a representation of the cock which crowed after Peter had denied Our Lord. Quite probably the sailors of Cork, like their Spanish counterparts also suspended an image of Judas from their rigging on Good Friday. It should be remembered that there were close links in former times between Cork and Spain. No bird appears in the contemporary arms.

25.04: The arms of Galway

The town of Galway has used various coats of arms over the years. They are discussed below in chronological order:

(*a*) The first coat of arms used by the corporation of Galway was that of the Burkes, earls of Ulster: *Or a cross gules* (§23.02). Those arms were, it seems, adopted during the fourteenth century. Much of Connacht was controlled by the Burkes at the time and Galway was the largest town in the province.

(*b*) The Burkes ceased to be earls of Ulster on the death of William, the third earl, in 1333. He was treacherously killed in his castle in Carrickfergus. William left as heir his daughter Elizabeth. She married Lionel, Duke of Clarence, the third son of Edward III. Lionel acquired the earldom of Ulster by right of his wife. The couple had only one daughter, Philippa, and in 1368 she married Edmund Mortimer, earl of March. Mortimer was earl of Ulster and Baron Trim and Connacht by right of his wife. At that point the corporation of Galway adopted the arms of the Burkes quartering Mortimer: *Quarterly 1 and 4 Or a cross gules; 2 and 3 barry of six Or and azure on a chief of the first two pallets between a dexter and sinister gyron all of the second overall an inescutcheon argent.* The civic authorities in Galway seem to have used those arms until 1485. Indeed there is some evidence that the arms remained in occasional use until the eighteenth century. Notice that Anne Mortimer (†1411), Edmund Mortimer's granddaughter, used a version of those arms

(§22.00). A version of the same coat of arms was used at one time by Drogheda also (§25.13).

> NOTE: There are several ways to blazon the arms of Mortimer. Another blazon which is based on a French version runs as follows: *Barry of six azure and Or a chief party per pale in three pieces the first per bend of the first and second the third per bend sinister of the same the second Or with a pale azure overall an inescutcheon argent.*

(c) The third arms used by the corporation of Galway was: *Azure a chevron Or between three castles triple-towered argent.* Hardiman believed that these arms were adopted in 1396, but it seems more likely that they date from the period when Galway received its first charter. This was granted by Richard III in 1485. The charter stated that the Burkes were to have no power or authority over Galway. It was time therefore to rid the town of the arms of the Burkes and to adopt new arms. The castles triple-towered are presumably a reference to the walls built round Galway at the end of the fourteenth century. The Lynch family provided a number of early mayors of Galway and it is likely therefore that the chevron *Or on a field azure* is in imitation of the arms of Lynch: *Azure a chevron Or between three trefoils slipped of the same.*

(d) The arms which are currently in use by the city of Galway have varied over the years. The most basic form is blazoned as follows: *Argent an ancient ship of one mast the sail furled sailing on waves of the sea all proper on an inescutched the royal arms of England.* It is not possible to say when those arms were first used, though it is probable that they were adopted when the town received its second charter from Elizabeth I in 1578. Clearly the ship was placed in the arms to emphasize the town's importance as a port.

The "royal arms of England" in the blazon refer to the following: *Quarterly 1 and 4 Azure three fleurs-de-lis Or (France modern); 2 and 3 Gules three lions passant guardant in pale Or.* Cf. the dexter side of the arms of Anne Mortimer (§22.00). On the common seal of Galway, however, it seems that the arms in the first and fourth quarters France ancient is depicted, that is, *Azure semée of fleurs-de-lis Or.*

The arms on the inescutcheon used today are *Sable a lion rampant Or.* The lion is the lion of England on the inescutcheon. The royal arms on versions of these arms as well as the English lion on this variant are intended to represent loyalty to the English crown.

Papworth cites yet another form of these arms: *Azure a ship sable adorned Or* (PO: 1089), though he cites no authority. These arms in all probability derive from the same seal from which the various forms of coat of arms *d*) also derive.

25.05: The arms of Derry

The arms of the City of Derry are unusual in that they depict a human skeleton. The arms are blazoned as follows: *Sable a human skeleton Or seated upon a mossy stone proper and in dexter chief a castle triple-towered argent on a chief also argent a cross gules thereon a harp or and in the first quarter a sword erect gules.* Motto: *Vita veritas victoria* 'Life truth victory'. The arms on the chief are those of the City of London.

Although the arms were not confirmed officially until 1613, they had been in use minus the chief for some time previously. The arms of London on the chief are a reference to the the London companies who were involved in the plantation of Derry; as a result the city was officially renamed Londonderry or in Irish *Londan-doire*, a name well attested in Irish:

> *A Londain-Doire, bolgach chughatsa*
> *Ar nós na scáile ar lasadh le púdar*
>> 'Curse upon you, O Londonderry, burning with powder like a shadow'
>> from "*Slán le Pádraig Sáirséal*" 'Farewell to Patrick Sarsfield'.

It is sometimes said that the skeleton refers to the death of Cathaoir O'Doherty, the great enemy of the planters of Derry. It was believed that he was immured in his own tower and so died of hunger. O'Doherty, however, did not die that way and he was still alive when the arms were granted. Other commentators claim that the skeleton has to to with an incident in the history of the Burkes, earls of Ulster. It was the Burkes who constructed Greencastle on Lough Foyle.

25.06: The arms of Armagh

The city of Armagh was without arms until the middle of the twentieth century. Before that Armagh used the arms of Ireland: *Azure a harp Or stringed argent.* Those arms could be seen until recently on banknotes in Northern Ireland. The arms were intended, it seems, to belong to County Armagh rather than the city of Armagh.

The urban district of Armagh was granted the following armorial bearings by the College of Arms in London in 1958: *Azure on a bend embattled between in chief a primatial cross and in base a harp Or a bendlet gules.* Crest: *On a wreath of the colours An ancient Irish crown gold.* Motto: *In concilio consilium.*

25.07: The arms of Limerick

The arms at present in use by Limerick are blazoned as follows in the Genealogical Office: *Gules a castle of two towers argent and between them an obtuse spire proper ensigned with a cross flory argent*. The city used at one time to quarter those arms with the three lions passant guardant of England. Burke blazons the those arms as follows: *Quarterly 1 and 4 Gules a castle on each tower an obtuse spire with a weathercock on an arch over the curtain wall a cross flory argent; 2 and 3 Gules three lions of England Or* (BGA: 609).

A version of those arms were seen in the arms of the Midwestern Health Board (§13.06).

25.08: The arms of Waterford

The arms currently in use by Waterford are: *Azure in base waves of the sea proper and above them three barges in pale Or*. These arms were confirmed by the Chief Herald in 1953. There was a time when the arms contained more than that. Burke gives the arms of the city of Waterford as follows: *Per fess gules and argent in chief three lions passant guardant in pale Or in base the sea proper three barges of the third* (BGA: 1081). The lions are those of England. A carved version of those arms can be seen in Main Street, Waterford. The arms have a harp as crest and a lion and dolphin as supporters. The motto is *Urbs intacta manet Waterfordia* 'The city of Waterford remains untouched' and was given by Henry VII for resisting the army of Perkin Warbeck.

25.09: The arms of Dundalk

The arms in use by the town of Dundalk are: *Or a bend gules between six martlets of the same*. In origin those are simply the arms of Thomas de Furnivall, who possessed Dundalk in the fifteenth century. A seal survives on which those arms are depicted although the date of the seal is uncertain. The Office of the Chief Herald confirmed those arms and granted a Crest: *A lion passant guardant Or*; and Supporters: *On the dexter side a boar rampant ermine and to sinister a Norman footsoldier armed and holding in the dexter hand a spear all proper*. The boar is a reference to the arms of O'Hanlon, lord of Orior. The motto used with the arms is *Mé do rug Cúchulainn códha* 'I bore courageous Cuchulainn'.

Another coat of arms was used by Dundalk in the sixteenth and seventeenth centuries: *Azure three martlets argent*. That seems to be a simplified or corrupted version of the Furnivall arms.

Some commentators have suggested that the arms of Dundalk derive from the armorial bearings of Dowdall, another family closely connected with medieval Dundalk. The arms of Dowdall of Oriel were: *Argent a fess gules between three martlets of the same* (BGA: 296). It has also been suggested that the martlets were doves at one time and that the coat of arms was a canting one: *Dove-dall > Dowdall.*

25.10: The arms of Port Laoise

Port Laoise was incorporated under the name *Maryborough* in 1553 in the reign of Mary Tudor. It seems that the town received its arms at that time: *Per fess gules and azure in chief two lions passant guardant in pale in base two fleurs-de-lis fesswise all Or.* We have no reference to the arms, however, until Richard Carney, Ulster King of Arms confirmed them in 1656. The arms are based on Mary's own arms, that is, France modern quartering England (§25.04).

25.11: The arms of Dún Laoghaire

Arms were granted to Dún Laoghaire at the end of the nineteenth century which are a good example of the indifferent heraldry of the period: *Purpure on a base barry wavy of nine azure and argent to dexter a grassy headland thereupon a tower embattled to sinister a Viking ship sail set all proper on a chief per pale argent and vert dexter an ancient mitre proper sinister an ancient crown Or.* That is a landscape/seascape for the most part. The crown is a reference to the name of Dun Laoghaire from 1821 to 1920, Kingstown. These arms became obsolete with the creation of Dunlaoghaire-Rathdown in 1986.

25.12: The arms of Naas, County Kildare

The arms of Naas, County Kildare are *Argent a serpent erect wavy proper.* There is, however, no evidence that the arms were ever granted or confirmed. Some commentators assert that the coat of arms is a canting one since the Hebrew word for a snake is *nahash*, which is close to the name of the town. I remain unconvinced by that explanation. Naas in former times was in former times the seat of the kings of the *Laigin* or Leinstermen, and the arms are almost certainly connected with the importance of Naas as a royal settlement in pagan times. The serpent, although absent from Ireland, was a cultic creature to the pagan Celts. It is noteworthy incidentally that Bridget the goddess/saint of Leinster is also connected with the serpent in early poetry.

25.13: The arms of Drogheda

Reference has been made above to the arms of Burke quartered with Mortimer, which was use for a time as the arms of Galway (§25.04*b*). It seems that a coat of arms was used by the town of Drogheda in the period 1368-1425 and beyond, perhaps, which was very similar to those arms of Galway. The only way in which the two coats differed was that the Mortimer arms were in the first and fourth quarter in the arms of Drogheda and Burke in the second and third, but the

Mortimer arms were in the in the second and third quarter in the arms of Drogheda.

Roger Mortimer, the first earl of March, Joan de Grenville, the grand-daughter of Maud Lacy, one of the joint heiresses of Hugh Lacy, lord of Meath. Mortimer obtained through Joan a large portion of the Lordship of Trim, of which Drogheda was part. It seems that Drogheda north of the Boyne used the arms of Mortimer until 1369. In that year Edmund Mortimer married Philippa, the heiress of Lionel, Duke of Clarence and earl of Ulster. Unlike the position in Galway, the Mortimers rather than the Burkes were the more important family in Drogheda. It was for that readon that Mortimer appeared in the first quarter in the arms of the town.

Drogheda had another coat of arms which was registered in the Office of Ulster King of Arms: *Azure per pale dimidiated on the dexter side three lions passant guardant in pale Or on the sinister as many hulls of ships of the last over all a castle of two towere triple-towered argent* (BGA: xcviii).

25.14: The arms of Youghal

The arms used by Youghal in the middle ages was de Clare dimidiating Fitzgerald (§22.03). Another coat of arms that was never matriculated survives in the Office of the Chief Herald. It is blazoned as follows: *Sable an ancient ship of one mast the sail furled the yard set square all Or*. Those arms were probably based on an old seal.

25.15: Other towns

Many other towns in Ireland have been granted arms or have been using unregistered arms for a long time, e.g. Gorey (§06.02), Kinsale (06.04) and Athlone (§16.04).

The Chief Herald of Ireland has granted arms to many towns since his office was established in 1943. For such arms wide use has been made of distinctively Irish charges and Gaelic tradition. Among the arms of towns discussed in this book one must include Trim (§16.02); Balbriggan (§07.09); Loughrea (06.03); Shannon (§16.05); Bundoran (§06.01); Castlebar (§10.03); Newcastle West (§06.01); Kells (05.03); Killarney (§07.09); Wicklow (§12.04); Kilrush (§10.07); Greystones (§07.01); Clonmel (§11.06); Arklow (§10.12); Letterkenny (§16.05); Fermoy (§13.01); Sligo (§10.12) and Tullamore (§12.08).

Among the arms granted to towns in Northern Ireland since 1943 that are mentioned in this book one can include Castlereagh (§15.06), Dungannon (§17.30), and Larne (§20.02).

26.00: The arms of some famous people

In this section the arms of some famous people in Irish history will be discussed.

26.01: Narcissus Marsh (1638-1713)

Narcissus Marsh was born in England and was educated in Oxford. He was ordained and came to Ireland in 1678/9 to take up the post of Provost of Trinity College. He was consecrated Church of Ireland bishop of Leighlin and Ferns in 1683, archbishop of Cashel in 1690, archbishop of Dublin in 1694 and was elevated to Armagh in 1704. He was intimately involved with the publication of the Bible in Irish. When he was archbishop of Dublin he founded Marsh's Library next to St Patrick's Cathedral. The library is still there.

These are the arms he used when he was archbishop of Dublin: *Azure a bishop's staff Or, ensigned with a cross patty also Or overall a pallium argent edged and fringed Or charged with four crosses patty fitchy sable* (the see of Dublin) impaling *Gules a horse's head couped argent between three crosses crosslet fitchy Or* (Marsh).

26.02: Jonathan Swift (1667-1745)

When Jonathan Swift was given the freedom of Dublin his arms were: *Or a chevron vair between three stags at speed proper*. These are also the arms on his tombstone in St Patrick's Cathedral. Burke ascribes another coat of arms to him: *Per pale Or and vert a on a chevron between three stags at speed three broad arrows the points downwards all counterchanged* (BGA: 990). These appear to be a slightly different version of the first arms. The "swift" stags are a canting allusion to the name.

26.03: Henry Grattan (1742-1820)

Henry Grattan was of importance in the Irish parliament at the end of the eighteenth century. His family were from Dublin. His great-grandmother, Grissel Brereton from County Cavan, was a heraldic heiress. Henry Grattan therefore bore the arms of Grattan quartered with Brereton: Quarterly 1 and 4 *Per saltire sable and ermine a lion rampant Or* (Grattan); 2 and 3 *Argent two bars sable* (Brereton).

26.04: John Henry Newman (1801-1890)

The arms used by John Henry Newman when he was made cardinal in 1879 were: *Or a fess dancetty gules between three human hearts of the same*. His motto was: *Cor ad cor loquitur* 'Heart speaks to heart', a statement from St Francis de Sales, to whom Newman had great devotion. Those arms can be seeen in several places in both England and Ireland, for example in the porch of the University Church, Stephen's Green, Dublin.

The same arms without the motto were in use by John Newman, the cardinal's father, before John Henry was born. The father adopted the arms in 1799 when he married. The truth, however, is that Newman's father had no right to the arms at all. Although Newman was made cardinal at the request of the Duke and Norfolk, a Roman Catholic layman, and the patron of the College of Arms, Newman's right or lack of right to armorial bearings was never examined. Newman's arms therefore were of no authority.

26.05: Charles Stuart Parnell (1846-1891)

The following arms were granted in Enlgand in 1846 to Henry Brooke Parnell, Baron Congleton, and to the other descendants of his father, John Parnell, baronet: *Gules two chevronnels argent and in chief three scallops of the same.* Henry Brooke Parnell had a younger brother called William Parnell Hayes. He was the father of John Henry Parnell of Avondale. This John Henry Parnell was the father of Charles Stuart Parnell, the celebrated politician. William Parnell Hayes, the grandfather of Charles Stuart Parnell, was thus a second son. Charles Stuart Parnell himself was the second surviving son of his father. Charles Stuart Parnell, therefore, bore the arms of Parnell, barons Congleton, with a crescent on a crescent.

26.06: Éamon de Valera (1882-1975)

The arms of the Presidents of Ireland can be seen together in the Heraldic Museum in Kildare Street. The arms ascribed to de Valera can be blazoned as follows: *Quartery 1 and 4 Argent a lion rampant Or; 2 and 3 Or a lunel gules within a bordure of the same charged with eight saltires couped gold.*

Those arms are Spanish in appearance. The quartering without function as a means of marshalling, is distinctively Iberian (§22.06 note). The bordure charged with eight charges is also a Spanish feature. The lunel is an Iberian feature, and was common in the heraldry of Spain and Portugal during the Reconquest. The crescent is a symbol of Islam and to allude to the defeated Moors four crescents were placed together. As the Christian leaders pushed the Muslims out of the Iberian peninsula, they placed the lunel in their arms to indicated their victories (§17.17).

Although de Valera used those arms, they were never granted. De Valera was born in the United States and his father was a Spaniard. The family of de Valera or Valera, from whom de Valera descended, were well known in Spain. When de Valera became president of Ireland, the Spanish ambassador provided a coat of arms. This was not a grant. The Spaniards simply provided a description of the de Valera arms and a depiction of them.

It is remarkable that de Valera was never advised to apply for arms from the Chief Herald of Ireland. The President is the first citizen of Ireland and it was de Valera himself who founded the Office of the Chief Herald. If de Valera was not within the jurisdiction of the Chief Herald, then nobody was. It seems likely that de Valera and his advisers did not really understand the question of heraldic jurisdiction.

26.07: John F. Kennedy (1917-1963)

The Chief Herald of Ireland ratified arms to President John Fitzgerald Kennedy on St Patrick's Day 1961. The arms are blazoned as follows: *Sable three helmets in profile Or within a bordure per saltire gules and ermine.* Crest: *Between two olive branches a cubit sinister arm in armour erect the hand holding a sheaf of four arrows the points upwards all proper mantled gules doubled argent.* There is no motto.

Those arms are interesting in themselves. The helmets on the sable field are the arms ascribed to Kennedy. President Kennedy descended from the Fitz-geralds of Desmond also and the *bordure per saltire gules and ermine* was placed on the shield as an allusion to the saltire gules on ermine of the Geraldines of Desmond (§23.01). The crest was based on the arms of the United States of America. The arms are usually depicted on the breast of a bald eagle which bears a branch of olive in its beak and a sheaf of arrows in its claws.

There is no official heraldic authority in the United States (§29.05). It was for that reason that President Kenedy got arms from Ireland, the land of his ancestors. It was indeed an unprecedented event when the government of Ireland presented arms to the head of another government, the President of the United States of America.

26.08: Lord Killanin (1914-1999)

The arms of Michael Morris, third baron Killanin were: *Ermine a fess dancetty sable in base a lion rampant of the same, armed and langued gules.* Crest: *On a fasces proper a lion's head erased argent goutté de poix.* Motto: *Si Deus nobiscum quis contra nos* 'If God is with us, who is against us?' The motto is a quotation from the Vulgate, Romans 8.31. Michael Morris inherited rank of baron in 1927, when his uncle Martin Morris died without issue.

The Michael Morris (1826–1901) first baron had supporters: *Two lions gules gorged with a chain Or pendant therefrom an escutcheon ermine charged with a sword erect proper pommel and hilt gold and standing on a fasces also proper.* These supporters were granted to him in 1889 with his life peerage as a lord of appeal. They did not descend with his hereditary peerage (1900). The second baron (1900-1927) bore the supporters, though it seems that he had no right to them. The third baron did not use any supporters until 1985, when the Chief Herald of Ireland granted him as supporters the lions gules which his uncle, the first baron, had borne. They, however, were not granted to him by right of his peerage, which was of no effect in Ireland, but because of his work as Chairman of the International Olympic Committee.

26.09: Charles J. Haughey (1925-2006)

The Chief Herald of Ireland granted arms to Charles Haughey in 1966: *Per pale Or and gules on the dexter a lion rampant of the second facing to the sinister on the sinister a stag rampant of the first holding a fasces of the third.* Crest: *Issuing from an ancient crown Or a demi-horse argent.* Motto: *Marte nostro* 'By our own struggle'.

27.00: Ecclesiastical heraldry

Although heraldry was in the beginning associated with the field of battle and with tournaments, it was not long until clerics began to practise arms. Their coats of arms were often displayed in cartouches rather than in the warrior's shield. Nowadays, however, priests, bishops, etc. use shields.

27.01: Protestant and Roman Catholic bishops

In Ireland among the ordained ministry bishops are the most frequent users of heraldry. The arms of bishops are frequently seen carved on tombs, etc. In Ireland the question of bishops is particularly complicated, since there exist in the country two hierarchies side by side, the bishops of the Church of Ireland and the bishops of the Roman Catholic Church. They often have dioceses that bear identical names. Usually, however, the external trappings of the arms indicate to which denomination a bishop belongs: the Roman Catholic bishops displays a tasselled hat, for example, while the Anglican bishop has a mitre. There is thus no danger of confusion.

> NOTE: In the period 1960-1970 the arms of the following Protestant and Roman Catholic dioceses were the same: Armagh, Dublin, Meath, Ardagh, Kilmore, Clogher, Clonfert, Cork, Down (§17.14), Leighlin, Limerick, Elphin, Waterford and Raphoe.

27.02: Protestant Clergy

The bishops and archbishops of the Church of Ireland have as external ornaments to their arms only the mitre above the shield. At one time it was customary for the bishops to impale their personal arms on the dexter side with the arms of their diocese to dexter. If a bishop is not armigerous when he is consecrated, he does not usually trouble to acquire personal arms, since new grants are so expensive. As bishop he displays therefore only the arms of his diocese or dioceses. It is also often the case that more than one historical diocese is under the *episcope* of a single bishop. It is a well-established practice that the arms of the various diocese are marshalled on a single escutcheon.

Take, for example, the arms of the bishop of Cork, Cloyne and Ross. Reference has already been made to the arms of the diocese of Cork (§09.03). The diocese of Ross, which was amalgamated with Cork in 1582/3, never possessed arms. The arms of Cloyne, which was amalgamated with Cork in 1835, are: *Azure a mitre proper the labelled Or between three crosses patty fitchy argent.* The bishop of the three dioceses bears a shield party per fess with the arms of Cork above and of Cloyne beneath.

If a priest of the Church of Ireland has arms he will bear them with helmet, mantling and crest, as does an ordinary layman. Since 1976 priests of the Church of England may display a special ecclesiastical hat instead of helmet and crest. That practice among Anglican clergy has not appeared in Ireland yet.

27.03: The Roman Catholic clergy

Apart from the Pope, who displays the papal tiara with his arms, all Roman Catholic clergy use a round wide-brimmed hat over their arms. A red hat with 15 tassels is borne by cardinals. A green hat with 15 green tassels appears over the arms of primates. A green has with ten tassels is borne by archbishops, a green hat with six tassels by bishops. A priest bears a black hat with one tassel over his arms.

Primates and archbishops place behind their arms a cross with two cross-pieces. Bishops use a cross with one crosspiece. Roman Catholic bishops in Ireland impale their personal arms with the arms of the diocese, that is, the arms of the diocese to dexter and the personal arms to sinister (§22.02).

27.04: Archiepiscopal sees of Armagh and Dublin

The arms of the sees of Armagh and and Dublin are very similar. Armagh is blazoned as follows: *Azure an Archiepiscopal staff in pale argent ensigned with a cross paté Or surmounted by a pallium of the second, fimbriated and fringed Or and charged with four crosses paté fitchy sable.* Those arms are identical with the arms of the see of Dublin, except that the pallium is charged with five crosses. See, for example, the arms of Narcissus Marsh when he was archbishop of Dublin (§26.01). The arms of the see of Armagh are incidentally identical with the arms of the see of Canterbury.

Those two coats of arms, of the sees of Armagh and Dublin, are in use today by the two denominations. In 1805, when the Catholic Petition was being discussed in the Westminster parliament, the question of the arms of the Roman Catholic archbishop, Dr John Troy, was raised. He was accused of having adopted the arms of the archbishop of the Established Church, and had placed a cardinal's hat over it. Troy denied that his armorial bearings and the arms of the Church of Ireland archbishop were the same. The coat of arms was the same, however, although the correct Roman Catholic ornaments had been placed round his arms by Troy, namely a double cross and a green hat. He also used to impale the arms with his own personal arms: *Azure a fess Or between three towers proper.*

27.05: Some Irish dioceses

It is probable that some of the arms being used today by Irish bishops are in origin non-heraldic seals. The Church of Ireland bishop of Waterford, for example, uses: *Azure a bishop in full canonicals holding in front of him a crucifix argent with the figure of Our Saviour thereupon proper.* That is in origin a pictorial representation of the Holy Trinity, the Eternal Father and the Son crucified. The Holy Spirit would originally have been a dove hovering above the figure of the bishop. It seems that the dove has in error been omitted.

The arms of the diocese of Tuam are: *Azure under an architectural canopy of three arches three human figures: in the middle a representation of the Blessed Virgin Mary holding in her arms the Holy Child between on the dexter side the figure of a bishop in full canonicals in the act of benediction and to sinister a representation of John the Baptist holding in his arms a lamb argent each figure in the appropriate raiment Or the faces hands and feet proper.* It is apparent that those arms are in origin an ancient seal.

The arms used by the Church of Ireland bishop of Derry are: *Gules in base two swords crossed in saltire proper pommelled and hilted Or on a chief the arms of Ireland, namely Azure a harp Or stringed argent.* Those arms minus the chief are the arms of the diocese of London. These arms are unusual in that they are the only coat of arms registered in the Office of the Chief Herald. The diocese had another coat of arms which was confirmed by Daniel Molyneux, Ulster King of Arms in 1613: *Gules three mitres Or.* Before that again another coat of arms was used: *[Argent] a church [proper].* It seems that those arms derive from a non-heraldic seal. On the seal of the chapter of the cathedral of St Columba in 1778 a representation of the cathedral minus spire but with a dove hover above it. The dove does not represent the Holy Spirit but St Columba, the patron saint of Derry.

27.06: Ecclesiastical blazons in Irish

Before leaving the matter of Irish ecclesiastical heraldry, it is perhaps worth mentioning that the arms of four Irish diocese are blazoned in Irish in manuscript 24C5 in the Royal Irish Academy, Dublin. The manuscript was written in 1842 and the scribe was Eamon O'Mahony. It is probable, however, that he was not the originator of the blazons. *Bairrín* is the Irish word for 'mitre' in these blazons rather than the expected *mítéar*. This is how the manuscript blazons the arms of a) the diocese of Cork and b) the diocese of Waterford:

(*a*) *Cros lán tiugh agus baruighion 'na lár agus tríd sin fós bachal eascoip agus baruighin an uachdar* 'A cross fully thick and a mitre in the middle and through that a bishop's staff and a mitre above'

(b) *Eascop 'na éide eascoip acht amháin an bharuighin agus cros láimh aige agus baruighion os cionn na sgéithe mar chách* 'A bishop in his episcopal raiment except the mitre and the hand cross and a mitre over the shield like the others'.

As can be seen, these blazons are neither exact nor explicit. The modern blazons for the above are cited above (§§09.03, 27.05).

27.07: Papal arms: Paul VI (1897-1978)

The Pope's arms are surmounted by a papal tiara rather than a hat. The crossed keys of St Peter apper behind the arms. Italian popes as a rule bore their arms in what is known as a "horse head shield". A good example of this can be seen in Galway Cathedral, where the arms of Paul VI (Giovanni Battista Montini) are carved on the outer west wall. The Pope's arms were: *Gules six stylized hills in base one two and three argent in chief three fleurs-de-lis one and two of the same*. The stylized hills are a distinctively Italian charge and in the present case they are canting charges on the surname, *Montini*. Paul VI was of noble origin and he used those arms before he became Pope.

27.08: John Paul II (1920-2005)

When John Paul II (Karol Woytyła) was Pope his arms were in the public eye: *Azure a cross Or the upright placed to dexter and the crossbar enhanced in sinister base an M of the same*. Woytyła bore the same arms as archbishop of Kraków, although with different tinctures: the field was azure but the cross and the letter M were both sable. This violated the tincture rule. Archbishop Bruno Heim, the leading expert on heraldry at the time in Roman Catholic Church, recommended when Woytyła became Pope that he should replace sable of the charges with gold. He also suggested that the letter M representing *Maria*, the Blessed Virgin Mary, should be replaced by a heraldic symbol, e.g. a rose (*Rosa mystica*), a fleur-de-lis (*Flos florum*), a crown (*Regina coeli*) or a tower (*Turris eburnea*). Heim's advice was not followed in this matter. As a result perhaps the best-known coat of arms in the world at the time was an example of rather indifferent heraldry. It should be pointed out, howeve, that in Polish heraldry house marks are common, that is to say charges, many of which resemble letters. It is generally believed that such figures derive ultimately from Norse runes.

28.00: The Heralds

To begin with the heralds were messengers and announcers in wartime. When in western Europe tournaments began to be held, the heralds organized them for the most part. Then they began to prepare lists of the various contestants and to record them in books, that is to say, the rolls of arms and armorials. It was not long then until the heralds became expert in heraldry in general. It is from that function that the term *heraldry* derives.

Gradually difference of rank arose among the heralds. The chief among them was known as "king of arms", above the ordinary heralds. Under them again were the pursuivants, junior heralds or apprentices. To begin with the heralds were independent and operated rather like troubadors. Then the greater nobility began to keep their own heralds and by the sixteenth century kings and emperors had their own heralds.

28.01: Heralds in Ireland; early references

Like heraldry itself the Irish heralds were to found among the Anglo-Norman colonist. The first herald in Ireland for whom we have any evidence was John Othelake, who was personal herald to Edmund Mortimer, third earl of March and lord deputy. Othelake was known as March herald. Edmund Mortimer died in 1381 and his son Roger became lord deputy after him. When Richard II came to Ireland both Roger and March Herald were with him (§01.05). There is also some evidence that there was someone else with the title March Herald who was in Ireland in the times of Edmund Mortimer, the fifth earl (†1425).

There are occasional references in the state papers from the end of the fifteenth century to Dublin Pursuivant, Ormond Pursuivant and Kildare Pursuivant, but it is not known what precise functions they may have had. It is likely that Ormond Pursuivant and Kildare Pursuivant were private heralds of the earls of Ormond and Kildare respectively.

The first reference to an Irish king of arms occurs in Froissart's Chronicles under the year 1392, where he speaks of Chandos, Irish king of arms. It is not certain, however, whether Froissart is can be trusted here. It is possible that he is simply referring to John Othelake, who has been mentioned above.

At some point during the reign of Henry V, James Butler, earl of Ormond had John Kitely appointed as Ireland King of Arms. James Butler was very interested in heraldry, and this move of his agrees with what is known about him from other sources. Although the office of Ireland King of Arms persisted until 1485, it is not certain exactly what connection, if any, John Kitely had with this country.

THE HERALDS

28.02: Ulster King of Arms and his office

A new chapter in the heraldic history of Ireland in the reign of Edward VI, for in 1552 a king of Arms was appointed for Ireland. The whole country was to be his heraldic province and his headquarters was to be in Dublin. His title was Ulster King of Arms. Given that Ulster was the province of Ireland over which the English government had least control, quite probably the mention of Ulster in the title was largely aspirational.

In the same year the first Athlone Pursuivant was appointed as an assistant for the king of arms. Bartholomew Butler (1552-1566) was the first Ulster King of Arms and his natural son, Philip Butler, was the first person in the office of Athlone Pursuivant.

It seems that there was some connection between the the Ulster King of Arms and his office and the College of Arms in London, although that did not last more than a few years. The office of Ulster King of Arms survived until Cromwell's time. In 1655 Richard Carney was appointed "Principal Herald for Ireland". The office of Ulster King of Arms was re-established in 1660, when Carney lost his job. Sir Richard Carney, son of Richard, Principal Herald, was Ulster King from 1683 to 1692. His son was Ulster King from 1692 to 1698.

When the Order of St Patrick was established in 1783, two new posts were created to administer the new order, that is, Dublin herald and Cork Herald. Those two positions survived until the post of Ulster King of Arms was abolished in 1943.

28.03: The Chief Herald of Ireland

When the Irish Free State was founded in 1922, the Office of Arms remained under the Crown and was not transferred to the native government. The Ulster King of Arms, Nevile Wilkinson, died in 1940, and was succeeded by his deputy, Thomas Sadleir, who was head of the office for three years, although he was not appointed king of arms. In 1943 the Irish government took over the office and Edward MacLysaght was appointed Principal Herald. Shortly thereafter his title was changed to Chief Herald of Ireland. He had the same duties and functions as the Ulster King with respect to granting and confirming arms. There are, however, two fundamental differences between the Ulster King of Arms and the Chief Herald of Ireland. In the first place the Chief Herald has no connection with the Order of St Patrick, which was allowed to wither after 1922. In the second place, he grants new arms with the authority of the Irish government, not with the authority of the Crown.

The official title of the office of the Chief Herald is the Genealogical Office and he and his staff are civil servants who are employed within the National Library, under the aegis of the Department of Arts, Heritage and Gaeltacht. The

Office was situated in Dublin Castle until the mid 1980s whern it was transferred to Kildare Street.

Edward MacLysaght retired as Chief Herald in 1953 and was succeeded by Gerard Slevin until 1981. Donal Begley was Chief Herald from 1982 till 1995. Fergus Gillespie was Chief Herald from 2005 to 2009. The current Chief Herald is Colette O'Flaherty.

An act was passed by the Oireachtas in 1997 to give a firm legal basis to the heraldic functions of the Office. The provisions of this act were the subject of review in 2006-07 when granting of arms was temporarily discontinued. The matter has now been resolved and grants are again being made.

28.04: Heraldic visitations

It was the custom for heralds of the College of Arms in London from *ca* 1530 to go round England and Wales examining the use and misuse of arms, that is, to discover whether people who were using arms actually had the right to them. A similar practice was begun in Ireland from 1567 onwards. It is clear that the use of arms without authority was common in Ireland in the sixteenth century. Only a few visitations were completed, however, apparently because the country was so disturbed. The results of visitations are preserved in the Genealogical Office from the following places: Counties Dublin and Louth (1568-1570); Drogheda and Ardee (1570); Swords (1572); Cork (1574); Limerick (1574); Dublin (1607, 1610); and Wexford (1610). The visitations were made under Nicholas Narbon, Ulster King of Arms (1568-1574) and Daniel Molyneux, Ulster (1607-10). It would seem that the visitations were confined to the Pale and the major cities. Of course it is possible that further visitations were made but evidence for them does not survive. As can be imagined, the records of the visitations are a very valuable source for the state of heraldry in Ireland at the time.

No heraldic visitation appears to have been made in Ireland after the beginning of the seventeenth century. From 1586 onwards, however, Ulster King of Arms registered funeral entries and this practice lasted for a long time. Funeral entries are reports on the funerals of important people, and contain the name of the deceased, his wife and relatives together with a coloured picture or trick of his arms. The practice of making funeral entries had ceased by the middle of the eighteenth century but Bernard Burke (§28.06) revived the custom for a while when he was in the Office of Arms. The funeral entries are also a valuable source for the practice of heraldry at the time.

Since it was not possible to carry out heraldic visitations in much of Ireland because of the disturbed state of the country, there were always gaps in what Ulster King of Arms knew about the use of arms in many places. As a result a practice arose which is still in force. If a man can show that he and his

antecedents have borne a coat of arms for one hundred years or three generations, he may get a certificate from the heraldic office confirming him in those
arms.

28.05: James Terry (1660-1725)

In June 1690 James II appointed James Terry as Athlone Pursuivant. When the
king fled to France Terry followed him. Terry took overseas a many documents
belonging to the Office of the Ulster King of Arms. Terry functioned as a
pursuivant of arms in the court of the Stuarts in St Germain and when he died
in 1725, Charles Hozier, a *juge d'armes* of the king of France, acquired the
documents that were in Terry's possession. They remained in his family until the
French Revolution, when they were placed in France's *Archives Nationales*.

James Terry was born in County Clare, in 1660. He married Mary Stritch in
1687. He had a difficult time in exile trying to record titles and genealogies. He
was more despised than rewarded.

Arms of Irish Families was Terry's great work. He finished the manuscript in
1712, which is preserved in the British Library in London.

28.06: Sir John Bernard Burke (1814-1892)

Sir John Bernard Burke was probably the most famous holder of the title of
Ulster King of Arms. He was son of Sir John Burke of Elm Hall, County
Tipperary, although he was born in London. He went to school in England and
then attended the University of Caen in France. He could not register in an
English university because he was a Roman Catholic. He was appointed Ulster
King of Arms in 1853 as successor to William Betham. He was knighted in the
next year. He lived in Leeson Street, Dublin and remained Ulster King of Arms
until his death. Betham had been Ulster King of Arms from 1820 to 1853 and he
achieved much in sorting out and classifying the genealogical and heraldic
manuscripts in the office. Burke outdid him, however.

Not only did Burke continue with the cataloguing that Betham had started,
he also published many substantial works. Among them one can include the
regular editions of the *General and Heraldic Dictionary of the Peerage and
Baronetage* or *Burke's Peerage* as it is usually known. Burke published a new
edition every year from 1847 until his death. The regular publication continued
thereafter (cf. BP in the Bibliography). Burke also published *The General Armory
of England, Scotland and Ireland* in 1842. He published many emended editions
thereof (BGA) until 1884.

BGA is a comprehensive work, but it cannot claim to be reliable. J. Brooke-
Little, Norroy and Ulster King of Arms says of it:

That this book was edited by a herald has given rise to the belief that it is an authoritative work of reference. Unfortunately such is not the case; it is but a collection of blazons of arms, crests and supporters arranged alphabetically under the names of those who are supposed to have borne them. Many of the coats given are inaccurately blazoned, wrongly attributed, borne without authority or just plain bogus.... Although Burke's work is unreliable, nonetheless it is valuable if used critically. Where the date of a grant or visitation is mentioned as authority for the arms given, the coat is usually genuine. (*Boutell's Heraldry*, 307) .

28.07: Native scholars: Roger O'Feral (*fl.* 1709) and Dermot O'Connor (before 1712-ca 1730)

In the first quarter of the eighteenth century there were a few scholars in Dublin working in the field of genealogy and heraldry, independently of the Office of the Ulster King of Arms. Among them were Roger O'Feral, Dermot O'Connor and Aaron Crossly.

Little is known about Roger O'Feral other than that he was a genealogist and that he wrote the first large collection of Gaelic genealogies and arms with the title *Linea Antiqua* (1708). The manuscript is preserved in the Genealogical Office. It is in that collection that one finds the bulk of the arms associated with Gaelic families and it is upon them that MacLysaght based most of the coats of arms he published in IF.

More is known about Dermot O'Connor. Indeed he was one of the most interesting con-men in the history of Ireland. It seems probable that he was born in Limerick, although in which year is not known. He was working as a scribe in the years 1712-16. He was in Dublin in 1719 and 1720 and from 1720 till his death some time after 1730 he was living in London. He is chiefly remembered today as the man who translated Keating's history of Ireland, *Foras Feasa ar Éirinn*, into English. He did not do the translation himself, however, though he claimed to have done it. He did publish it, however, along with plates showing the arms of the subscribers. It is obvious that he was a competent artist and heraldist.

O'Connor liked to claim that he had authority to grant arms. At all events it seems that he prepared a grant of arms in 1724 for Matthew Quilty, an Irishman living in Malaga, Spain. It seems that Quilty was anxious to marry a Spanish noblewoman and he therefore needed a certificate of nobility. The certificate which O'Connor drew up for him is in Latin, and he refers to himself in it as *Antiquarius pro regno Hiberniae electus et juratus* 'Elected and sworn historian for the Kingdom of Ireland'.

O'Connor is interesting from the linguistic point of view, since there survives from him a document written in Irish in which he attempts to blazone arms in the language. It seems that O'Connor himself invented the terminology he uses, and though the language is neither clear, complete nor consistent, it does represent an attempt to use Irish to discuss heraldry.

Here are a number of O'Connor's Irish language blazons followed by i) a literal translation and ii) a modern blazon in English:

(a) *Leathleoghan dubh air bhuidhe a leath bheas, sa leath oile bán le hermín fá chevron bán; er sin trí réalta órdha an uaithne* (MacShanly)

    i) 'A demi-lion sable on yellow in base in the other half white with ermine under a white chevron on that three stars Or in vert'

    ii) *Per chevron vert and the base per pale Or and ermine a chevron argent between in chief three estoiles Or and in dexter base a lion rampant gules.*

(b) *Chevron dearg armen idir thrí treafoyles slipt argent.* (Miach)

    i) 'Chevron red ermine between three trefoils slipped argent'

    ii) *Gules a chevron ermine between three trefoils slipped argent.*

(c) *Dhá leoghan chuthach ór ar dhearg, trí chloidheimhe crosda, an dornchla órtha.* (Ó Braonáin)

    i) 'Two angry lions Or on gules, three swords crossed the hilt Or'

    ii) *Gules two lions combatant holding between them a sheaf all Or in chief three swords argent pommelled and hilted Or two crossed in saltire the points upword the third fesswise point to dexter.*

28.08: Aaron Crossly (*fl.* 1694-1724) and William Hawkins (1670-1736)

Little is known about Aaron Crossly. He called himself a "heraldic painter" and he had a shop at the corner of Thomas Street and Bridgefoot Street. We know, however, that he published the first Irish peerage, *The Peerage of Ireland*, in Dublin in 1723. At the back of the book he published an outline of heraldry and he admits that he got assistance with both genealogy and heraldry from Irish scholars, including Dermot O'Connor.

Crossly had a long dispute with William Hawkins, Ulster King of Arms from 1698 to 1736. Hawkins was rather irascible and he annoyed many people, something which did not help him in his dispute with Crossly. Hawkins complained that Crossly was providing armorial bearings for funerals of the nobility. That business of Crossly's was a source of vexation to Hawkins, because he believed it was an insult to himself and to the dignity of the Office of Ulster King of Arms. Hawkins believed that only he himelf had the right to give permission for such funeral arms. On one occasion in the year 1711/12 Hawkins saw a funeral passing by, the deceased being Richard Boyle. Artwork by Crossly was clearly visible on the funeral coach and Crossly immediate proceeded to pull off the coach as much as he could of the heraldic insignia. Hawkins was thereafter brought before the magistrates to explain his behaviour. Hawkins did not succeed in hindering Crossly's activity, because Crossly had powerful friends, Robert Dale in the College of Arms in London, for example, and Sir Richard Cox, one time Irish Chancellor.

Oddly enough the funeral entry in the Genealogical Office for the funeral of Richard Boyle is in Crossly's hand or at least in the hand of one of his assistants.

29.00: Heraldic jurisdiction in the modern world

As a result of revolutions and the spread of democracy, there are many countries that lack an official heraldic authority. In France since 1872, for example there has been no heraldic administration for private persons. The heraldry of the old aristocracy remain, of course. Anyone in France, however, who wishes to adopt arms may do so. Such do-it-yourself arms are known as "burgher arms". If a man adopts arms of someone else, the original armiger can take him to court. Civic heraldry in France is regulated by a government commission.

Burgher arms are the rule for citizens of Germany, Switzerland, and Austria. In those countries, however, there are private institutions which assist people in devising suitable arms and they also register such arms.

The Netherlands, Belgium, and Denmark are monarchies and they have offices which control the arms of the aristocracy. If an ordinary citizen, however, is not armigerous and desires arms, he may adopt arms.

29.01: England and Wales, Scotland

Great Britain and Ireland are exceptional from the heraldic point of view, since heraldic jurisdictions exist in them to control arms of all kinds. Inside the United Kingdom there are two authorities: the College of Arms in London and the Court of Lyon King of Arms in Scotland.

There are three kings of arms in the College of Arms in London: Garter, Norroy and Clarenceux. Garter King of Arms is the chief heraldic officer in England and Wales. The other two kings have a local jurisdiction, Norroy King of Arms north of the river Trent and Clarenceux to the south of it. There are six heralds in the College and four pursuivants. The Duke of Norfolk, the Earl Marshall, is the patron of the College, though not a member of the corporation. As a general rule people are not prosecuted if they use arms without authority. There was, however, a famous case in 1954 when a theatre in Manchester was prevented from using the arms of the City of Manchester. In order to try the case the ancient Court of Chivalry had to be resurrected.

There is only one king of arms in Scotland, the Lord Lyon, who has three heralds and three pursuivants as assistants. The Lord Lyon is a civil servant and he has behind him the authority of the law. Historically Lord Lyon's position is a Gaelic one. The chief ollave of Scotland it was who installed the King of Scotland and it seems that the office of chief ollave or shanachie of Scotland survives in the Lyon King of Arms.

29.02: Northern Ireland

When the office of Ulster King of Arms was abolished in 1943, the jurisdiction of the erstwhile king of arms was given to Norroy, who became Norroy and

Ulster King of Arms. His heraldic province is the North of England and Northern Ireland. The Irish constitution of 1936 claimed that the six counties of Northern Ireland were a detached part of of the Irish state. That meant that two separate authorities claimed jurisdiction inside Northern Ireland, the Chief Herald of Ireland and Norroy and Ulster King of Arms. Both grant arms to individuals and corporations within Northern Ireland.

29.03: The Commonwealth

The College of Arms in London grants arms to individuals and to institutions in the countries of the Commonwealth. When British colonies gained independence in the nineteen-fifties and nineteen-sixties, for example, the College of Arms granted them official arms. Individual citizens in Commonwealth countries who desire arms, can get them them from the English kings of arms. People of Scottish origin, however, apply to Lyon King for arms. Citizens of Commonwealth countries who are of Irish origin sometimes apply to the Chief Herald of Ireland for arms.

South Africa left the Commonwealth in 1961. Shortly thereafter the State Heraldic Bureau was established in South Africa, so that the republic could continue to have a heraldic authority. Until the advent of majority rule in South Africa some citizens, who were unwilling to accept recognition from the state's heraldic bureau, applied to the English kings of arms for new grants.

Corporations and individuals in Canada had always applied to the College of Arms in London or to the Lyon King in Edinburgh for new grants. The Canadians, however, are very jealous of their own sovereignty and in 1988 an official Canadian heraldic authority was established. An individual Canadian citizen or corporation now applies to the Office of the Chief Herald of Canada for a new grant.

29.04: Spain

There are kings of Arms in Spain who grant arms with the authority of the king and under the aegis of the Spanish Department of Justice. These have been known officially as *cronistas de arms* since 1951. Spanish heraldry has its own distinctive features (§26.06) and the Spanish *cronistas* grant arms still to Spaniards and to people living in parts of what was once the Spanish empire.

29.05: The United States of America

Many citizens of the United States of America are anxious to acquire arms, although they have not inherited any. Although is no public authority in the United States that grants arms, if a coat of arms is well publicized, it has the protection of law, exactly like a trademark.

HERALDIC JURISDICTION IN THE MODERN WORLD

There are a number of ways for an American citizen to acquire suitable personal arms. In the first place he may receive an honorary grant from the College of Arms in London, if he can show that he is descended from someone resident in the United States before the War of Independence in the eighteenth century. He does not of necessity have to be of English descent. If he is of Irish or Scottish descent he may apply to the heraldic authorities in Dublin or Edinburgh respectively. A noteworthy example of an Irish grant to an American citizen are the arms of President Kennedy which have been mentioned above (§27.07).

An American citizen may also apply for arms from Spain. If he can show that his paternal or maternal ancestors bore Spanish arms, the Spanish *cronista de armas* can register those arms for him. He may also request a new grant if he lives in a part of the United States that was at one time under Spanish jurisdiction, New Mexico, for example, California or Florida. Grants of that kind are becoming increasingly popular. The Chief Herald of Ireland and the Lyon King recognize such arms. At the moment the English kings of arms do not.

An American citizen who wishes to acquire armorial bearings does not need to go to any of the heraldic authorities in Europe. There are a number of private institutions in the United States that provide arms for individuals and corporations. The American College of Heraldry and Arms was established in Maryland in 1966 and granted arms to both individual citizens and to institutions. Lyndon Johnson and Richard Nixon obtained arms from the College, as did Spiro Agnew. The American College of Heraldry, however, ceased activity in 1970.

President Dwight D. Eisenhower obtained arms from Denmark in an unusual way. He was awarded the Order of the Elephant by the Danish king after the Second World War, which was the greatest honour which the Kingdom of Denmark could bestow upon him. Since Eisenhower was not already armigerous, the authorities of the order designed arms for him. His arms show a simple field with an anvil, a canting reference to his surname *Eisenhower* 'striker of iron'.

Since neither the federal government nor the governments of the indivual states of the United States concern themselves with personal arms, there is nothing to prevent a citizen of the United States from devising a coat of arms for himself. If he does so, he should of course avoid using arms already in use by any European or American armiger. He should also consult an experienced heraldist, so that his arms do not violate the basic rules of heraldry. There exist in the United States institutions that register arms that have been legitimately granted or arms which have been designed by the bearer and are different from any other armorial bearings.

29.06: Devisal of arms

Since arms are granted in the United Kingdom under the authority of the Queen and under the authority of the Irish government in Ireland, neither can legitimately grant arms to American citizens, who are outside both their jurisdiction. If therefore arms are devised for American citizens by the College of Arms or the Chief Herald of Ireland they are honorary grants. Honorary grants cannot be made to corporations and towns in the United States, however. The College of Arms in London, however, have adopted another practice, that of *devising* arms. Brooke-Little describes the matter thus:

> Some years ago, an American town wanted to be granted arms by the English Kings of Arms, but, as the Queen's Writ did not run in the United States, such a grant could not be made. However, an arrangement was reached whereby the Kings of Arms were empowered, by an Earl Marshal's Warrant dated 25th July 1960, to devise, that is design and record, arms for towns in the United States. Then, by another Warrant dated 1st February 1962, the permission to devise arms in the United States was extended to include corporate bodies other than towns. Before a devisal is made in the United States, the consent and approval of the Governor of the sovereign state in which the devisal is to be made is always obtained.
>
> (*Boutell's Heraldry*, 268).

Devisals of arms to American towns and institutions by the English kings of Arms are becoming more common. In 1986 the College of Arms devised arms for the native American people, the Mescalero Apache of New Mexico. The Chief Herald has not devised arms for an American corporation, but he did devise arms for the Chair of Irish Studies in St Mary's University in Halifax in Nova Scotia in 1987. The legal basis of such a devisal is not certain. The Chief Herald of Ireland can no longer devise arms for any Canadian corporation since the establishment of the Canadian Heraldic authority in 1988.

There also exists in the United States an institution known as the College of Arms Foundation. This promotes and disseminates knowlege of English heraldry in the United States.

29.07: The basis of heraldic jurisdiction

It is apparent from what has been said above that the criteria used to determine heraldic jurisdiction are uncertain. If one is talking about personal heraldry, the criteria can be classified into three sections:

(*a*) The Chief Herald of Ireland grants arms to Irish citizens or to people who are domiciled in Ireland, that is, within his heraldic province. Similarly Lyon King of arms grants arms to Scots and the English kings of arms to Englishmen and Englishwomen.

(*b*) The European heraldic authorities grant arms to Americans of European origin. An example of such a grant is the arms granted to President Kennedy. He obtained honorary arms from the Chief Herald of Ireland, because he was a descendant of people who were domiciled at one time in Ireland, that is, within the present-day province of the Chief Herald. Similarly Lyon King will grant arms to Scots who live within the heraldic province of the English kings of arms. This is done on the understanding that such arms will be used only within Scotland. Theoretically speaking if such a grantee of the Lyon Kings wishes to use the arms in England, he should first of all register the arms with the College of Arms.

(*c*) The Spaniards and the English heraldic authorities grant arms to Americans who are domiciled in areas that once formed part of their respective heraldic provinces.

Since coats of arms developed in the first instance in order to distinguish knights in armour from one another, it is clear that (*a*) is the only criterion that has any historical validity. A king of arms cannot ensure that the arms he grants are different from all other arms, if such arms are to be used outside his own heraldic province. The reality, however, is that the fees paid to the heraldic administrations are very welcome. It is likely therefore that the uncertainties in current heraldic jurisdictions are likely to persist.

29.08: Arms as a sign of nobility

In Scotland it is assumed that the right to a coat of arms is in some sense an affirmation of nobility. Some commentators claim that in England also a grant of arms from the monarch gives the grantee some kind of nobiliary status. It cannot, on the other hand, be argued that a continental European citizen has any claim to nobility, if he adopts and and uses burgher arms.

The question is more controversial in Ireland. There is an express prohibition in *Bunreacht na hÉireann* 'the Irish Constitution' on noble titles of any kind: "Titles of nobility shall not be conferred by the State" (*Bunreacht na hÉireann* 40.2.1). On the other hand the state grants arms to its citizens in exactly the same way that the English monarchs granted arms to Irishmen and Irishwomen in the past. The Chief Herald of Ireland grants arms to American citizens and the American Constitution also forbids titles of nobility also. One can claim that the Chief Herald of Ireland grants arms only to worthy men and women, but that is not the same as saying that they are in any sense noble. For the question of so-called "Gaelic titles" see §31.05

.

30.00: Unauthorized arms

The citizen of a country that lacks a heraldic administration are fully justified in adopting burgher arms. In Ireland and in other countries where a heraldic authority does exist, the citizen can obtain a grant or confirmation of arms from the relevant authority on the payment of the required fee. Many Irish people, however, believe that coats of arms and surnames go together. If a man is called O'Sullivan, for example, all he needs to do is to find out the arms of the O'Sullivans and those are his authentic and legitimate arms. This opinion is a serious fallacy, as we have seen. If a man called O'Sullivan were to petition the Chief Herald of Ireland to devise arms for him and to grant them to him, it is very likely that his personal arms would be based on the O'Sullivan arms, but the armorial bearings granted to O'Sullivan, the petitioner, would be different from all other arms granted previously.

Unfortunately there are companies that make a profit out of the ignorance of the general public. They survive on the widespread ignorance of heraldry and the belief that arms somehow belong to surnames. If it is possible to show that the coat of arms X belonged at one time to somebody called Y, and if the customer bears the surname Y, then such companies are prepared to provide the arms X to the customer on a certificate, a wall-plaque, on a ring or anything else, if they see the colour of the customer's money first of all.

Companies advertise in print and on-line at both the Irish and the American market. Their basic assumption is that surname = coat of arms and that "your family coat of arms" or worse still "your family crest" is one which has been in use by someone who bore the same surname as you. One company says: "We have researched and filed over 500,000 coat of arms [sic!] for families of European origin. If in the unlikely event that your name is not on our files we will undertake the necessary research to locate a documented source containing an authentic coat of arms upon receipt of a firm order for same."

It would be easy to defend such business on the grounds that the United States lacks a heraldic authority and that customers of such companies do not really believe that they own the arms of others which are supplied to them. This defence is invalid, however. Bogus heraldry of this kind pushes out real heraldry. Customers are satisfied with worthless falsehood when for a relatively small cost genuine heraldic practice waiting for them in the Genealogical Office. "Heraldic" companies do great damage to the standing of heraldry and to the understanding of heraldry among the general public. Worse still the examples of heraldic art which they peddle are often of very poor quality.

30.01: Heraldic honesty

It should be mentioned here that there are heraldic companies which do inform their customers of the right to use arms. They explain that buying a plaque with a coat of arms painted on it does not entitle the purchaser to use those arms as his own. One company operating in the United Kingdom, for example, has gives this warning to potential customers:

> In consultation with and as advised by a Herald of the College of Arms we draw particular public attention to the following facts:
>
> First, it will be clearly understood that the Armorial Bearings we provide are those which have been in the past, or are at present associated with particular family surnames. Accordingly, there is no reason why you should not display these as decorative reproductions with pride derived from association with your name. However, by doing so it is not possible to claim these arms as your own as, for example, by using them as a personal mark of distinction on writing paper, seal, rings and so forth. To do so in England and Scotland would not be in accordance with the Laws of Arms.

It is interesting that Ireland is not mentioned in that warning. Lyon King of Arms in Scotland has the power of the law behind him. In England the medieval Court of Chivalry was revived in order to adjudicate in a case of the unlawful use of arms. The status of arms in Ireland is uncertain, and their use or misuse has never been tested in an Irish court of law. The warning for England and Scotland cited above is greatly to be welcomed. It is probable however that the warning would not have been issued but for the complaints made by the College of Arms.

30.02: "Arms of the name"

Oddly enough it seems that the association of arms with surnames is a very old practice in Ireland. O'Connor Don and O'Connor Sligo are two branches of the same kindred. There was a connection also between the arms born by members of the two branches. O'Connor Don bears an oak tree on a silver field (§16.00). O'Connor Sligo impaled the oak tree with a lion: *Per pale vert and argent to dexter a lion rampant to sinister Or to sinister on a mound in base of the second an oak tree proper* (IF: 212). The oak tree can also be seen in the arms of chiefs who were connected with the O'Connors, e.g. O'Concannon and O'Donnellan (§§09.03, 15.01).

The oak tree also appears, however, on the arms of O'Connor Faley, although he was not related to nor had any dealings with the O'Connors of

Connacht. His arms were: *Argent on a mount in base vert an oak tree fruited proper* (IF: 212).

The arms ascribed to the Fagans, a family of Norman origin are: *Per chevron gules and ermine in chief three covered cups in fess Or* (§17.07). There are people called Fagan, however, whose name in Irish is *Ó Faogáin*, a variant of the Gaelic name *Ó hAogáin*. Some commentators believe that *Ó hAogáin* is itself a variant of *Ó hÁgáin* (*O'Hagan*). It is interesting therefore that the arms of Fagan appears in its entirety in the arms of O'Hagan (§17.03). The two families are of completely different origins, one Norman, the other Gaelic, but somebody at some point thought the two surnames, *Fagan* and *O'Hagan*, were sufficient close as to warrant incorporating the arms of the one in the arms of the other.

31.00: Miscellany

31.01: Hatchments

When discussing Crossly and Hawkins above (§28.08), we pointed out that the two of them were in dispute over heraldic decorations during funerals. It was a common practice to prepare *hatchments* or funeral arms and to hang them outside a house when one of the inhabitants died. After a period of mourning the hatchment would be taken down and hung up in the church.

The hatchment was painted on a square of wood approximately four and half feet square, but the wood was always turned sideways to form a lozenge. The arms of alliance were usually used in the case of a married person. The colour of the background behind the shield determined whether the wife or husband had died. If the dexter side was black, the man had died. If the arms themselves appeared on a lozenge, that meant that the wife became a widow on his death.

The painting of hatchments is no longer practised, but examples are frequently seen in old churches.

31.02: Trade union banners

When members of trade unions march in processions or demonstration, they often carry their banners. These hang from a wooden cross-piece attached at right angles to the upright post. Technically speaking they are not banners but *gonfalons*. At one time such gonfalons displayed the arms of the trade union. As has been demonstrated by T. P. O'Neill (1976), the trade unions during the nineteenth century attempted to prove that there was continuity between trade unions and medieval guilds. This meant that the unions not infrequently used the arms of the guilds, when they began creating gonfalons for the new unions.

The heraldry of the union gonfalons in Ireland is interesting in itself, for it seems that the artists who created the banners used without authority the arms of the guilds of the City of London. O'Neill publishes depictions of the gonfalon of the Guild of Weavers of Drogheda and of the gonfalon of the Union of Silk Weavers of Dublin (*ca* 1880). Both show variants of the same arms: *Azure on a chevron argent between three leopard's faces each holding in the mouth Or as many roses gules*. The supporters are two wyverns in both cases. The arms are in fact those of the Worshipful Company of Weavers of the City of London, which were first granted in 1490 (CCH: 406).

31.03: Badges

Heraldic badges have little status in Irish heraldry, although they are becoming increasingly important in England. In Scotland the crest is often used as a badge. The badge in essence is a charge taken from the arms or from the crest which has been specified for use when the whole arms are not necessary. The harp which can be seen on Irish government documents is thus a badge.

A good example of a heraldic badge was the griffin within a circle of bezants that was used by the Northern Bank until the end of the twentieth century. In fact the badge had been designed for the Midland Bank in England in 1952. When the ownership of the Northern Bank passed to an Australian firm, the griffin disappeared from Irish streets.

The heraldic badge must be distinguished from the non-heraldic logo. Again at the end of the twentieth century Allied Irish Bank adopted such a non-heraldic symbol in unheraldic colours. It was a pity at that time that the bank did not consult with the Chief Herald for a tasteful heraldic badge.

31.04: Orders of chivalry

Orders of chivalry are not allowed in Ireland, because of an express prohibition in the Constitution. Other European republics, however, do bestow titles of honour on their citizens and on foreigners also. There were several functioning orders of chivalry under British rule in Ireland before 1922.

> *Fuair tar oilbhéim bheith 'na Threisinér*
> *ós Iath inisréidh Fhéidhlime.*
> *Fuair sé d'airdchéim Ridireacht Gáirtéir,*
> *ainm nár ghnáth ar Éirionnach.*
>
> 'In spite of censure he achieved the post of Treasure over Ireland of the smooth plains. He was awarded knightship in the Order of the Garter, a title not common for Irishmen' (J. Carney, *Poems on the Butlers*, 74).

When an example appears anywhere in Ireland of the royal arms was painted or carved under British rule, the arms are shown within the circlet of the Order of the Garter. The circlet is a representation of the garter itself with the words in French written around: *Honi soit qui mal y pense* 'Shame on him who thinks evil of it'.

A special order of chivalry was created for Ireland in 1783, the Order of St Patrick. From the beginning, until the disestablishment of the Church of Ireland in 1870 St Patrick's Cathedral, Dublin, was the chapel of the order. The stall plates of the knight can still be seen in the choir of the church and the banners of the knight of the order when the order moved its headquarters from the cathedral. From 1870 until 1922 Dublin Castle was the headquarters of the order and the banners of the last members of the order are still displayed in St Patrick's Hall in the Castle.

The Order of Malta is active in Ireland and their headquarters are in Clyde Road, Ballsbridge, Dublin. Cardinal Cathal Daly was made a bailiff grand cross of honour and devotion of the order there on the second of June 1992.

The Pope recognized the Sovereign Military Hospitaller Order of Saint John of Jerusalem in 1113. When the Crusaders lost the Holy Land, the order retreated to Rhodes and later still to Malta. The headquarters of the order are in Rome. Members of the order usually place the badge of the order behind their personal arms, that is, a cross of eight points argent, and they usually place round their arms the circlet of the order, that is, a rosary with a Maltese cross pendant from it. The higher ranks in the order also place the arms of the order (*Gules a cross argent*) on a chief within their arms. This usually appears on a chief, or on a quarter for the highest ranking officers of the order.

In 1990 the Chief Herald of Ireland granted supporters (*two knights in complete armour*) to Michael Joseph Egan, Knight Grand Cross of Obedience and Bailiff of the Order of Malta. This was because Michael Egan was according to the practice of the order entitled to use supported by right of his high position in the Knights of Malta.

31.05: Gaelic nobility

Certain survivals of the Gaelic nobility have persisted into our own times. Several chiefs of the name used supporters by right of their nobiliary status, which put them on the same level as peers (§20.01). When the Office of the Chief Herald was established, MacLysaght allowed supporters to such chiefs as by right.

Although the practice of allowing supporters to "chiefs of the name" did not continue, the Genealogical Office showed great interest in chiefs of this type. From time to time the Chief Herald would recognize someone as the chief of his name and would present him with a certificate. Since this constitutes the recognition of an existing status, rather than conferring a new rank on him who was so recognized, it did not violate the provision in the Irish Constitution which forbid the state to grant titles of nobility.

Unfortunately false claims have been made which were not properly investigated. Susan Hood writes:

> Chiefs-of-the-name controversies have arisen again in recent years as a result of the well publicised bogus claimes of Terence McCarthy. In the 1980s he presented a pedigree without genealogical integrity to gain recognition as the MacCarthy Mór, Chief of the Name, and to support his claim to be Prince of Desmond and Lord of Kerslawny. Extensive genealogical research commissioned by the current Chief Herald, Brendan

O Donoghue, subsequently established that McCarthy's claims were false and the courtesy recognition was declared to be 'null and void' in 1999. The MacCarthy Mór hoax has brought into question other courtesy recognitions, which the G[enealogical] O[ffice] with expert assistance from leading genealogists is currently endeavouring to resolve (Hood, 208).

In 1990 William Marmion-Kalmbach, or "Lord of Duhallow", an associate of Terence McCarthy, published a little book about Gaelic nobility called *Gaelic Titles and Forms of Address: a guide in the English language* (Kansas City 1990). Although there is a certain amount of historical fact in the book, most of it is pure fiction. The author claims, for example, that there were four "orders of chivalry" in Gaelic Ireland: Clann Deagh or Knights of Munster; Clann Baoiscne or Knights of Leinster; Clann Mhorna or Knights of Connacht; Heroes of the Red Branch (presumably Knights of Ulster); and knights of the Niadh Nask. The author says:

> The Niadh Nask today is referred to as a "Nobiliary Fraternity" – not as an "Order". As such, it is totally recognized by the prestigious International Commission for Orders of Chivalry. Again, there never was, nor is there now, any intention to imitate Orders of Chivalry, which the Gaelic Knighthoods *predate*. Obviously, however, many Niadh Nask are also knights of recognized Orders of Chivalry and thus do have prefix titles of "Sir" or "Chevalier," etc., from those orders, though all recognize that those prefixes are non-Gaelic honours. Admission to Niadh Nask is not at all sectarian, and the Fraternity includes Scottish and English peers, and European and crowned heads.

Although the honour called Niadh Nask (Nia Naisc) is pure fantasy, it is not difficult to see where the basic idea originated. Geoffrey Keating says that a certain druid evicted Eochaidh, king of Leinster from Tara and from the kingship of Ireland in the time of Niall of the Nine Hostages, because he was not wearing the collar of a champion round his neck. Keating says:

> *Ionann sin ré a rádh agus go ngabhadh grádha Ridire Gaiscidh. Óir amhail adeirthear miles torquatus ré ridire gaiscidh, is mar sin adeirthear nia naisc i nGaedhilg ris an ngaisceadhach do ghabhadh nasc nó slabhra fá 'n-a bhrághaid. Ionann iomorro nia is gaisceadhach nó tréinfhear, agus is ionann nasc is slabhra* 'This was the same as to say that he should have received the degree of Knight of Chivalry. For as the knight of chivalry is called *miles torquatus*, so also Nia Naisc is applied in Irish, to the champion

who wore a nasc or chain round his neck. For *nia* means "champion" or "valiant man" and *nasc* means "a chain."'

If Ireland is indeed a modern republic in which all citizens are equal and nobiliary titles are expressly forbidden, it was perhaps unwise for Chief Heralds, as employees of the state, ever to have given official "courtesy" recognition to Gaelic titles. Such a controversial activity detracts from the legitimate function of the Office of the Chief Herald in the fields of genealogy and heraldry

Abbreviations

AF	A. C. Fox-Davies, *Armorial Families: a Directory of Gentlemen of Coat Armour* (5th edition London 1905)
AH	A. C. Fox-Davies, *The Art of Heraldry* (2nd edition London 1986)
AWW	Gayre of Gayre and Nigg, *The Armorial Who is Who 1979-1980* (Edinburgh)
BGA	Bernard Burke, *The General Armory of England, Scotland, Ireland and Wales* (final edition 1884, reprint Ramsbury 1989)
BP	Bernard Burke, *Peerage and Baronetage* (London 1908)
CCH	Geoffrey Briggs, *Civic and Corporate Heraldry: a Dictionary of Impersonal Arms of England, Wales and N. Ireland* (London 1971)
CGH	A. C. Fox-Davies, *A Complete Guide to Heraldry*, revised by J. P. Brooke-Little (London 1985)
FCA	Joseph Foster, *The Dictionary of Heraldry: Feudal Coats of Arms and Pedigrees* (2nd edition London 1989)
FNMI	John T. Gilbert, *Facsimiles of the National Manuscripts of Ireland* (London 1874-82)
GO	Any manuscript in the Genealogical Office
HHB	Anthony R. Wagner, *Historic Heraldry of Britain* (London 1939)
HIF	G. A. Hayes-McCoy, *A History of Irish Flags* (Dublin 1979)
IF	Edward MacLysaght, *Irish Families: Their Names, Arms and Origins* (4th edition Dublin 1985)
IH	Christopher and Adrian Lynch-Robinson, *Intelligible Heraldry* (London 1948)
K	Cecil R. Humphery-Smith, *Kennedy's Book of Arms*, a facsimile edition of *Sketches Collected chiefly from the Records in Ulster's Office and other authentic Documents* [1816] (Canterbury 1967)
PO	J. W. Papworth, *Ordinary of British Armorials* (London [1874], reprint 1985)
TH	Michel Pastoureau, *Traité d'Héraldique* (Paris 1979)
THBF	J. Woodward agus G. Burnett, *A Treatise on Heraldry British and Foreign* (reprint Rutland, Vermont 1967)

Bibliography

Armstrong, E. C. R. (1913): "A note as to the time heraldry was adopted by the Irish chiefs", *Journal of the Royal Society of Antiquaries of Ireland* 43, 66-72.

Barry, J. (1970): "Guide to the records of the Genealogical Office, Dublin, with a commentary on heraldry in Ireland", *Analecta Hibernica* 26, 3-41.

Blake, M. (1905-06): "The Arms of the Corporate Town of Galway", *Journal of the Galway Archaeological and Historical Society* 4, 45-48.

Brooke-Little, J. P. (1983): *Boutell's Heraldry* (London).

Butler, T. B. (1943-55): "The Officers of Arms of Ireland", *The Irish Genealogist* 2, 2-12, 40-47.

Butler, T. (1980-81) "Heraldry of the Butlers in Ireland", *Journal of the Butler Society* 2, 86-101.

Butler, T. (1991): "Some Heraldic Shields of the Butlers in Ireland with Source References", *Journal of the Butler Society* 3, 363-375.

Chorzempa, Rosemary A. (1987): *Design your own Coat of Arms* (New York).

Collins, S. M. (1941): "Some English, Scottish, Welsh and Irish Arms in Medieval Continental Rolls", *The Antiquaries Journal* 21, 203-210.

Crossly, Aaron. (1724): *The significance of most Things that are born in Heraldry* (Dublin), ceangailte lena *Peerage of Ireland* (1723 Dublin).

De Breffny, B. (1982): *Irish Family Names: Arms, Origins and Locations* (Dublin).

Du Noyer, G. V. (1868a): "Catalogue of 101 drawings of coats of arms from original sketches from tombstones", *Proceedings of the Royal Irish Academy* 10, 179-188.

Du Noyer, G. V. (1868b): "Catalogue of 103 drawings of coats of arms from original sketches from tombstones", *Proceedings of the Royal Irish Academy* 10, 402-412.

Galloway, P. (1983): *The Most Illustrious Order of St Patrick* (Chichester).

Garstin, J. R. (1908-11): "The Arms and Seal of Dundalk", *Journal of the County Louth Archaeological Society* 2, 205-207.

Heraldic Artists Ltd (1980): *The Symbols of Heraldry Explained* (Dublin).

Heim, Bruno B. (1981), *Heraldry in the Catholic Church* (Gerrards Cross).

Hickey, Elizabeth (1982-84): "Arms of the Earls of March and Ulster on the tower of the Cathedral of Trim, Ireland", *The Coat of Arms*, N.S., vol. V, No. 126, 148-152.

Hickey, Elizabeth (1988-89): "Royal Heraldry and some Irish Arms at Trim, County Meath", *Ríocht na Midhe* 8, 129-140.

Holland, M. (1916): "Sketch of the Cork City Arms by Daniel Maclise", *Journal of the Cork Historical and Archaeological Society* 22, 85-88.

Hood, Susan (2002): *Royal Roots – Republican Inheritance: The Survival of the Office of Arms* (Dublin)

Jackson, V. (1940-42): "The Armorials of the City of Dublin", *Dublin Historical Record* 3-4, 33-38.

Lart, C. E. (1938): *The Pedigrees and Papers of James Terry, Athlone Herald at the Court of James II in France, 1690-1725* (Exeter).

Lyall, Andrew (1993-94): "Irish Heraldic Jurisdiction", *The Coat of Arms* N.S. vol. X, No. 164, 134-142, No. 165, 178-187, No. 167, 266-275.

BIBLIOGRAPHY

Mac Lochlainn, A. (1953): "Rex v. Crossly: a lecture with manifestations", *County Kildare Archaeological Society Journal* 13, 193-200.

Mac Lochlainn, A. (1954): "A Gaelic Armory", *Journal of the Royal Society of Antiquaries of Ireland* 84, 68-71.

MacLysaght, E. (1949): "Some observations on the arms of the four provinces", *Journal of the Royal Society of Antiquaries of Ireland* 79, 60-63.

Meek, D. E. (1986): "The Banners of the Fian in Gaelic Ballad Tradition", *Cambridge Medieval Celtic Studies* 11, 29-69.

Murphy, Sean J. (2004): *Twilight of the Chiefs: The MacCarthy Mor Hoax* (Bethesda)

Ó Comáin, M. (1991): *The Poolbeg Book of Irish Heraldry* (Dublin).

Ó Conluain, P. (1990): "The Red Hand of Ulster", *Dúiche Néill* 5, 24-38.

O'Neill, T. P. (1976): "Irish Trade Banners", in C. Ó Danachair, *Folk and Farm* 177-199 (Dublin).

Pye, R. F. (1970), "The Armory of the Western Highlands", *The Coat of Arms*, vol. XI, No. 81, 3-8, No. 82, 51-58.

Reeves, W. (1853): "The Seal of Hugh O'Neill", *Ulster Journal of Archaeology*, 1st series, 1, 255-258.

Roelofsma, D. K. (1982): "A Sketch of the Gaelic Elements in Irish Heraldry", *Communicaciones al XV Congreso de Ciencias Genealógicas y Heráldicas* (Madrid), 367-379.

Skey, W. (1846): *The Heraldic Calendar: a list of the nobility and gentry whose arms are registered and pedigrees recorded in the herald's office in Ireland* (Dublin).

Slevin, J. Gerard. (1955-56): "The heraldic practice of the Archbishops of Dublin", *Repertorium Novum* 1, 470-476.

Vinycomb, J. (1895, 1898): "The Seals and Armorial Insignia of Corporate and other Towns in Ulster", *Ulster Journal of Archaeology* 1, 36-46, 111-119; 4, 23-32, 103-111.

Vinycomb, J. (1896-97): "Arms of the Bishoprics of Ireland", *Ulster Journal of Archaeology* 3, 2-12, 98-112.

Went, E.J. (1952): "Fishes in Irish heraldry", *Journal of the Cork Historical and Archaeological Society* 57, 110-120.

Williams, N. J. A. (1989): "Of Beasts and Banners: the origin of the heraldic enfield", *Journal of the Royal Society of Antiquaries of Ireland* 119, 62-78.

Williams, N. J. A. (1990a): "Dermot O'Connor's Blazons and Irish Heraldic Terminology", *Eighteenth-Century Ireland* 5, 61-88.

Williams, N. J. A. (1990b): "Irish Heraldry: Facts and Fallacies", in William Nolan, ed., *The Heritage Business* Centre for Local and Heritage Studies, University College Dublin, 119-129.

Williams, N. J. A. (1992): "A Seal of an Irish Regiment in the Service of the King of France", *Journal of the Royal Society of Antiquaries of Ireland*, vol. 122, 146-149.

Williams, N. J. A. (1994): "Computer Graphics and Heraldry", *The Coat of Arms* N.S. vol. X, No. 168, 310-317.

Woodward, J. (1894): *A Treatise on Ecclesiastical Heraldry* (Edinburgh and London).

Index of illustrations

The letter *F* preceding a number refers to the greyscale Figures. The letter *P* preceding a number refers to the colour Plates. *Mac* and *Mc* are interfiled.

INDEX OF ILLUSTRATIONS

General index

bishops: 22.02, 27.00, 27.05, 27.06
  Catholic bishops: 27.01, 27.03
  Protestant bishops 27.02
Blackwood, Baron Dufferin: 19.05
Blake: 10.06, 11.04, 19.02, 19.06
blazon: 03.02, 05.08, 18.00-18.04
Blessed Virgin Mary: 15.03
bleu céleste: 05.02
Blood: 16.03
boar: 11.07, 18.00, 23.08
Bog rosemary: 16.08
bomb: 17.16
book: 17.19
Book of Kells: 05.03
bordure: 05.06, 10.01, 10.02, 14.07, 18.02,
  18.03, 23.06, 23.07, 24.03, 24.05,
  26.06, 26.07
bow and arrow: 17.02
Boylan: 12.00
Boyle, Earl of Cork: 08.00
Boyle, Richard: 28.08
Boyne: 24.05
Bradshaw: 07.03
branches and leaves: 03.03, 16.02
  elder branch: 16.02
  oak branch: 07.01
  olive branch: 03.03, 12.06, 12.10, 25.01,
    26.07
Bréifne: 02.00
Brennan: 01.06
Brereton: 26.03
Brian Ború: 24.01, 24.04
Bristol: 25.03
Britannia: 02.01
British Library: 28.05
broad arrow: 17.25, 26.02
Brookeborough; *see* Brooke
Brooke-Little, J.: 19.05, 26.06
Brooke of Brookeborough: 20.02
Browne, Earl of Kenmare: 11.05, 21.02
Browne, Marquis of Sligo: 21.02
Brownlow, Lord Lurgan: 10:01, 10.02
Brutus: 02.01
Buaidh na Naomhchroiche: 09.00
bugle horn: 17.04
Bundoran: 06.01, 25.15
burgher arms: 29.00
Burke: 11.05, 22.00
Burke, J: 28.06
Burke, Sir J.Bernard: 28.06
  his visitations: 28.04
  crest for corporations: 19.08

Burke, Richard: 23.02
Burke, Walter: 09.01
Burke, William: 23.02
  Elizabeth his heiress: 23.02
Burkes: 19.06, 23.02, 24.06, 25.13
  Earls of Ulster: 25.04, 25.05
Burke's Peerage: 28.06
Busch: 16.01
Butler, Bartholomew: 28.02
Butler, James, 4th Earl of Ormond: 00.02,
  01.06
  his quarrel with Talbot: 01.06
  appoints a king of arms: 28.01
Butler of Lanesborough: 21.02
Butler, Pierce: 01.09
Butler, T.: 23.03
Butler, Theobald: 00.02
Butler, Thomas Bacagh: 01.07
Butlerabo: 21.00
Butlers: 17.07, 23.03
  crest: 12.07
  motto: 21.00
Butlers of Dunboyne: 23.03
Butlers of Ormond: 21.00, 24.10

cadrúca: 13.06
caduceus: 13.06
Caen: 28.06
Caithréim Thoirdhealbhaigh: 01.00
Calais, siege of: 00.02
California: 29.05
Calvert, Lord Baltimore: 21.02
Cameron, Alexander: 03.01
Canada: 29.03
canting arms: 03.03
cap of maintenance: 17.11
Carden, Templemore, Co. Tipperary:
  10.05
Carney, James: 31.04
Carney, Richard: 25.10, 28.02
Carney, Sir Richard: 28.02
Carolan: 01.06
Carrickmacross: 21.03
cartouche: 04.01, 22.01, 27.00
Castlebar: 09.05, 10.03, 16.00, 21.03,
  25.15
Castlereagh: 15.05, 17.11, 25.15
castles *&* towers: 17.05
cat-a-mountain: 11.04, 11.05
  domestic cat: 11.05
Catherine wheel: 17.26
Cecil, William: 01.00

Plates

P27   County Dublin, Four Impossible Crests—Blackwood, Baron Dufferin, Tabuteau, Portarlington, Fizmaurice, Lord Lansdowne, Wingfield, Viscount Powerscourt

P28   Dublin, Belfast

P29   Anne, Countess of Cambridge †1411, Linnea M. Mangan (née Aitchison), Narcissus Marsh †1713, Archbishop of Dublin, Margaret, Viscountess Ferrard †1824, The Provost of Youghal, McGrath, O'Riordan

P30   The Fitzgeralds, the Burkes

P31   Miscellaneous Butlers: Thomas Walter †1206, Earls of Ormond from the fifteenth century, Thomas Butler, 1st Earl of Dunboyne †1329, Butler, Baron Cahir, The Butlers of Dunboyne from c. 1660, James Butler, 2nd Baron Dunboyne †1624, Thomas Butler, 10th Earl of Ormond 1532-1614, John Butler, 2nd Marquis of Ormodn 1805-54, Thomas Butler, Clogrenan, Baronet 1628

P32   Fitzroy, Duke of Grafton, FitzClarence, Earl of Munster, Wellesley, Duke of Wellington, Gough, Viscount Gujerat and Limerick

P33   The King of Ireland according to the Wijnbergen Roll (thirteenth century), The Province of Leinster, The Province of Leinster in the seventeenth century, The arms of Ireland (1413), Robert de Vere, Duke of Ireland (1386), The Province of Munster in the seventeenth century, The Province of Connacht, The Irish Monastery, Regensburg, The arms of Ireland according to Conrad von Grünenberg 1483

P34   The Province of Connacht in the seventeenth century, Munster according to the Uffenbach Roll, c. 1440, The arms of Meath according to W. Hawkins, Ulster King of Arms 1698-1736, The Province of Ulster, The original arms of Ulster according to W. Hawkins, Northern Ireland, The King of Ireland as found in armorials of the fifteenth century, The Republic of Ireland, County Meath (1988)

P35   County Kilkenny, County Tipperary, County Carlow, Galway 1368-1485, Galway 1485-?1578, Galway ?1578-, Dublin (original arms; see PO: 365), Limerick, Cork

P36   Armagh, Waterford, Dundalk, Port Laoise, Drogheda, Dún Laoghaire, Naas, Gorey, Youghal

P37   Jonathan Swift, Henry Grattan, Charles Stuart Parnell, Lord Killannin, Éamon de Valera, John Fitzgerald Kennedy, President of the USA, Charles Haughey

P38   Some Dioceses of the Church of Ireland   Armagh, Derry and Raphoe, Kilmore, Elphin and Ardagh, Meath, Clogher, Cashel and Waterford, Cork and Cloyne, Limerick, Killaloe and Clonfert

P39   Pius XII (Eugenio Pacelli), Peter Creagh †1707 Archbishop of Dublin, John XXIII (Angelo Giuseppe Roncalli), Paul VI (Giovanni Battista Montini), John Paul II (Karol Wojtyła), John Paul I (Albino Luciani), Sovereign Military Order of Malta, Cardinal John Henry Newman, The Dominicans

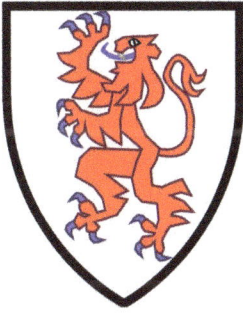

Talbot   O'Carolan (Co. Meath)   Dease (Co. Meath)

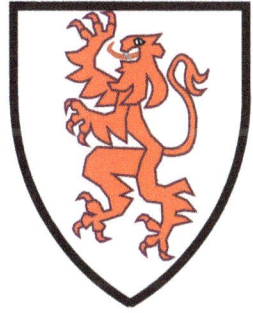

MacEgan (Westmeath)   O'Kearney (Co. Offaly)   McAuley (Co. Offaly)

Keogh (Co. Roscommon)   O'Shiel (Co. Offaly)   Crosbie (Laois and Offaly)

Brennan (Co. Roscommon)   O'Daly (Co. Westmeath)

Arms of some chiefs of the Irish Midlands

Plate 1

Ahern (*heron*)

Creagh (*craobhacha* = 'branches' in Irish)

Hackett (*hake*)

Harte (*heart*)

Barry (*bars*)

Griffith (*griffin*)

Sheehan (*síoth* = 'peace' in Irish)

Purcell (*porcell* = 'young pig')

Synnot (*cygne*, *swan*)

Nine Examples of Canting Arms

Plate 2

Crest

Cap of maintenance

Mantling

Helmet

Coronet

Dexter supporter

Sinister supporter

Shield

Compartment

Motto

ESSE QUAM VIDERI

Brownlow, Lord Lurgan

THE ACHIEVEMENT

Plate 3

Above: Standard of Gerald FitzGerald, Earl of Kildare (1611-12)

Right: Standard of Thomas Butler, Earl of Ormond and Ossory (1615)

Plate 4

 Argent [Ar.]

 Or [Or]

 Gules [Gu.]

 Azure [Az.]

 Sable [Sa.]

 Vert [Vt.]

 Purpure [Purp.]

 Sanguine

 Murrey

 Tenné

 Ermine

 Ermines

 Erminois

 Pean

 Vair

Heraldic Tinctures

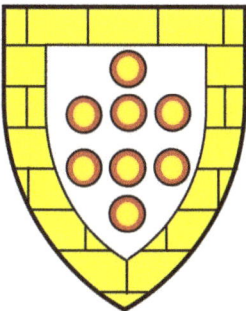 Kells, Co. Meath

 Victoria College, Belfast

 Meredith

Plate 5

Adair

O'Cassidy

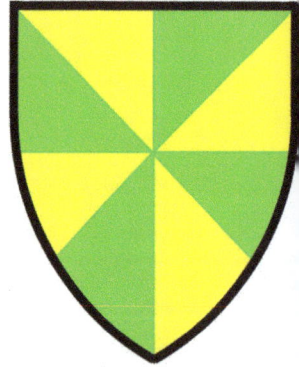

Crotty

Doyle

O'Higgins

Poyntz

Stephenson

Tallant

Tuite

Plate 6

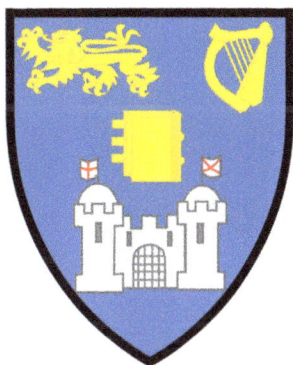

Trinity College, Dublin

The Ulster Bank

County Offaly

Balbriggan

Loughrea

Bundoran

Newcastle West

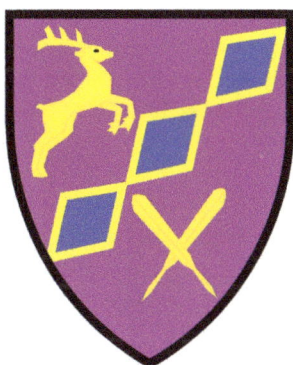

Killarney

Greystones

Plate 7

Bradshaw

Lecky

Maginn

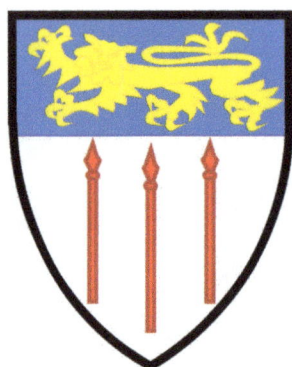

MacLysaght

MacGilfoyle

Jordan

Myler

Nugent

Rowley

Plate 8

O'Shea

Morris of Galway

O'Connolly (Kildare)

McDonagh (Connacht)

Clements

Boyle, Earl of Cork

Ankettle

O'Hara

Domhnall Ó Beaglaoich,
Chief Herald of Ireland

Plate 9

Warner

O'Donnell

Martin (Galway)

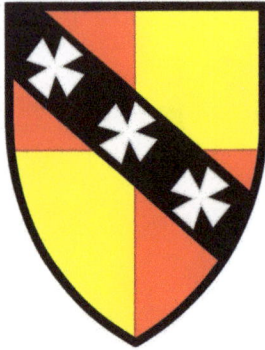

O'Hannon

Vesey

Wall

Drury

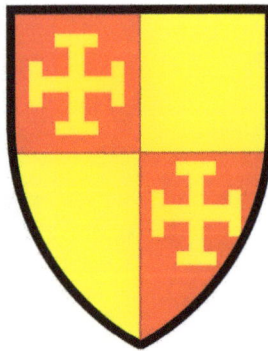

Cross

Molyneux

Plate 10

O'Flanagan

O'Mara

O'Quigley

Molesworth

Crowe

Castlebar

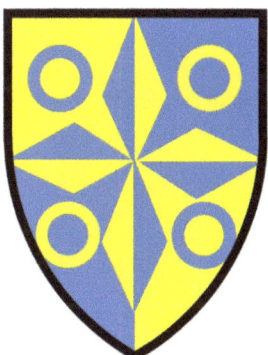

Peacocke

Carden

Costello

Plate 11

Blake

Taaffe

Kilrush

Garda Síochána
College

Devereux

Staples

Hogan

Sligo Town

Arklow

Plate 12

Lacy

O'Lalor

O'Hynes

O'Toole

O'Rourke

McMahon

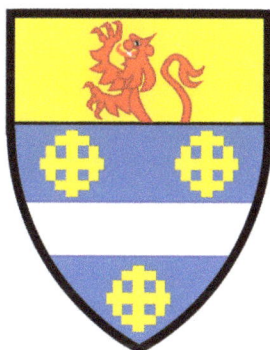

Terry

Parsons

Tenison

Plate 13

O'Doherty

Clonmel

O'Hanley

Mulrooney

O'Fallon

Wolsely

O'Donoghue

O'Quin

Pratt

Plate 14

Boylan

Browne (Galway)

O'Casey

Wingfield

O'Gormley

O'Madden

Tullamore

Wicklow Town

O'Kirwan

Plate 15

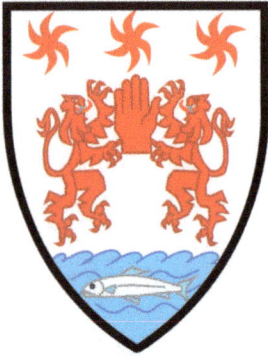

O'Neill

Fermoy

O'Cahill

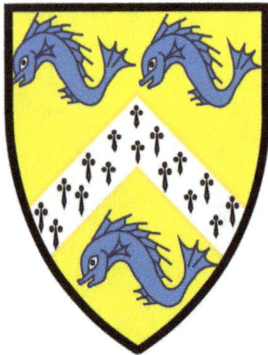

O'Regan

O'Dea

Mid-Western Health
Board

O'Corrigan

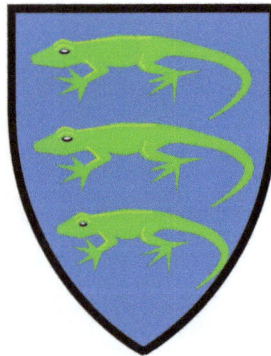

MacCotter

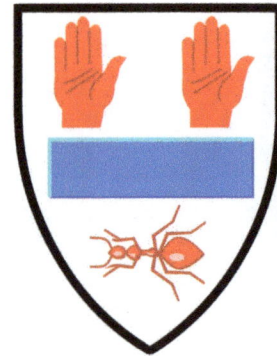

Ballymena Academy

Plate 16

MacGillycuddy

Hanratty

Ryan

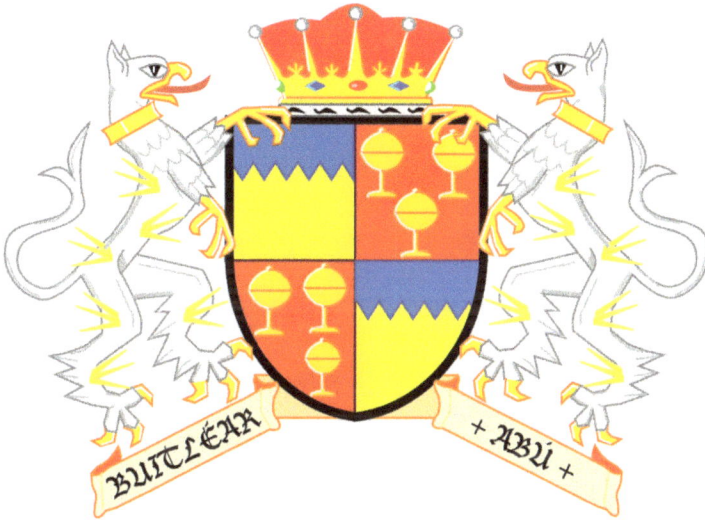

Earls of Ormond

O'Neilan

MacAuliffe

Gerard Slevin

Plate 17

O'Donnellan

O'Loughlin

The Diocese of Tuam

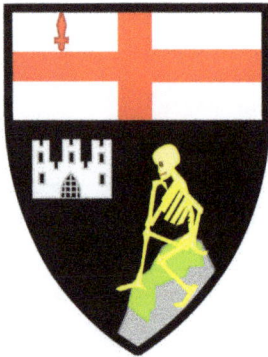

Derry

MacBrady

O'Donovan

O'Mangan

Goan

Crean

Plate 18

O'Dowling

O'Callaghan

O'Clery

Blood

Darcy

National University
of Ireland

Athlone

Shannon

D'Olier

Plate 19

Maloney

Fagan

Bellingham

Tralee

O'Shaughnessy

Plunkett

O'Coffey

Lightburne

O'Dowd

Plate 20

O'Davoren

O'Finnegan

University of Dublin

O'Mulvihill

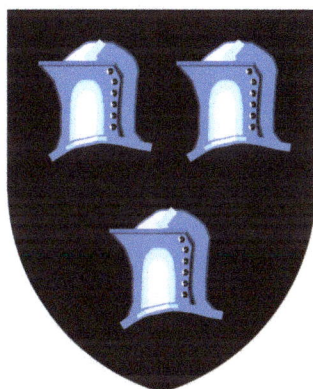

O'Kennedy

Association of Municipal
Authorities of Northern Ireland

Castlereagh

Ferrers

Sir John W. Moore

Plate 21

Diocese of Down

Granville Lord
Lansdowne

Ball

Lally

MacGovern

MacDonnell
(Co. Clare and
Co. Galway)

Conroy

O'Driscoll

O'Flaherty

Plate 22

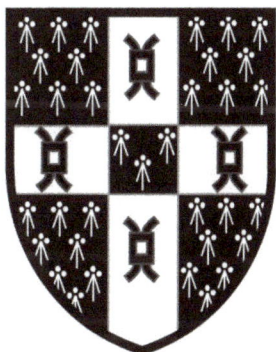

Winterton

Redmond

Maunsell

O'Moran

MacKeown

O'Shanley

O'Duggan

Walsh of Iverk

MacColgan

Plate 23

Scott

Hay

Macnamara

Leeson,
Earl of Miltown

Dungannon

O'Sheehy

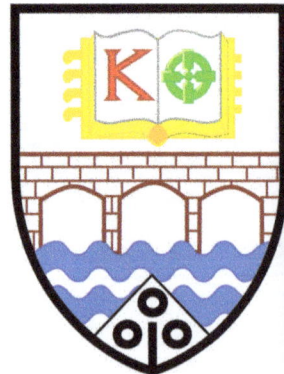

St Killian's Community
School, Bray

Plate 24

Barret

O'Scanlon

Sarsfield

Cusack

V. J. S. Doddrell

Oadby U.D.C.

Mrs H. M. Laing

J. Berger-Carrière

Borough of
Wandsworth

Plate 25

Edward Festus Kelly

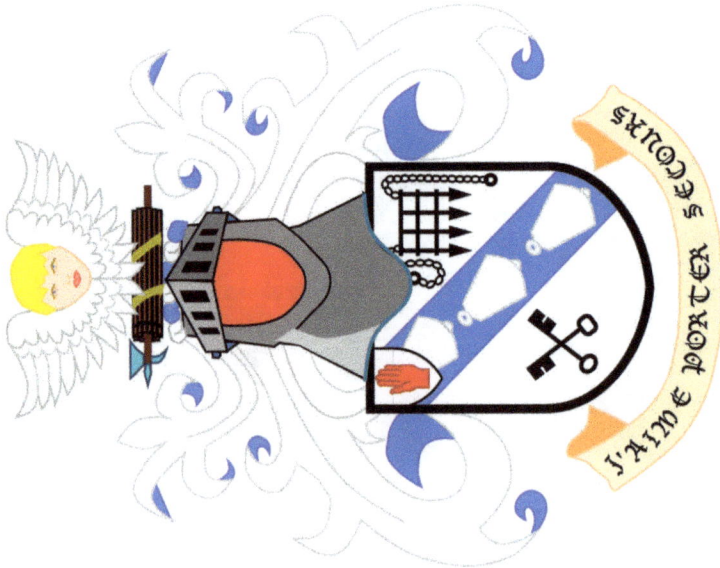

Andrew Marshall Porter, Baronet

Plate 26

Tabuteau,
Portarlington

Wingfield,
Viscount Powerscourt

Blackwood,
Baron Dufferin

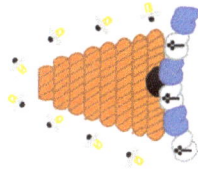

Fitzmaurice,
Lord Lansdowne

Four Impossible Crests

County Dublin

Plate 27

OBOEDENTIA CIVIUM URBIS FELICITAS

Dublin

PRO TANTO QUID RETRIBUAMUS

Belfast

Plate 28

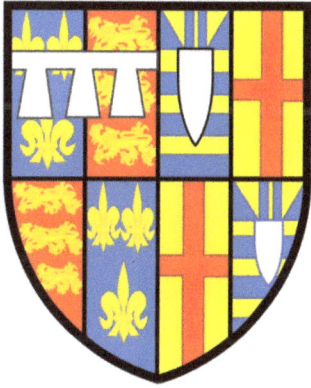

Anne, Countess of
Cambridge †1411

Linnea M. Mangan
(née Aitchison)

Narcissus Marsh †1713,
Archbishop of Dublin

Margaret, Viscountess Ferrard †1824

The Provost of Youghal

McGrath

O'Riordan

Plate 29

Maurice Fitzgerald
†1177

Gerald †1203-04

Thomas, Lord of
Shanaid †1213

John †1261

Gilbert

John FitzThomas,
Earl of Kildare †1316

Maurice,
Earl of Desmond †1356

The Fitzgibbons

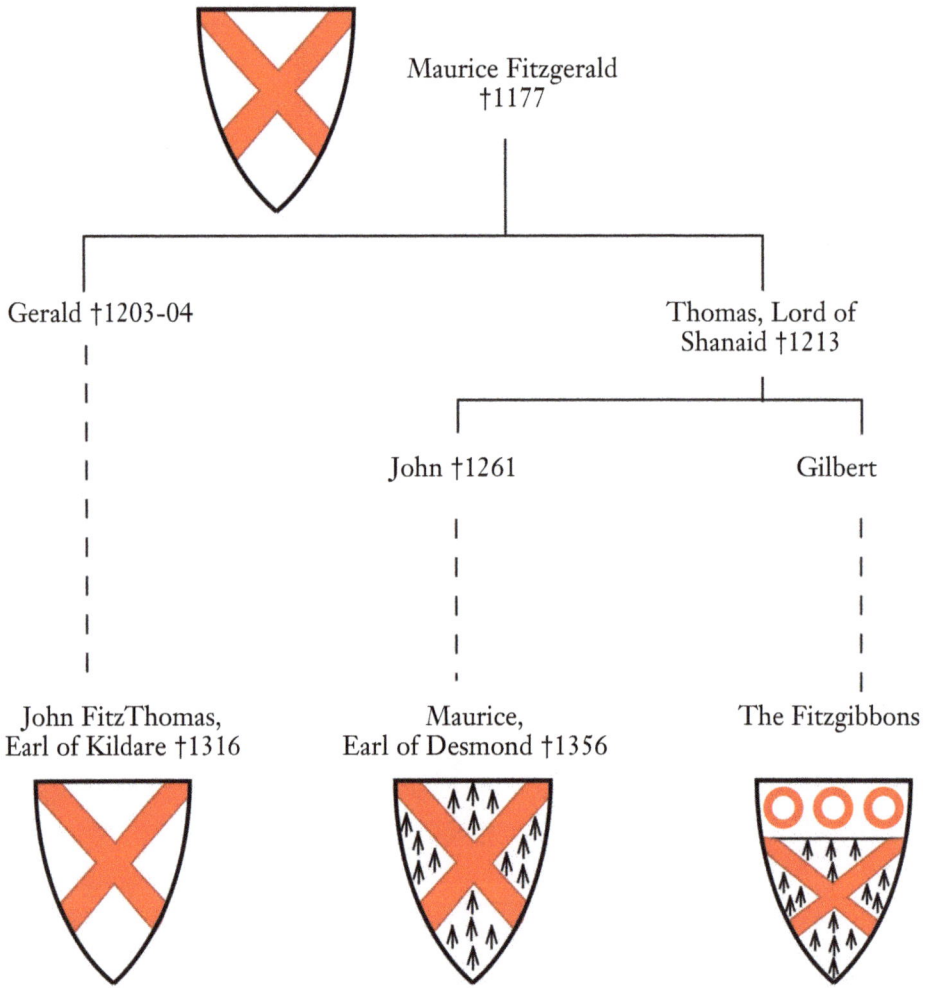

The Fitzgeralds

The Burkes of Ulster

Lacy

The Burkes of
Connacht

The Burkes

Plate 30

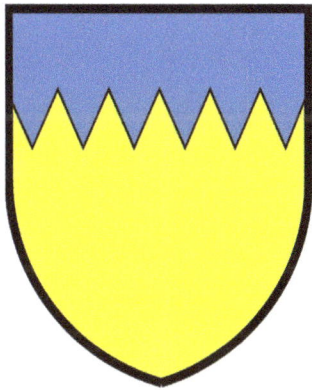

Theobald Walter †1206

Earls of Ormond from
the 15th century

Thomas Butler, 1st Earl
of Dunboyne †1329

Butler, Baron Cahir

The Butlers of
Dunboyne from *c.* 1660

James Butler, 2nd Baron
Dunboyne †1624

Thomas Butler, 10th Earl
of Ormond 1532-1614

John Butler, 2nd Marquis
of Ormond 1808-54

Thomas Butler,
Clogrenan, Baronet 1628

Miscellaneous Butlers

Plate 31

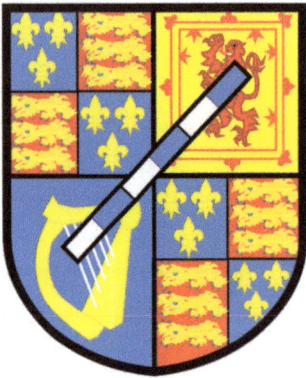

FitzRoy,
Duke of Grafton

FitzClarence,
Earl of Munster

Wellesley,
Duke of Wellington

Gough, Viscount Gujerat and Limerick

Plate 32

The King of Ireland according to the Wijnbergen Roll (13th century)

The Province of Leinster

The Province of Leinster in the 17th century

The arms of Ireland (1413)

Robert de Vere, Duke of Ireland (1386)

The Province of Munster in the 17th century

The Province of Connacht

The Irish Monastery, Regensburg

The arms of Ireland according to Conrad von Grünenberg 1483

Plate 33

The Province of Connacht
in the 17th century

Munster according to the
Uffenbach Roll *c.* 1440

The arms of Meath accord-
ing to W. Hawkins, Ulster
King of Arms 1698-1736

The Province of Ulster

The original arms
of Ulster according to
W. Hawkins

Northern Ireland

The King of Ireland
as found in armorials
of the 15th century

The Republic of Ireland

County Meath (1988)

Plate 34

County Kilkenny

County Tipperary

County Carlow

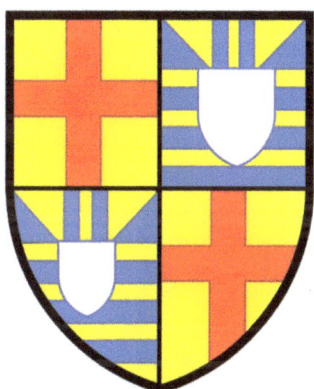

Galway 1368-1485

Galway 1485-?1578

Galway ?1578-

Dublin
(original arms; see PO: 365)

Limerick

Cork

Plate 35

Armagh

Waterford

Dundalk

Port Laoise

Drogheda

Dún Laoghaire

Naas

Gorey

Youghal

Plate 36

Jonathan Swift

Henry Grattan

Charles Stuart Parnell

Lord Killannin

SI DEUS NOBISCUM QUIS CONTRA NOS

Éamon de Valera

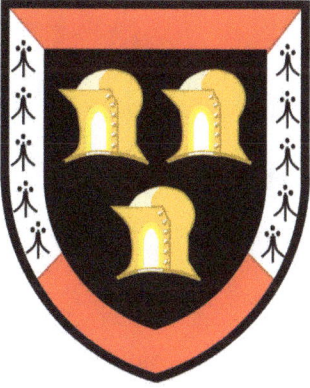

John Fitzgerald Kennedy,
President of the USA

Charles Haughey

Plate 37

Armagh

Derry and Rafoe

Kilmore, Elphin,
and Ardagh

Meath

Clogher

Cashel and Waterford

Cork and Cloyne

Limerick

Killaloe and Clonfert

Some Dioceses
of the Church of Ireland

Plate 38

Pius XII
(Eugenio Pacelli)

Peter Creagh †1707
Archbishop of Dublin

VIRTUTE ET NUMINE

John XXIII
(Angelo Giuseppe Roncalli)

Paul VI
(Giovanni Battista Montini)

John Paul II
(Karol Wojtyła)

John Paul I
(Albino Luciani)

Sovereign Military
Order of Malta

COR AD COR LOQUITUR

Cardinal John Henry
Newman

The Dominicans

Plate 39

www.ingramcontent.com/pod-product-compliance
Lightning Source LLC
Chambersburg PA
CBHW040140270326
41928CB00022B/3275